MARIA
THERESA

Books by Edward Crankshaw

Joseph Conrad: Aspects of the Art of the Novel
Vienna: The Image of a Culture in Decline
Britain and Russia
Russia and the Russians
The Forsaken Idea: A Study of Viscount Milner
Gestapo: Instrument of Tyranny
Russia Without Stalin
Khrushchev's Russia
The New Cold War: Moscow v. Pekin
The Fall of the House of Habsburg
Khrushchev: A Biography
Maria Theresa
The Habsburgs
Tolstoy: The Making of a Novelist
The Shadow of the Winter Palace
Bismarck
Putting Up with the Russians

Novels

Nina Lessing
What Glory?
The Creedy Case

MARIA THERESA

Edward Crankshaw

'*They condemn the past for its ignorance and prejudice, while knowing nothing at all about the past and not much more about the present.*'

(Maria Theresa on the exponents of the 'new philosophy', 1774)

New York   1986   *Atheneum*

LIBRARY OF CONGRESS CATALOGING-IN-PUBLICATION DATA
Crankshaw, Edward.
Maria Theresa.
Reprint. Originally published: London: Longmans, 1969.
Bibliography: p.
Includes index.
1. Maria Theresa, Empress of Austria, 1717-1780.
2. Austria—Kings and rulers—Biography.   3. Austria—
History—Maria Theresa, 1740-1780. I. Title.
DB71.C7   1986   943'.053'0924 [B]   85-28678
ISBN 0-689-70708-8

Manufactured by Fairfield Graphics, Fairfield, Pennsylvania
First Atheneum Paperback Edition

For
Margaret Stephens
with love and gratitude

Contents

RUSSIA

Moscow •

Riga •

IC SEA

Dvina

EAST
PRUSSIA

THE HABSBURG EMPIRE
and Central Europe 1740

Vistula

Warsaw •

P O L A N D

Kiev •

Dnieper

Cracow •

be

• Budapest

Odessa •

H U N G A R Y

TRANSYLVANIA

TIA

Belgrade •

Bucharest •

Danube

B L A C K   S E A

O T T O M A N

E M P I R E

Constantinople •

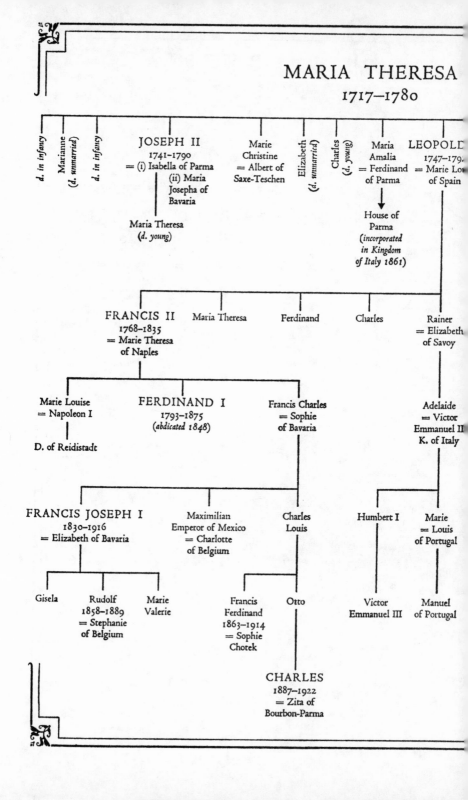

MARIA THERESA
1717–1780

d. in infancy

Marianne *(d. unmarried)*

d. in infancy

JOSEPH II
1741–1790
= (i) Isabella of Parma
(ii) Maria
Josepha of
Bavaria

Maria Theresa
(d. young)

Marie
Christine
= Albert of
Saxe-Teschen

Elizabeth *(d. unmarried)*

Charles *(d. young)*

Maria
Amalia
= Ferdinand
of Parma

↓

House of
Parma
*(incorporated
in Kingdom
of Italy 1861)*

LEOPOLD
1747–179.
= Marie Lo
of Spain

FRANCIS II
1768–1835
= Marie Theresa
of Naples

Maria Theresa

Ferdinand

Charles

Rainer
= Elizabeth
of Savoy

Marie Louise
= Napoleon I

D. of Reidistadt

FERDINAND I
1793–1875
(abdicated 1848)

Francis Charles
= Sophie
of Bavaria

Adelaide
= Victor
Emmanuel II
K. of Italy

FRANCIS JOSEPH I
1830–1916
= Elizabeth of Bavaria

Maximilian
Emperor of Mexico
= Charlotte
of Belgium

Charles
Louis

Humbert I

Marie
= Louis
of Portugal

Gisela

Rudolf
1858–1889
= Stephanie
of Belgium

Marie
Valerie

Francis
Ferdinand
1863–1914
= Sophie
Chotek

Otto

Victor
Emmanuel III

Manuel
of Portugal

CHARLES
1887–1922
= Zita of
Bourbon-Parma

RANCIS OF LORRAINE
1708–1765

Joanna *(d. young)*

Josepha *(d. young)*

Marie Caroline
= Ferdinand I
of Naples

Ferdinand
= Marie
Beatrix d'Este

→ House of Modena
*(incorporated in
Kingdom of Italy
1861)*

Marie Antonia
(Marie Antoinette)
= Louis XVI

Maximilian *(d. unmarried)*

---

ancis I
Naples
Maria
Spain

Maria
Theresa
= Francis II
of Austria

Marie Amélie
= Louis
Philippe
(K. of the French)

Louis
Joseph

Charles
Louis
(Louis XVII)

Marie
Thérèse
= Duke of
Angoulême

---

ristina
dinand VII
Spain

Ferdinand
(King Bomba)

*(incorporated
in Kingdom
of Italy 1861)*

Ferdinand
D. of Orleans

Louise
= Leopold I
of Belgium

Clementine
= Augustus of
Saxe-Coburg

---

sabella

Comte de
Paris

*(Pretenders to the
French throne)*

Leopold II

Philip

Charlotte
= Maximilian
of Austria

Ferdinand
of Bulgaria

---

onso **XII**

Stephanie
= Rudolf
of Austria

Albert I

---

onso XIII

Albert II

Chronological Outline

1717 *Born*   Eldest daughter of Emperor Charles VI and Elisabeth Christina of Brunswick-Wolfenbüttel.

1738   Married Prince Francis Stephen of Lorraine, Grandduke of Tuscany.

1740 *November* Death of Charles VI.

    December Frederick II of Prussia invades Silesia.

1741 *April*   Defeat of Austrian forces at Mollwitz.

    June   Maria Theresa crowned Queen of Hungary.

    July   Elector Charles Albert of Bavaria challenges succession and invades Austria in conjunction with the French.

    September Maria Theresa successfully appeals to the Hungarians.

    November Fall of Prague.

    December Charles Albert crowned King of Bohemia.

1742 *February* Charles Albert crowned Emperor Charles VII at Frankfurt.
Khevenhüller takes Munich for Austria.

    June   Treaty of Breslau, Prussia withdraws from war, taking most of Silesia.

    December Austrians recapture Prague.

1743 *May*   Maria Theresa crowned Queen of Bohemia.

1744 *May*   Frederick attacks again, invading Bohemia and taking Prague.

1745 *January*	Death of Emperor Charles VII.	
October	Francis Stephen crowned at Frankfurt, Emperor Francis I.	
December	Treaty of Dresden ends second war for Silesia.	
1748 *November*	Treaty of Aix-la-Chapelle ends War of Austrian Succession.	
1746–56	Period of domestic reforms. Haugwitz.	
1753	Kaunitz becomes Chancellor.	
1756–7	Reversal of the Alliances: England and Prussia now allied against France, Austria and Russia.	
1756 *September*	Seven Years War begins with Frederick invading Saxony.	
1763 *February*	Peace of Hubertusberg ends Seven Years War.	
1765 *August*	Death of Francis. Joseph II Emperor and Co-regent.	
1767	Promulgation of Theresian Legal code, in preparation since 1749.	
1770	Marriage of Marie Antoinette to Dauphin of France.	
1772 *August*	First Partition of Poland.	
1773–80	Constitutional, educational, judicial and economic reforms.	
1778–9	War of Bavarian Succession.	
1780 *November*	Death of Maria Theresa.	

PART ONE

A Sea of Troubles

Chapter One

The Inheritance

In the autumn of 1740 the courts and chancellories of Europe were shocked out of their routine bickering and intrigue by an event of the first magnitude. The Emperor Charles VI had died suddenly at the Favorita Palace in Vienna. He was only fifty-five; and he was the last male Habsburg. He had come home from hunting across the Hungarian border, soaked through and chilled to the bone after a typical day in the wettest and coldest October in memory. They brought him back to Vienna in a high fever; and within nine days he was dead. Perhaps the mushrooms he ate for his last meal, Voltaire's 'pot of mushrooms which changed the course of history', had something to do with it. Perhaps not. History was in any case changed by his death; it released forces of ambition and greed which were to transform the face of Austria, of Europe and, indeed, of the world.

The immediate fact was that the line of male succession in Europe's greatest dynasty, a five hundred-year-old chain, was snapped. With it ended the almost automatic right of the Habsburgs to the Crown of what was left of the Holy Roman Empire. Worse still, the Habsburg properties, sprawling and incohesive, almost bankrupted by Charles's foolish and unnecessary intervention in the War of the Polish Succession and the Russian war against the Turks, were vulnerable and beset by predatory and unscrupulous neighbours.

During his lifetime Charles had done his best to insure against this contingency, but his best was uninspired and insufficient. With the Habsburg dominions now defended only by the Emperor's

3

daughter, Maria Theresa, inexperienced, untaught and very young, it looked like the beginning of the end. Many stood to gain from the dismemberment of the Austrian possessions. England alone stood to lose.

It was thus an uneasy accession. Only the new young queen appeared confident. She was twenty-three, married five years to the personable and kindly Francis Stephen of Lorraine, whom she loved deeply and passionately, but of whom she expected little. The great thing was that she had God on her side; of this she had no doubt. And she, with God, would do what was necessary once she had learnt the techniques of government and diplomacy. Her courtiers and ministers, frightened and old, did not see matters in this light. They bowed deeply but thought it was bound to end badly. Maria Theresa was impatiently aware of their inadequacy. Soon she would have to find new advisers to replace the men who had grown old in her father's service: some of them had served her uncle, Joseph I, and even her grandfather, Leopold II, in the struggle with Louis XIV. But for the time being she had to make do with what brains and experience they could muster and herself supply the courage and the resolution. She had not the faintest idea how much of these she would need.

The old men saw a young woman, to them a child, upright, with level eyes of a very clear blue; strikingly good looking, sometimes beautiful, with her height, her corn-coloured hair – great masses of it, her only known vanity. They had known her as an extremely determined young girl, who was also gay and high-spirited to the point of frivolity, with a passion for dancing and card-playing all through the night. Now she was pale, but the remarkable thing was that only a few hours before she had been prostrate with grief, her doctors prepared for a miscarriage; and now here she was, very much a queen, having summoned them to her first audience – not seated on the throne to receive them, but standing on the steps that led up to it, wonderfully fair in her mourning, framed by the heavy purple canopy. She stood alone and with perfect self-possession, her husband, now Grand Duke of Tuscany, on her left, but outside the frame. It was to go on like this.

She spoke of her father through tears, but then, commanding herself, commanded the old men, telling them that she proposed to confirm them all in their appointments for the time being. They in their turn kissed her hand and bowed to her as Queen of Hungary, Queen of Bohemia, Archduchess of Austria, Duchess of Milan, Statthalter of the Netherlands, and all the other titles that accrued to the House of Habsburg. The transition from one reign to the next was thereby formally achieved and with the traditional lack of emphasis.

The new reign was to last forty years. In the course of this time Maria Theresa revealed in herself as an individual a natural force no less valid and a good deal more benevolent than any of those more impersonal natural forces, economic forces, social forces, which we are nowadays inclined to think of as the exclusive agents of history. She was not a conquering queen, or even a warlike one: she could fight like a tiger and was at war for a large part of her reign; but she never fought for aggrandisement, always, sometimes in vain, to preserve her inheritance. Her sole gain, Austria's share of Poland in the first partition of that doomed land, was the fruit of the only completely disreputable action of her life, and this was committed reluctantly under pressure from her son and co-regent and with bitter regret, Frederick the Great's facile jibe notwithstanding. She was not a zealously reforming queen. Her reforms were radical and far-reaching, but she reformed, as she fought, because she saw what had to be done, even while she resisted to the end the logic of the Enlightenment. Her own force was directed, precisely, to countering the forces of ambition and greed which threatened her frontiers from without and the forces of inertia and disruption from within stemming on the one hand from feudal traditions and on the other from the excesses of the Age of Reason. By the inspired deployment of her extremely powerful individual force she did far more than conduct a holding action which gave her realm a breathing space in a violently changing world. She achieved for her realm of many lands a sort of balance, a synthesis, which was to enable it to survive into the twentieth century as a viable and more or less coherent society.

Perhaps most important of all, she was to offer the world an example of what may be achieved in the way of good guidance by an individual of moderate, peaceable and benevolent temperament standing up against the greed of violent and ambitious men and the impatience of doctrinaire idealists. She was fallible, limited, often blind; but her heart was in the right place and she used her head to obey it. She had the supreme gift of discerning first-class advisers and sticking to them. She was not a leader. She was, as observed, a force, instinctively content to interact with other forces.

All this is hindsight. Maria Theresa did not share it. Her whole life, from the moment of her accession, was spent grappling with the urgent problems of the day, more rarely with those of tomorrow. It was concerned, year in year out, first with the survival of Austria as a power, then with strengthening it, then with the amelioration of the lives of her subjects, then with bringing up her many children. On the face of it, her accession was the start of a new chapter in a familiar story. Neither she nor anybody else in Europe knew that the story she thought she was continuing had already ended.

2

Her inheritance was a dynasty without a firm base. It was not a country, rather a princely house holding disputed sway over many lands and many peoples: Germans, Magyars, Rumanians, Italians, Flemings, a wide and bewildering variety of Slavs. At the time of her accession it included the Germanic hereditary lands, corresponding roughly with present-day Austria in addition to certain areas since lost to Italy and Yugoslavia; the lands of the Bohemian crown, which consisted of Bohemia, Moravia and Silesia; the lands of the Hungarian crown, which included Hungary and Croatia (but not Transylvania, which was governed from Vienna); various minor enclaves in southern Germany, known collectively as the Vorlande; and, more far-flung, the Austrian Netherlands (Belgium), the duchies of Milan and Mantua, together with Piacenza and Parma. Tuscany came to her through her husband. It is worth mentioning at this moment that the capital of Hungary was not then Buda-Pesth, but Pressburg, just across the Danube from Vienna, which is now, as Bratislava, the capital of Slovakia.

'In other countries dynasties are episodes in the history of the people; in the Habsburg Empire peoples are a complication in the history of the dynasty.' This observation by a distinguished English historian is true up to a point; but it would be truer still to say that the Habsburg dynasty differed from others in being a common passage in the history of many peoples. A critical passage into the bargain; some of them it saved, until the age of the dictators, from being engulfed by Germany and Russia, perhaps gave them the necessary maturity to survive the great twentieth-century tidal movements when they came. It is certainly true to say that the Habsburgs themselves until Maria Theresa were interested scarcely at all in the countries over which they ruled. On the part of the monarch there was no sense of identification with the nation. How could there be, when there were so many peoples with such differing outlooks and traditions? The whole contraption of the Habsburg empire was a unique personal estate which took its peculiar colour from two distinct and sometimes contradictory lines of historical development. As a family the Habsburgs, Counts of the Holy Roman Empire with possessions in Alsace and what is now south-east Germany, had a devouring passion for landed property supported by a genius for acquisition. This operated preferably through marriage, which among Catholics was calculable and safe, rather than through war, which was neither. This passion and this genius from 1273 onwards, when Rudolf of Habsburg was crowned Holy Roman Emperor at Aix-la-Chapelle, operated almost without intermission under the aegis of the imperial crown. Beginning with the acquisition of a handful of mountainous provinces roughly identical with present-day Austria, successive Habsburgs, as emperors, set out on their long course of family aggrandisement which culminated in the dazzling imperium of Charles V, who ruled the Netherlands, Burgundy, the Habsburg German lands, Spain, a great part of Italy and the vast Spanish Empire in the Americas. This was too much, even for this extraordinary family; and, after the abdication of Charles V in 1556, Spain and all her possessions went to his son Philip, while his brother Ferdinand I took the German lands and the imperial crown. The Spanish branch went down; the Austrian branch prospered. In those pre-Reformation days the Roman Empire was still a reality, if only a shadow of what it once had been, and the Emperor was a power.

Ferdinand now began the eastward drive and, through marriage, incorporated Bohemia and Hungary into his personal realm. The House of Austria was thus established as a power in its own right. From the sixteenth century it had two main foes: the Ottoman Empire and France. As the defender of Christendom against the Turk Vienna was in the battle-line and the house of Habsburg justified its imperial pretensions. As 'the eternal counterpoise' to France it played a less spectacular but no less vital role. The lines were frequently crossed: thus we find the Christian king, Louis XIV, aiding the barbaric host of Kara Mustapha in the last and most dangerous attempt to take Vienna and destroy the Christian emperor, Leopold II.

The Turkish threat was broken at last in 1683. This was the year of the Turks' deepest, as it turned out their last, incursion into central Europe. They laid siege to Vienna, still as it had been for centuries an outpost city, and for months the armies of Kara Mustapha lay elaborately encamped under the walls of the city which had been founded by the Romans to deal with just this sort of contingency. It looked like the end. But on the very day that they finally broke through the walls succour arrived at the hands of the legendary and brilliant Polish king, Jan Sobieski, and the imperturbable Duke of Lorraine, whose grandson was to marry Maria Theresa. The Grand Vizier's army was destroyed. Fourteen years later in two triumphant campaigns Prince Eugene of Savoy at the head of the Austrian forces took the war into the Balkan strongholds of Islam, won the famous victory at Zenta and captured Belgrade. Although Maria Theresa's father at the end of his reign was to forfeit Eugene's most spectacular gains and ruin the Austrian economy as a result of his ill-advised and bungled participation in a Russian campaign against Turkey, there was no question by then of a renewed threat to Vienna. Austria was no longer an outpost. She was looking westwards. And it was Eugene, in his joint campaign with Marlborough in the War of the Spanish Succession, who turned her into a great power, breaking the pretensions of Louis XIV and establishing the conditions necessary for the victory of England in her struggle with France for overseas empire.

3

It is the War of the Spanish Succession which introduces us to Charles VI, Maria Theresa's father. With the death of the imbecile Charles II of Spain, Louis XIV, then at the summit of his glory, was determined that the Spanish crown should go to his own son Philip. Austria also laid claim to that crown. England could not tolerate a union of France and Spain beneath one sceptre, a union, moreover, which threatened the existence of Holland. Thus the last act of William of Orange was to call into being the Grand Alliance against France which was to bring together the two soldiers of genius, Marlborough and Eugene. Blenheim, Oudenarde, Malplaquet, Ramillies – all the battle honours – and the capture of Turin by Eugene were the milestones of this astonishing campaign. But no sooner did England see France punished than she reacted sharply against a new danger: the accession of Spain to the Habsburgs. She pulled out of the war, leaving Austria high and dry. Certainly by the elaborate series of agreements known as the Treaty of Utrecht Austria won a coveted foothold in Italy (Naples, Milan and Sardinia – Sardinia later exchanged for Sicily – all taken from Spain) and also a white elephant in the shape of the Spanish Netherlands. Her exclusion from Spain was a blessing in the long run, but to Charles it was the hardest blow. He might have said that 'Spain' was written on his heart. As a second son it was to have been his own inheritance. When he was called to Vienna to succeed his elder brother, Joseph, who died suddenly of smallpox in 1711, he was engaged in making a last stand in Catalonia against the Bourbon forces. He left his young wife in Barcelona as a pledge that he would soon be back. But he never went back, and all Spain, including Catalonia, which detested the Bourbons, went to Philip on the understanding that no man should ever be king of France and king of Spain. To the end of his days, however, Charles behaved like a Spanish monarch, and his court at Vienna was distinguished by the stiff Spanish ceremonial. He himself wore the dress of the Spanish grandee: black doublet and hose, black shoes and scarlet stockings. His worrying, alarmist mind found refuge in the sombre impassivity, the unsmiling features, the slowly pacing gait of a Spanish convention which was very much at odds with the less pretentious, more spontaneous mood of the Vienna court; at odds, too, with certain strong elements in the emperor's own character.

He would have been happier as the younger son he was born to be. He enjoyed the graces of life. To look at him on his public appearances nobody would have guessed that this emperor had ever been acquainted with emotions arising from warmth, kindness, impulsiveness. When Jonathan Swift wanted a model for his king of Lilliput he thought at once of the dark features of the Emperor Charles VI: 'His features were strong and masculine, with an Austrian lip and arched nose, his complexion olive, his countenance erect . . . his deportment majestic.' But behind this image of imperial *gravitas* was an odd mixture of timidity and warmth. He had, in the words of Archdeacon Coxe, 'the art of seeming well pleased with everything without so much as smiling once'. He loved music and was an assiduous and by no means ungifted composer, though less accomplished than his father, Leopold II. He had accepted that his marriage must be an affair of state, and he left the choosing of his bride to his father, Leopold, and his advisers. For a variety of reasons they picked on Elizabeth Christina of Brunswick-Wolfenbüttel, a child of fourteen who was to grow into a beauty of extreme tenderness and charm. The two were married by proxy and Charles, in Barcelona, continued placidly in an affair of some standing with the Countess Althan, whose husband was later to exercise a sinister influence at the Court of Vienna. He was prepared to be kind and polite to his young bride when she should be sent out to him, but in the event he was startled by her beauty:

Although on every side [he wrote to Elizabeth's father] I had been told in advance of the exceptional beauty and remarkable qualities of my angelic queen and consort (who is winning all hearts here), now that I have seen her everything that has been said about her is but a shadow devoured by the light of the sun. I have no words to express my exceeding happiness and satisfaction. I shall be eternally grateful to you for making it possible that this angel should become my queen. I only wish she had a consort worthy of her merits; but I will do my best to be to her a faithful husband. The treasure that has been committed to my care shall be truly guarded.

The angel was to have a difficult time. She could not produce a male child (when at last she did, it died) and she was never allowed to forget it. It was not that Charles heaped reproaches upon her: it was, rather, that for years to come, from 1713 until his death in 1740 in fact, the greater part of his energies and ingenuity were directed to the supreme task of achieving a son to succeed him – and, failing that, of ensuring that his line should be perpetuated by his daughter and his possessions settled irrevocably upon her.

But, until the end, he could never bring himself to recognise Maria Theresa, much as he loved her, as his inevitable heiress. Long after it was clear that the unfortunate Elizabeth Christina could never have another child, boy or girl, he went on hoping. Elizabeth Christina was ill: she might very well die; sad though this would be, Charles could marry again, a lusty, younger woman, as young as he could find; a simple, child-bearing girl. But Elizabeth Christina outlived him; and Maria Theresa was called to the throne which, for some time, she had been convinced would one day come to her, but for which she had not been trained. Her father's legacy was a run-down empire and a sacred document. His elder brother, Joseph, high-spirited, quick, imaginative and bold, would have managed things very differently. But he reigned for only six years and had no time to do anything but carry on with the War of the Spanish Succession and, by putting down the Hungarian peasant rebellion, secure Hungary for the Crown. Had he lived, on the other hand, Maria Theresa would never have been Queen.

4

The sacred document which was to secure the Emperor's realm to his successors for ever was known as the Pragmatic Sanction of 1713. This term was used for a certain kind of imperial decree which could be promulgated by the emperor in his own right without the necessity of first obtaining the agreement of the Electoral Diet. There had been other pragmatic sanctions, but the one we remember was devised by Charles VI to ensure European recognition of the indivisibility of the jumble of Habsburg lands and the right of a female to inherit – a specific female, indeed, for one of the articles of the decree provided that his own daughters should have precedence over those of his dead elder brother, the Emperor Joseph I. One of his nieces, thus arbitrarily disinherited, was married to Charles Albert, Elector of Bavaria, who was to dispute the succession and cause Maria Theresa much woe.

Nothing more clearly illustrates Charles's character. In 1713 he was twenty-eight; he had been married for only five years to a beautiful and highly nubile bride, and for more than two of those years they had been separated by the Spanish War. There was then no reason at all to suppose that Elizabeth Christina would not soon bear him a son. Yet here he was, back in Vienna to take over from his brother, fussing like an old man as though the whole future of the realm hung on his infant daughter, as yet unborn. In fact it did thus hang. Charles's fears turned out to be fully justified. Only the method he chose to ensure against their realisation was at fault.

Charles was by all means a failure; but in fairness to him we should remember that the expectation of life was not in the early eighteenth century what it is today. The hazards were various and harsh. His brother Joseph had died at thirty-three. The smallpox might strike at any moment from one day to the next. Not to have had smallpox as a child was at that time a distinct barrier to an advantageous marriage, the risks later in life were so great; for those whose minds were fixed on heirs a wife with a pock-marked countenance was more promising than beauty unscarred. In fairness, also, we should understand what Charles was, above all, trying to achieve. By the time of his death the question of the female succession was indeed all important, but in 1713 it was only secondary. The main object of Charles's magic paper, for which he was made to pay a very high price, was to ensure for all time that the Habsburg lands should be indivisible.

Some such insurance was badly needed, was indeed overdue. As Roman Emperor, which for long had meant no more than Emperor of the Germans, Charles enjoyed great prestige but little real power. To exert the united forces of the Empire he had to carry with him the rulers of many Teutonic fractions, some of them jealous and strong, and such unanimity was hardly ever achieved. As head of the House of Habsburg he had his base in Vienna, capital of an Austria which was only an Archduchy. He was King of Bohemia and King of Hungary only by consent of the Bohemians and the Hungarians. He was King of Naples (until he lost it in 1738) and Duke of Milan only by agreement with the European powers. His Austrian inheritance, which included the dukedoms of Tirol, Styria, Carinthia, etc., he held together under one crown only because his forebears had somewhat belatedly seen the sense of the law of primogeniture and insisted that the head of the House should hold all these lands. There was nothing to stop the fragmentation of the greater part of the Habsburg possessions but the strength, prestige and character of the monarch himself. When Charles died, as the last male Habsburg, there would be nothing to stop quarrels breaking out within the family itself, ending in the division of the Austrian lands; there would be nothing to stop the secession of Bohemia, of Hungary, of the Italian possessions; there would be nothing to stop rival powers from detaching whole provinces, kingdoms indeed, on quasi-legalistic grounds. There would be nothing, that is to say, to stop the total disintegration of the Habsburg inheritance.

This was agreed by Charles's most valued advisers. Incomparably the greatest of these, Prince Eugene of Savoy, diminutive in his grandeur, the saviour of the dynasty, told Charles that he must not set too much store by treaties, which might be torn up: if he wanted to secure the future integrity of his House there was only one thing for it, a full treasury and a powerful army. These things were hard to come by. Charles had little understanding of finance. He had also inherited the family trust in treaties. He made the mistake of seeing himself as a gifted diplomat and a skilled negotiator. He did not see that treaties are licences for the strong, but only traps for the weak.

In the light of what was to happen after his death, it has often been said that Charles's obsession with his Pragmatic Sanction, at which he was to work and worry away for three decades, was wholly wasted effort. No sooner was the young Queen on the throne than signatory after signatory broke his pledged word; the sacred document might never have existed. But in fact it was not wholly wasted effort. Certainly the Pragmatic Sanction proved to be useless in the

European power struggle: it stopped neither the French nor the Bavarians from trying to break Maria Theresa; it did not deter Frederick II (the Great) of Prussia from an act of calculated and unprovoked aggression; but without this document to uphold her the new young queen would have had no firm base on which to stand. She needed, too, as few monarchs needed in those days, the bastion of legality; such was her temperament that in her early days only the assurance that honour and legality were on her side could have given her the strength and fortitude to resist the various pressures, insidious from her allies, violent from her foes, which threatened the Habsburg lands with dissolution. The Pragmatic Sanction proclaimed the unity of these lands: this unity was her inheritance to defend, and all the more so because of the very high price paid by her father – by her husband too – to secure formal recognition of this unity by the European powers and the principalities of the Empire. The Pragmatic Sanction was her fortress and her rock.

But it was also more than this. For the first eight years of her reign she was fighting, first against Prussia, then against France and Bavaria, Saxony, Spain and Sardinia, then against Prussia again. Then there was a lull. She had lost to Frederick the rich provinces of Upper and Lower Silesia, but the rest of her possessions were intact and it was now her great task, with the help of a most remarkable collection of supremely able advisers, to turn the Habsburg Empire into a centralised state with an appropriate bureaucratic machine and a properly organised army – and the schools and academies capable of supplying the needs of the bureaucracy and the army. The formal unity established by the Pragmatic Sanction was the indispensable foundation upon which she was able to construct an organic unity.

Chapter Two

Heiress Apparent

It was not until her nineteenth year that Maria Theresa became a person to be reckoned with. Then, in 1735, foreign diplomats in Vienna began to report with some excitement the rise of a new star. What impressed them above all was the stubbornness and spirit she brought to bear on her father in her determination to marry Francis Stephen of Lorraine, with whom she had been in love since childhood. They say then that she had a mind of her own in other matters too, that although she loved her father she had the clearest eye for his shortcomings, and, though her father might still hope for a son, she herself was already quietly convinced that she would one day rule. In the words of the prosing English ambassador, Sir Thomas Robinson, later Lord Grantham, she was 'a princess of the highest spirit. She reasons already. Her father's losses are her own. She admires his virtues, but then she condemns his mismanagement, and is of a temper so formed for rule and ambition, as to look upon him as little more than her administrator.' The Venetian ambassador reporting at the same time thought that no woman in the world could be so well fitted to succeed her father. No woman in the world could have so humoured her father in his obsession with male heirs without for a moment relinquishing her own claims. She was a model of tact and discretion. But, with all this, 'she never loses sight of her future position, and, when she comes into her inheritance, those who are summoned to her councils will find that the decisions rest with her and not with them'.

The general effect, however, was a good deal more sympathetic than these images of a masterful, ambitious and self-centred young woman could suggest. Masterful she was, but it was not until later that she allowed this quality to show; she would rather plead than command, and she put all her charm and dignity and natural humility into her pleading. Ambitious in the normal usage of the word she was not: she had a sacred inheritance to defend, and she would defend it. She was self-centred only in the sense that she saw herself as the trustee upon whom all depended. The critical eye she turned upon her father, whom she dearly loved, held no malice. She was one of those uncommon creatures who can view with almost perfect detachment the weaknesses and shortcomings of the beloved without being affected by them in her emotions or her conduct. It was to be the same with her husband. She adored him. She discovered his limitations very soon – and still adored him: he was clever in money matters, but he was valueless as a counsellor in affairs of state; more disappointingly, as a military commander he was inept. By the time she was twenty-five the young queen had registered these facts and digested them. She employed her husband's financial talents but looked elsewhere for political advice and generalship. She also found before long that he was fairly systematically unfaithful. She continued to adore him and to make herself available to him every night of her life, consulting, much later, when she found her responses flagging, her celebrated physician and mentor Gerhard van Swieten, who advised her in straightforward terms of a clinical precision undreamt of by bourgeois societies until the advent of Dr Kinsey. She had a passion for staying up all night dancing and playing cards. At a time when outside observers were recording with some awe the toughness and virility of her mind, they were also amazed at the perfect freshness and lack of inhibition of the expression of her love for Francis Stephen. Robinson, who had an ear for Court gossip, after his account of her attitude towards her father, could add: 'Nothwithstanding this lofty humour by day, she sighs and pines all night for the Duke of Lorraine. If she sleeps, it is only to dream of him; if she wakes, it is but to talk of him to the lady-in-waiting.' In little notes to Francis Stephen on the eve of their marriage she would burst out of the frame of formal betrothal, add postscripts of the most tender and eager affection, calling him her 'little mouse' and signing herself with perfect abandonment:

'je vous embrasse de tout mon cœur; menagez vous bien, adieu caro viso

'je suis la votre sponsia dilectissima.'

2

This gifted and extremely complex young woman had behind her a comfortable but lonely childhood. She was born in 1717, two years after the death of Louis XIV in France, and the year of Eugene's capture of Belgrade. She was born in the Hofburg in Vienna, but the best days of her childhood were spent in the Favorita Palace, which she was later to turn into the Theresian Academy, or Theresianum, on a hill overlooking the city and just outside the old walls. Here, very close to the great Belvedere Palace, Lukas von Hildebrandt's masterpiece of baroque, begun three years before she was born and finished in 1723 to house the art treasures of Prince Eugene, her father preferred to stay from early spring until late autumn. It was a good and comfortable home, but she was short of youthful company, the family, for those days, being very small. Her infant brother, the longed-for heir, died when only weeks old. A small sister died at five. This left her with her younger sister, Marianne, as the only children in the nursery. And it was this loneliness which encouraged her when still a child to fall head-over-heels in love with Francis Stephen, the heir to Lorraine, nine years older, when he was brought to Vienna by her father to be educated at the Austrian court.

The first intention had been to marry Maria Theresa to Francis's elder brother, Clement, a youth of outstanding talent and address. Nothing had been formalised when the boy died of smallpox on the eve of his first visit to Vienna. After some hesitation Charles decided to try out Francis instead. Maria Theresa fell in love with him as a child and stayed in love with him as a young woman. As soon as she was old enough to make her views felt she refused to hear of anybody else: but she was given some bad times by her father in his determined search for a better match, any match which would reinforce his Pragmatic Sanction. She knew quite early that her beloved hero was not very good at book-learning. His spelling and grammar were atrocious (they remained so all his life) and the despair of his parents in Lorraine, who feared that his inability to write literate German or French might lose him an empire. But he endeared himself to the Emperor by his keenness at hunting and shooting; the clerks could spell. He was a first-class shot and good at fencing and dancing. He could be relied upon always to keep the Emperor company in the worst weather, rising in the dark to shoot duck in the Danube marshlands, tireless in his riding, passionate for the Emperor's most favourite sport of hawking.

The Court itself was a characteristically Viennese mixture of grandeur and cosiness. The stiff, slow Spanish ceremonial was for show. Off duty there was a good deal of informality and a good deal of boisterous cheerfulness. Papa, the Emperor, was never known to smile in public, but he was kind enough behind closed doors. The private apartments in the Leopold *Trakt* of the Hofburg, called the *Retirada*, were fairly homelike, and the Favorita Palace, on its hill, had a large and pleasant garden with a great view over the city, well-timbered, with bosky grottoes, and two lakes to delight a child. It was here that the Emperor liked to put on his grand alfresco spectacles, which cost more than the privy purse could well afford. Then the larger of the two lakes might be turned into a set-piece for a lavish marine display. In the year before Maria Theresa was born Lady Mary Wortley Montagu attended one of these performances:

Nothing of that kind was ever more magnificent; and I can easily believe what I am told, that the decorations and habits cost the emperor thirty thousand pounds sterling. The stage was built over a very large canal [*sic*], and, at the beginning of the second act, divided into two parts, discovering the water, on which there immediately came, from different parts, two fleets of little gilded vessels, that gave the representation of a naval fight. It is not easy to imagine the beauty of this scene, which I took particular notice of. But all the rest were perfectly fine in

18

their kind. . . . The theatre is so large, that it is hard to carry
the eye to the end of it; and the habits in the utmost magnificence, to the number of one hundred and eight.

Of course, it rained. Only the imperial family was protected by a
canopy. The opera had to be broken off. 'The company crowded
away in such confusion, I was almost squeezed to death.'

The title of that opera was *Angelica vincitrice d'Alcina*, rendered by
Lady Mary as 'The Enchantments of Alcina', and the music was by
the new Court musical director, Johan Josef Fux, the author of the
famous treatise on counterpoint, *Gradus ad Parnassum*, which was to
hold its own for more than a century to come. This sort of spectacle
was one of the last manifestations of that baroque splendour which
transformed Vienna and made the city one of the glories of the
world during the latter part of the seventeenth century. Even as
Maria Theresa was growing up, taste was beginning to change, and
long before she was queen the state of the economy alone forbade the
continuation of such grand extravagance except on the part of the
richer of her subjects.

The enjoyments of her girlhood were more modest. She shot
arrows at a target, but she was not allowed to ride. She was a sensitive
musician. She sang, appearing with other members of the Court and
the imperial family in quite elaborate productions of opera. But she
was more than a tolerated amateur. When, before her accession, she
lived briefly in Florence as Grand Duchess of Tuscany, she performed
in a duet with the famous Italian tenor Senismo, then old (earlier he
had been brought to London by Handel to sing in many of his
operas), who was so enchanted by the beauty of her voice and the
steadiness of her musicianship, that he had to break off in tears.
Quite a number of connoisseurs, Italian and English, with no axe to
grind, reported with astonishment that the young queen in Vienna
sang so well in a voice both strong and fine that she might have made
a career on the operatic stage. She also played the clavier extremely
well. Music was indeed in the blood: Maria Theresa's father had
composed quite well, her grandfather, Leopold II, more than well.
She liked to make a joke of her own musical gifts. Towards the end
of her life she said she must be the first, that is the senior, *virtuosa* in

Europe: her father had put her up on the stage in Vienna when she was only five and made her sing a song.

Virtually nothing is known of the child's relations with her mother. Elizabeth Christina was widely regarded as a woman whose only fault had been that she could not produce a son who lived. She was beautiful before she became very fat, and people spoke of her goodness and sweetness of nature. In a society of extravagant artificiality she preserved a naturalness which was rare indeed, and although the infant Maria Theresa had to be dressed in the manner of the day – her clothes being tiny replicas of the extravagant dresses then in fashion for her elders – little or no attempt seems to have been made by her mother to curb or restrain her childish high spirits: she was gay and exuberant to the point of boisterousness long after she became queen. From her mother, and in reaction from the society which filled her mother's court, she carried into later life her own carelessness in matters of dress. When it was necessary she could make herself look magnificent: with her natural taste and her eye for colour, her striking looks and splendid carriage, she could play anyone else off the stage; but, although she loved pretty things (in the Hofburg treasury there is an artificial posy of precious and semi-precious stones, starred with butterflies and brightly coloured beetles which is one of the most delicious objects ever made), as a rule she could not be bothered with them and, even at the height of her beauty, she must have left less time for dressing than any queen in the history of the world.

It has to be recorded, nevertheless, that the legend of the daughter's warm affection for her mother lacks evidence to sustain it. Indirect evidence, indeed, suggests the contrary. In later life Maria Theresa was to spend a good deal of time carefully recording the characteristics of those closest to her. She was also apt to burst out at any time, in speech or writing, expressing passionate gratitude to those who had helped her most. Not once is her mother mentioned in these or any other contexts. Her sister Marianne she adored, making the warmth of her feeling clear to all who would listen. About her mother she kept silent.

Her education was absurd. It was one thing to have a father who liked nothing better than to play the clavier or conduct whole operas with Maria Theresa and her sister Marianne in the cast. It was one thing to have Hasse and Wagenseil as her music teachers, but none of these had any voice in the dreary hours spent with tutors. These, with only one or two exceptions, were Jesuits. No doubt they were charming men, as Jesuits are; some of them were scholars and pedagogues of extreme distinction, but they worked from the *Ratio Studiorum* of 1599. They must have bored themselves as much as they bored their royal pupil, to judge by the questions and answers in exercise books religiously preserved: Which of the early patriarchs lived before the flood, which after? How much older was Methuselah than Adam? Where do we find a description of the building of Carthage by Dido? On, on and on, as the flies crawled over the window-panes of the Favorita Palace while the sunshine glittered on the lakes outside. There was no attempt at any time to prepare her for the position she must one day occupy – unless one counts the holding up as models of all the princely virtues romanticised images of past German kings. She is supposed to have been especially good at Latin; but here contemporaries who heard her making formal speeches in that tongue were misled by the charm and eloquence with which she spoke the words written out for her by Bartenstein, her first adviser. She had a good delivery and, with her musicianship, a good ear. But to the end of her days her spelling and grammar were wonderfully wild in German and fairly eccentric in French, which she used in almost all her letters.

Of all she was taught, the only things that remained with her were her manners, her music, a certain feeling for Italian poetry and her religion. Here the Jesuits wrought well. They were long past the peak of their influence in Austria, but they still held a monopoly of education. Maria Theresa's faith was absolute, and this was a great part of her strength. She moved and had her being in the festivals of the Church. For her First Communion she was taken to the pilgrimage church at Mariazell, nearly 3,000 feet up in the Styrian Alps, with its miracle-working Madonna to whom her father had prayed for a son. But her faith did not prevent her in years to come curtailing the powers of the Jesuits still further: she would declare her authority over any individual or any organisation which seemed to her to challenge with its pretensions her secular authority; but it is not too much to say that she lived in and through the Church. This had its drawbacks. Thus, for example, her great antagonist, Frederick the Great of Prussia, appeared to her not only as the unscrupulous foe he was but as a pretender in league with the Devil. Thus, too, even in the days of her alliance with England, the English appeared to her as dangerous heretics, to be kept very much at arms' length: she was to be appalled at the prospect of her son, Maximilian, visiting the nest of heretics and risking contamination. To the French King, on the other hand, she had no hesitation in recommending little Marie Antoinette as a suitable bride for the Dauphin. Louis XV, for so long the enemy of her house, was, after all, a Catholic, the Dubarry notwithstanding. The simplicity of her faith was to be a curiously complicating factor in the career of this born diplomat. It was one that lesser diplomats had to grasp as an important fact of life.

3

She was married at nineteen, and her marriage was a victory which cost her husband a good deal. Although since the death of his elder brother Francis Stephen had always been the candidate most favoured by the Emperor, others had thought differently. The various plans put forward, which caused Maria Theresa agonies of uncertainty and apprehension, reflected perfectly the restlessness of an age in which treaties seemed to be made to be broken, in which every ruler went in fear, always justified, that his neighbour had immediate designs on his territory, that his closest ally was about to betray him to the common enemy. Rulers were irresponsible as rarely before. Everywhere but in England the power of the aristocracy was broken, and nowhere but in England was mob opinion yet a force to be reckoned with, or at least evoked. The old dynamic movements had petered out, but the habits of mind produced by those movements still persisted.

After Utrecht, through which England effectively established the balance of power in Europe, there was to be no more question for a hundred years of France pursuing the dream of hegemony over

Europe by, as it were, frontal attack: she still wanted gains, but they must be had on the cheap. England's picture of the power balance was distorted by the overriding concern of George II for the security of Hanover. Nobody, with the exception of the ageing Prince Eugene, perceived the nature of the potential threat to the antique pattern from the rise of Prussia. Spain, in the person of the termagant Elizabeth Farnese, sought furiously to recover the Italian possessions, to say nothing of Gibraltar, taken from her at Utrecht. In Vienna purpose was hopelessly divided. Most of the Emperor's senior advisers looked towards Spain. The Spanish camarilla in Vienna, centred on Count Althan, was indefatigable in intrigue and only overreached itself when it set out to discredit Prince Eugene – at first with some hope of success. The Emperor had always been jealous of the grand old warrior's fame and resentful of his diplomatic acumen and his habit of being almost always right.

At a time when the salvation of Austria depended on a strengthening of the dynasty through absolute loyalty to the house of Habsburg, as opposed to the imperial idea, a large part of the nobility, many of them from families as antique as the Habsburgs themselves, had no desire to assist a process of centralisation which would inevitably lead to increased submission to the Crown. It was again only Eugene, the great outsider, who understood this reality. He had given his life not for the aggrandisement of the Empire but in the service of a dynasty. He would have liked to have seen the Habsburg possessions in the Netherlands, rich as they were, exchanged for at least a large part of Bavaria, thus augmenting the Habsburg heartland and at the same time removing from French influence a neighbour state which had become a Tom Tiddler's ground for Cardinal Fleury's intrigues. It was he, indeed, who gave Maria Theresa one of her bad moments by urging her betrothal to the Bavarian crown prince. Another came from Elizabeth Farnese's determined, but equally vain effort to win her for her son, Don Carlos of Spain.

Throughout all this period of more or less inconsequent manoeuvre almost the only fixed point in the entire European scene – unless one counts France's incessant intrigues among the German states and principalities – was Charles's Pragmatic Sanction. It was indeed a paradox that in this age when treaties were not worth the paper they were written on, when Charles himself had suffered at first hand from the unreliability of allies, a European monarch should have staked everything on paper promises, and on paper paid for very dearly in all directions. Each government which formally recognised the Pragmatic Sanction exacted a very heavy pound of flesh. England, for example, insisted on the dissolution of the Ostend Company, which threatened her own trading activities and was carrying Austrian commerce as far afield as China. It was equally paradoxical that through his fixed idea this monarch, who thought habitually in very broad imperial categories, who never surrendered his claim to the Spanish throne, should have set in motion the machinery which was in effect to transform the Empire as a concept into Austria as a centralised power.

Part of the price that had to be paid for the Pragmatic Sanction was paid by Francis. It was only when his betrothal with Maria Theresa was finally determined upon that the French put a spoke in the wheel. They wanted Lorraine, not to snatch crudely, but as part of a long-term operation. It was first to go to Stanislaus, the exiled king of Poland, whose daughter was married to Louis XV, then to revert to the Bourbon crown. Unless Francis would formally re-nounce his title to the succession France would refuse to recognise the Pragmatic Sanction. But of course she would not dream of making Francis the loser. On the contrary. In Florence the Medici line was on the point of final extinction: in return for Lorraine, Francis should inherit Tuscany.

Francis submitted, as his elder brother would certainly not have submitted. He was not made for conflict of this kind. It had seemed that the world was at his feet. He had lately been leading the sort of carefree existence that most suited him. He had visited the English Court where he had made useful friends and charmed everyone: in London this future Holy Roman Emperor had been inducted into freemasonry by Lord Chesterfield. He had gone on to Berlin to assist at the betrothal of the Prussian crown prince, and he had been him-self charmed and delighted by the man who was soon to emerge as the bane of his adopted home. He had surprised everyone by setting Lorraine's finances in order after his father's death. He was going to marry Maria Theresa, whom he loved. He was to be head of the House of Habsburg, which in future would be known as Habsburg-Lorraine, and he had every chance of being crowned Emperor. Now he was told that all was lost unless he signed away his own people and his own land. His mother was beside herself with fury and indignation; so was Maria Theresa. He was filled with shame at the prospect of surrendering his ancient inheritance into the hands of France. Being caught between the Emperor and the King of France was bad enough; being caught between two women was worse. He did not like being bullied, but bullied he was. He had plenty of spirit but no fighting stamina. The Emperor's only competent adviser, Bartenstein, rude, arrogant, overbearing, clever, but blinded by prejudice, stood over him with the celebrated ultimatum: 'No renunciation, no arch-duchess.' He gave in. It says a good deal for Francis that, as far as is known, he never in later life reproached Maria Theresa for demanding this sacrifice. It is a further indication of her own character that, although she came to detest Bartenstein during the course of this transaction, she later recognised his relative ability and employed him, not with the happiest results, as her mainstay during the first appallingly difficult years of her reign.

It might be thought that the first four years of her marriage were the happiest years of her life. It is to be doubted whether they were. She had possession of her beloved prince, she bore him three children, she had the privilege of royalty and none of the responsibilities of government; but she also found herself in a very hard school. These were indeed the character-forming years. She had to stand by and watch her father frittering away her inheritance in those two un-necessary wars. The children she gave birth to were all girls and she had to suffer her father's frequent outbursts of despair. Francis him-self got off to a very bad start. In 1738 he set off with his brother for the Turkish War, determined to make his name as a commander in the field. It was his first great opportunity and he failed to rise to it. Caught up in the ignominy of defeat, he broke down and returned to Vienna on sick-leave. Granted that he was not a military genius, this was not his fault. Once he had seen with his own eyes the true state of affairs he had done his best to convey to the Emperor the atrocious conditions and the weaknesses of supply and command which made defeat inevitable. He had shown personal courage but none of the leadership, resolution and clear-headedness required by his position. Maria Theresa had to suffer the sacrificial pangs of a bride sending her husband off to the wars, and these were not compensated by deeds of glory.

To the Viennese this failure only confirmed the view that Francis was a nonentity, and a feeble and foreign one at that. To get him out of harm's way the Emperor insisted it was time that he and the Archduchess should make their state entry into Tuscany. The only memorial to that visit, which was very short, was the great triumphal arch put up at the Porta Galla, which stands to this day. The visit was short because Francis was determined to return to the wars and do better than before, while the Emperor was seized with new fears. Supposing he died while his heiress was still in Tuscany? Would dissident elements grasp the opportunity to support the claims of Charles Albert of Bavaria to the Habsburg lands?

They returned to Vienna and renewed unhappiness. The Emperor refused to give Francis the command, and it was just as well. The summer campaign was a disaster, and the war ended with the loss of Belgrade and all Eugene's conquests in Serbia, Bosnia and Wallachia. The Viennese, who had been grumbling dangerously at the cost of the war, now boiled over. There was rioting in the streets and ministers went in fear of their lives. Popular feeling against Francis was more violent than ever before. He was incompetent, he was a coward, he was worse: he was in the pay of the French. (It had been Villeneuve, the French Ambassador to the Porte, who had manoeuvred the unfortunate Marshal Neipperg into disgraceful surrender at Belgrade, and Neipperg was known to be very close to Francis.)

The Emperor was indeed in fear of death. Such was his misery and shame, such his superstitious sense that all hands were against him, that he thought he might die, quite literally, of a broken heart.

So these, for Maria Theresa, were far from happy years. Nobody knows what arguments went on behind closed doors among the family. They must have been bitter at times. With Eugene gone, the emperor was very much under the thumb of Bartenstein, who was above all intent on appeasing the French. Not because he loved them but because he would have nothing to do with England after her treachery at the end of the War of the Spanish Succession. It had been Eugene who suffered most acutely from this treachery; but Eugene was a statesman and understood that France would never rest until she had undone Austria, no matter how benignly Fleury might smile, and that Vienna's only and natural ally was and must be England with her almost infinite financial resources, her great sea-power, and her ineradicable and inevitable rivalry with France. He was big enough to put his personal humiliation on one side and work for an even closer alliance with the English. Bartenstein was not. He was the sort of man who smarted for ever for revenge and allowed his emotions, misleadingly behind a front of icy calm, to wreck his judgment. He was also one of those strange but frequent creatures, the arch-flatterer and intriguer who is himself everlastingly deceived by flattery and intrigue.

Francis Stephen saw all this and argued as best he could to per-suade the Emperor. Maria Theresa naturally supported him. But publicly her conduct and bearing was impeccable. She gave no out-ward sign that she was aware of her great destiny. She formally sub-scribed, without a murmur, to an article in the Pragmatic Sanction which cut herself and her children out of the succession should her father yet achieve a male heir. She was later to say, and truthfully, as far as her future subjects were concerned, so long as the emperor was alive, no one as much as looked at her. Francis was unpopular: he talked and gesticulated like a Frenchman. She was nothing: rather the Bavarian elector as ruler than this chit of a girl. She was treated with a lack of consideration which was as abominable as it was shortsighted: on her way to Florence, six weeks after childbirth, she was held up for a fortnight in freezing lodgings at Verona in mid-winter because of quarantine regulations. But she bore it all with perfect dignity. Always she held herself back, whether in Vienna, in Pressburg, in Florence, allowing Francis Stephen to stand forward. For the greater part of these years she lived in her father's house, constantly subject to his moods of fury and desperation. There was plenty to cloud the relaxed enjoyment of submitting herself to her husband's will, the enthusiasm with which she threw herself into the business of bearing his children, helping him to shine, and com-forting him in adversity. There was a great deal of conscious waiting and watching – and learning. She learnt a good deal about her husband, whom she continued to adore as the illusions were stripped from her. But the one thing she could not learn was the mechanics of government. From this field her father excluded her entirely, so that when he died, after violent convulsions, and very bravely in his lucid intervals, as a result of chill and exhaustion in the hunting field, all she knew about government was that she was Queen to command.

Chapter Three

The Clouds Gather Round

The young Queen had no Melbourne to teach and advise her as she faced for the first time the task of being a ruler. But indeed, even a Melbourne would have been insufficient here. She needed, rather, a Disraeli: ten years were to pass before she found one. To begin with she had to make do with the material to hand. She was given scarcely two months to find her feet before she was all but overwhelmed by the first act of violent aggression, the start of an often desperate battle for survival which, with more or less intensity, was to devour most of her public energies for eight often desperate years. Because of this she turned very naturally to the few who were tough and possessed of fighting spirit, even though she had to put up with a good deal at their hands, and even though their conduct *vis-à-vis* both Austria and the outside world landed her in quite unnecessary difficulties.

She began with nothing but her character, her good nature, her religious faith, and her sense of the sacred nature of her imperial inheritance. She believed in the pledged word, in treaties, in loyalty, in goodness. She trusted in God. Her very gaiety and lightness of heart came from this trust. She had nobody but God to fear, and God she strove to obey. She did not take herself very seriously: then and for a long time afterwards she was the despair of those who demanded pomp and circumstance. Throughout her reign, she liked to disconcert the disapproving and delight her friends with a sudden, slyly cheerful remark in deprecation of her exalted self. Her duty, on the other hand, she took very seriously indeed. In this she was exactly opposed to her ministers, who took themselves more seriously than their duties — about the nature of which, moreover, they tended to be unclear.

She was given time for nothing. With his last hopeless military adventures her father had indeed run the Empire into the ground. Many years later, in one of her celebrated Memorials, recollecting peril in tranquillity, she was to complain of her father's failure to induct her into even the rudiments of politics and statesman ship. 'In these circumstances I found myself without money, without credit, without an army, without experience and knowledge, even without counsel, because all my ministers were wholly occupied in trying to discover which way the cat was going to jump.' She had nobody at all among her senior ministers who could advise her intelligently, which was why, very soon, she decided to repose her trust in the man who was technically only the secretary of the Secret State Council, Johann Christoph von Bartenstein, the son of a Strasburg University teacher, a born Protestant, whom she at first detested because of his arrogance, his ill-nature, his pompous schoolmasterly ways and his bullying of her husband in the matter of his renunciation of Lorraine. What she did not see was that precisely these qualities were also detested by those whose help she needed, above all the English, who found themselves sorely tried by this prosing, conceited little man, with the tight mouth and the popping eyes, who thought that diplomacy consisted in arguing like a seminarist, in making debating points, in forcing ideas down the throats of ambassadors and foreign governments. But at least Bartenstein had courage and resolution in adversity, and courage and resolution were qualities Maria Theresa needed above all. She continued to believe in God, but when God appeared to be on the side of Frederick of Prussia and Louis XV of France, as well as a choice assortment of minor jackals, she needed human help as well.

Her council of state must have looked to this imperious but diffident young woman of twenty-three like something out of a nightmare. Its members appeared to be embalmed. At first sight one might have said that their only distinction was that none of them had died of smallpox. Certainly from her first minister, or chancellor,

Count Sinzendorf, she received no comfort at all. He had immense experience, in the sense that he had been at the heart of European affairs for half a century; but experience teaches nothing to a fool and Sinzendorf in statesmanship was nothing but an extremely *rusé* fool. His chief skills lay in the direction of corrupt practice in the grand manner, particularly the exploitation of his high position to extract money and perquisites from friends and enemies alike. That position he owed to secondary talents for flattery and short-term intrigue. The Emperor Charles, to whom he owed his advancement, knew all about him and all about his background. Sinzendorf's father, the Emperor Leopold II's minister, had been broken and deprived of his estates for corruption and treachery. But the son was amusing and useful and seems to have been regarded by Charles with a sort of lazy contempt, as a foil to the demanding directness and honesty of Prince Eugene whose tiny but overwhelming presence filled the emperor with a sense of his own inferiority. Sinzendorf had been on the Spanish payroll; he had extracted grants from Lorraine in return for his championship of Francis Stephen's marriage with Maria Theresa; Maria Theresa herself was to suspect, more than suspect, that he took bribes from Frederick of Prussia, her arch-foe. In her memorandum, already cited, she was to say that she had never been able to trust him and that his relations with Prussia had been 'incorrect'. But she needed him as the man who knew all the tricks and had been at the centre of power long enough to show her the ropes. He was to die quite soon, rich and outwardly honoured. So perhaps he was not a fool after all. Yet who but a fool could have been at the Court of Versailles, as ambassador, in the time of Louis XIV, without understanding that Cardinal Fleury was not only the most gifted living statesman but also an intriguer who could outmanoeuvre a dozen Sinzendorfs before breakfast?

Fleury, now a very old man, was by all means intent on preserving peace; but he was still increasingly active in the interests of France, as expressed particularly in the weakening of Austrian influence in Germany. Sinzendorf thought he could manage France. He confused diplomatic scheming with policy. He was quite unable to perceive (he was not alone in this) the absolute validity of Eugene's policy of alliance with British sea-power, an alliance to be cultivated cost what it might and regardless of personal humiliation, the only security against French ambition. Instead, he was ready to turn from England and pin his hopes to Spain which he still thought of as a power. Superficial, irresponsible, the model of senile vanity, he was the last man in the world to serve as mentor, right hand, and stay of an honest and passionate young queen.

The only man she found she could trust absolutely was her finance minister, Count Gundacker Starhemberg. He was honest, loyal and steady. He also understood money (he had been head of the Vienna City Bank); but he, too, was old, seventy-eight, at that epoch antiquity itself. His understanding of politics had never been great, and his services to Charles had been chiefly financial and administrative. He had done his best to make the Emperor see (working with Prince Eugene, whom he disliked) the need to turn the monarchy into a more centralised state, and he had been staunch for the alliance with the Maritime Powers. But now he had shot his bolt, and his judgment was clouded by dabbling in the quasi-occult. These were the outstanding personalities. In addition there were the two Harrach brothers, Aloysius and Joseph, men of great wealth and ancient family, the first concerned with domestic affairs, the second president of the War Council: Charles had appointed him when the equally ancient Fieldmarshal Königsegg had been put in charge of the army in the field. There were not many to choose from, the Emperor had observed to Francis at the time. In fact he was better than most. Königsegg himself was still about and a member of the War Council, even though he had barely escaped a court-martial for his share in the Turkish débâcle; but as he spoke little and was incapable of committing himself in any discussion, nobody, apart from Francis Stephen, who liked him, ever listened to what he said. The two Harrachs were seventy-two and sixty-nine respectively, and Königsegg was older still. This is no denigration of age. Frederick the Great, Napoleon, Stalin, Mussolini and Hitler were all young, or youngish, when they appeared on the world stage – enough to make one think twice about the glorification of youth. But the young Queen's ministers were third or fifth-raters, and all were deeply embedded in the past. Between them, the members of this cabinet or conference had helped Charles to ruin Austria.

It was not merely that there was virtually no centralised administration. All the affairs of the realm were disastrous. Less than 100,000 florins were available to the young queen; the national debt was beyond reason; the sources of royal income – mines, timber, etc. – were mortgaged up to the hilt; loans from the great nobles had been spent. The army was supposed to number some 160,000 men in time of peace. Now it was barely half strength and neither officers nor men had been paid for several months. In the Turkish War sickness and disease had killed far more than had died in battle. Now in peacetime desertion was never ending. Most of the army was still in Hungary; the lesser part was scattered in small garrisons from Milan to Brussels, from the Tyrol to Bohemia and Silesia. When Starhemberg exposed these facts to Maria Theresa she kept a brave face, but when he had gone she was found by her lady-in-waiting, the Countess Fuchs, in tears.

Throughout the Habsburg lands disaffection was acute. It was to be expected that the Hungarians would think of seizing the occasion to start a fresh insurrection. But the trouble went deeper than that. In Vienna itself, among the common people, there was a widespread feeling that the Habsburgs and the Hofburg had had their day. Nobody really believed that the Emperor's daughter, this chit of a girl, could rule effectively: if she kept her throne it would be as her husband's consort, and the Lorrainer was disliked and distrusted: he was still thought to be under the thumb of France. Charles Albert of Bavaria, a good German, and married to a Habsburg, seemed the obvious person to carry on the great imperial tradition: he was strikingly handsome and also well liked. His own agents, and Fleury's agents too, swarmed in the city and the countryside, putting it about that Maria Theresa was under her husband's thumb and that Francis was no better than a traitor. Charles Albert seemed the obvious bet for all those who wanted security and peace. In the outlying provinces, of course, the common people hardly knew Austria from Bavaria, while the great families, who owed their positions, their privileges and their wealth to the Habsburgs, were already seeking to hedge their bets, to reinsure themselves. When, just under a hundred years later, after the crushing of the 1848 revolution, there was a move to set up a responsible upper chamber, the great aristocrat and prime minister, Prince Felix Schwarzenberg, replied:

> I consider it impossible to instil into our aristocracy true vitality and much-needed resilience, because, to this end, not only respectable individuals are called for, but also a politically trained, well-organised and courageous class. This class we lack completely. I do not know of more than a dozen men of our class in the entire monarchy who could in the present circumstances serve profitably in an upper chamber.

This appalling indictment of his fellow-nobles from the saviour of the monarchy was more or less deserved. With notable exceptions, the great landowners of the hereditary lands used the monarchy to secure their privileges and, ruling themselves like monarchs in their own territory, gave little or nothing in return. Hungary was a special case. The Hungarians had managed to hang on to their ancient ways under centuries of Turkish rule; with the Turks pushed back by the imperial armies, they proposed to go on as they had done before: only a handful of the greater magnates had the wit to perceive that, on the lowest level, Habsburg rule, intolerable as it might be in some respects, was at least a guarantee of survival. The most selfish and irresponsible of all – again with certain splendid exceptions – were the Catholic nobles of Bohemia and Moravia who had received colossal grants of land from Ferdinand after the Battle of the White Mountain which had destroyed the Protestant nobility. Their debt to the throne was absolute and comparatively recent. Instead of riding them on a tight rein Maria Theresa's predecessors, over several generations, had lavished privileges upon them. Now they had forgotten that they owed anything at all. So long as they were allowed to continue in undisturbed possession of their estates, their serfs and their wealth they did not care who was emperor. Some concealed their thoughts; others were shameless. A little later, when the young Queen was fighting for survival, one of the grandest of them had the effrontery to apply to the Queen whose cause he had sworn to uphold for a special dispensation: would she graciously, he petitioned, allow him to safeguard his Bohemian estates by acknowledging Charles Albert of Bavaria as his rightful sovereign? It was as though a divisional commander asked permission to desert in the middle of a battle. Those who deserted without asking permission at least showed the courage of their convictions.

It was no wonder that Maria Theresa wrote in later years: 'I do not think anyone would deny that history hardly knows of a crowned head who started his rule under circumstances more grievous than those attending my accession.' It was no wonder, either, that she turned to Bartenstein, who was at least industrious, competent and not primarily engaged in furthering the interests of his own relations and connections at the dynasty's expense.

She understood neither finance nor politics nor war; but she had seen what had happened to her father, who understood far more than she, as he moved through his last years with his head in the clouds, surrounded by a rabble of flatterers and deceivers. She was determined to understand all these things. Finance, for the moment, she left to Starhemberg and Francis, who had a head for business. To get the army behind her, as a first step to increasing it, she proclaimed immediate amnesty and reinstatement for a number of senior commanders who had been languishing in prison as a punishment for their share in the surrender of Belgrade. The amnesty was just, since her own father had been chiefly to blame for the disasters of the Turkish War; the reinstatement was more dubious. Wallis, the commander in that campaign, had the sense to retire to his estates; Schmettau entered the service of Frederick of Prussia; Seckendorf, who had been a successful general in his time, offered his services to Charles Albert of Bavaria, who was already preparing to contest Maria Theresa's succession. Nothing offers a clearer commentary on the Hofburg's lack of moral authority than the behaviour of these brave soldiers towards the young Queen to whom they owed their release from the damp and gloomy fortress at Peterwardein on its rock above the Danube opposite Novy Sad. Only one, Marshal Neipperg, very much a broken reed, who had actually negotiated the surrender of Belgrade, eagerly welcomed the opportunity to resume active service, with results most acceptable to Prussia, lamentable for Austria.

To get the people on her side Maria Theresa performed an imaginative act. It had been a terrible and dreary autumn, and the harvest everywhere was ruined. The peasants were hungry and desperate. One of their chief and most bitter complaints was that their meagre substance, what was left of it, was being consumed by the game which swarmed on the vast Crown estates for the delectation of the late emperor and his hunting companions. The young Queen shocked her entourage by giving orders for the immediate wholesale slaughter of the birds and animals — deer, wild boar and hares — so sedulously preserved by her beloved father.

She knew just how the people were grumbling. She had known of their discontents during all her father's 'last ten unhappy years', she was later to write, 'just as any private person would, without knowing whence they came, or what their causes were'. Now, to find out, she went behind her ministers and sent one of her ladies-in-waiting, Elisabeth von Friz, out into the streets, heavily cloaked, to mingle with the people and report what she heard in the way of grumbling and criticism, active sedition, too. In the days when ladies-in-waiting were never allowed into the city on foot, but went always in a carriage from the royal mews, chaperoned at that, this was a bold initiative. The people, she learnt, had nothing against her specifically, but her husband was distrusted and despised. Thus she knew already if she had not known before, that it was imperative for her to make it clear to all the world that she the Queen was the ruler. There would be time, later on, to make Francis Emperor and compel the people and the world to do him homage. Meanwhile she insisted on formally proclaiming him co-regent, an appointment without precedent — indeed, against the spirit of the Pragmatic Sanction.

It was not much that she could do in those first weeks. She was already looking out for a confidential adviser, and she knew the man she wanted. But at least she was clearing the decks for action when it came.

2

It came almost at once. All eyes were fixed on Bavaria, now challenging the succession on the strength of an ancient claim, which, when the documents were at last rooted out and examined, was proved to be unfounded. There was much despondency and alarm about the attitude of Versailles. Fleury, to the great consternation of the old men in Vienna, had omitted to declare his adherence to the Pragmatic Sanction. When pressed, he offered the insolent excuse that he had been searching the protocols in vain for the proper method of addressing the queen of Hungary. London was characteristically evasive. Newcastle, indeed, while proclaiming England's friendship with the house of Austria, made no reference to the Pragmatic Sanction and said 'the only attachment we have to the court of Vienna is on account of preserving the balance of power in Europe'. This was in contradiction to the observation of George II, who declared his intention of honouring 'the engagements I am under'. Only Holland, Russia, the joint kingdom of Saxony-Poland, Venice and the Vatican seemed willing to declare themselves unequivocally.

Only a few months before Maria Theresa's accession in Vienna the young Frederick had succeeded his intolerable father, Frederick William, in Berlin. Nobody foresaw the least danger from Frederick, widely known as the crown prince who despised warlike things and loved the arts of peace. He was a philosopher of sorts – at least the patron of philosophers; he wrote a great deal of bad verse; instead of reviewing troops he played the flute. He despised the Germans as uncouth barbarians and romanticised the culture of Versailles. Francis Stephen, attending his wedding in Berlin, had been enchanted by him and thought of him as a friend. More than this, Frederick owed a profound debt of gratitude to Austria: both the Emperor and Prince Eugene had protested sharply to Frederick William about his treatment of his son. The Emperor, moreover, had secretly advanced money to him.

Frederick William himself could, indeed, have been a great nuisance to Austria had he so desired. Besides establishing the Prussian economy and Prussian society very firmly on the lines first laid down by the Great Elector, he endowed his kingdom with the best disciplined and most coherent fighting force in Europe. But although grossly violent in temper and unrelievedly autocratic in his own household, he was clear-seeing and long-headed as a statesman. His only extravagance was the formation and nourishment of his famous grenadiers, a regiment of giants. These he drilled to the highest pitch of precision, but he would have cut off his own right hand rather than risk losing one of them in battle. He was not a coward. He had fought at Malplaquet. But he knew Prussia's limitations. And although he sensed that his small and scattered kingdom was moving towards the day when it would have to challenge Austria, that day was not yet. Even though, with some reason, he considered himself tricked by the emperor in the matter of his claims to two duchies on the lower Rhine, Berg, with Düsseldorf, and Jülich, he swallowed the pill. Prussia's continued existence depended on calculating manoeuvring between the great European powers – Hanoverian England, France, Austria and Russia. Furthermore, his resentments notwithstanding, he always considered himself a loyal servant of the Emperor and could never have contemplated open and armed defiance of his imperial master.

This attitude, together with enlightened domestic policies – the establishment of schools, the freeing of serfs, the efficient ordering of finances – was in perfect contrast to his ungovernable rage when crossed by those who owed him subjection and obedience. When Frederick, whom he regarded as soft and frivolous, showed his natural stubbornness by refusing to resign his rights to the succession, he fell upon him and nearly strangled him to death. When, as a result of this, Frederick tried to run away to Paris and was caught, he was tried by court martial and sentenced to death. The crown prince's companion, Katte, was actually beheaded outside Frederick's cell, and Frederick, compelled to watch the execution of his friend, fainted away.

If anyone might be expected to turn out a neurotic it was Frederick, and he amply fulfilled such expectations. After a period of rigorous imprisonment he understood that to survive in future he had to keep his thoughts to himself and outwardly obey. The climax of his obedience was his marriage at twenty-one to the unfortunate Elizabeth Christina of Brunswick of whom he wrote, before he had even set eyes on her, 'I pity the poor creature; there will be one more unhappy princess in the world.' He did his best to behave well by this colourless, timid, but gentle nonentity. 'I should be the most contemptible of men if I did not sincerely respect my wife; for she is the gentlest of creatures and is always seeking to please me.'

But he drew away from her with increasing aloofness and there were no children. In later life, he made it a rule to change out of his thigh-boots once every year to appear at his wife's court on her birthday.

But at first his marriage had its uses. It enabled him to set up house at Rheinsdorf and, forgetting his father, develop his own inclinations. It was at Rheinsdorf that he emerged as the philosopher-prince and developed his courtship of Voltaire, the start of a relationship which, far from spreading sweetness and light, was to bring out the worst in both men. It was here, too, that he scribbled away at his first writings (apart from the poetry which Sainte-Beuve characterised as his greatest sin): *Considérations sur l'Etat politique de l'Europe* and *L'Antimachiavel*. Both revealed the activity of a cool, calculating and original mind, sceptical and detached, showing an understanding of European politics remarkable in one who had been excluded by his father from any induction into affairs of state and was supposed to be an aesthete. *L'Antimachiavel* in particular, setting out the duties of a sovereign seen as 'the first servant of his people' should have been taken as a warning. While purporting to attack Machiavellian principles, it did nothing of the kind. On the contrary, it showed a perfect mastery of them. The only difference between the aspiring counsellor of Florentine princelings and the heir to the throne of Prussia was that the one concentrated on problems of government and aggrandisement in terms of an individual ruler, the other in terms of the hypothetical good of an individual state – the good of the state, of course, was what the ruler thought it was. It included, in Frederick's case, the aggrandisement of Prussia by whatever means came to hand.

His ambitions were strictly limited. He was determined to round off the Prussian estate sufficiently to make it permanently viable and to distinguish it sharply from the ruck of German electorates and principalities. It was already a kingdom; but its soil was thin and arid, its natural resources rare; and, scattered in its component parts, it was highly vulnerable. Prussia was to be the lodestone and leader of Protestant Germany, independent of the Catholic nexus in the south: indeed, but for the Reformation, it would never have got itself on the map as, in the current jargon, a historical necessity. But there was not even the faintest beginning of an idea in Frederick's mind of using Prussian power and Prussian aggrandisement to unify the limbs of Germany on racial or German nationalist lines.

To a perfectly reasonable desire to make Prussia large and powerful enough to establish and preserve its independence was added the personal and emotional determination of the young Crown Prince to make his mark on history (he was twenty-six). And it was one of those remarkable historical accidents that brought this misleading young man with a passion to prove himself to the throne in the very year that Vienna, his chief obstacle, was to be thrown into confusion by the premature death of the Emperor Charles. Frederick succeeded in May 1740; Maria Theresa in October.

Even while Charles was still emperor, Frederick knew what he wanted to do. He had spent long hours studying the map of Europe and working through past protocols and agreements. The emperor's questionable faith in the matter of the duchies of Berg and Jülich gave him a legalistic pretext for seeking a quarrel with Vienna; but what he wanted was Silesia, or part of it, conveniently adjacent to his own territories, relatively advanced in industry, rich in agricultural and mineral wealth, the most valuable province of the Habsburg Empire, but cut off from Bohemia by the difficult country of the Riesengebirge; it was Protestant into the bargain. He also had to guide him a document of which Vienna was happily unaware, nothing less than the Political Testament of the Great Elector, written down in 1672 and lost until nine years before Frederick came to the throne: here, a clear signal from the great Founder, was a plan for the conquest of Silesia.

The emperor died on October 20th. Immediately Frederick, guessing the state of panic in Vienna, guessing that other predators would at once be contemplating moving in to the kill, decided to act. 'It is only a question of executing designs I have long had in mind,' he wrote. And indeed he had already reorganised his army on a regional basis to make for the swiftest possible mobilisation. He had become his own foreign minister, though still using Podewils, inherited from his father, as his instrument. But he gloried in secrecy and dramatised and romanticised his own cunning, that first infirmity of the dictatorial mind: having nobody to answer them back dictators have to be constantly proving to themselves that they are

cleverer than other men, a necessity which soon leads them to
practise cleverness for its own sake. Thus Frederick on the necessity
for secrecy on the part of the ruler: 'If I thought that my shirt or my
skin knew anything of my intentions, I would tear them off.'

Only Podewils and his most trusted general, Schwerin, were told
of the plan to seize Silesia. They counselled circumspection, an
initial minor demand to Vienna, reinsurance all round. Frederick
was bolder.

Silesia is the portion of the imperial heritage to which we have
the strongest claim and which is most suitable for the House of
Brandenburg. It is consonant with justice to maintain one's
rights and to seize the opportunity of the Emperor's death to
take possession. The superiority of our troops, the promptitude
with which we can set them in motion, in a word, the clear
advantage we have over our neighbours, gives us in this unexpected emergency an infinite superiority over all the other
powers in Europe. If we wait until Saxony and Bavaria start
hostilities, we could not prevent the aggrandisement of the
former, which is contrary to our interests. If we act at once we
keep her in subjection and by cutting off the supply of horses
prevent her from moving.

And so on. England would counterbalance France; Holland would
not care; Russia would find herself embroiled in Sweden. . . . It was
all very carefully thought out. But nobody, least of all in Vienna,
must suspect. Even while he was deploying his army and giving it its
operation orders, he went through an elaborate show of diplomacy, a
finished operation in deceit. To Francis he wrote:

The great loss which your Royal Highness has suffered through
the death of the Emperor arouses my deepest sympathy. This
event will unsettle the affairs of all Europe, and its consequences
will be the more dire for its unexpectedness. You are aware of
the great esteem in which I hold you and the deep friendship I
have always felt for you. In accord with these sentiments, I beg
your Royal Highness to look upon me as your good and tender
cousin.

He went on to assure his support for Francis's claim to the imperial crown. Francis was moved. It is clear that Frederick was intent not only on putting Marie Theresa off her guard, but also on driving a wedge between her and Francis. Maria Theresa herself was alive to the danger very soon. As early as November 19th, long before Frederick ceased insisting on 'the purity of my intentions' in repeated letters, she was writing to the Austrian ambassador in Berlin in the blunt way which was to become so familiar, but which must have been startling indeed to the men of affairs who thought of her as an innocent young girl: 'In the interest of a proper understanding you had better realise that nobody is to be trusted less than a Prussian.'

By the end of November all the world knew that the young Prussian King was brewing mischief. His troop concentrations could not be concealed, but their purpose was disguised by deceptive movements. Not a word was breathed about Silesia. Fleury, exploiting Frederick's friendship with Voltaire, despatched this sycophant of genius on what was ostensibly a personal courtesy visit, really to spy out the land and report on Frederick's intentions – which, however, Voltaire was unable to penetrate. England initiated probing enquiries, only to be snubbed, Frederick drawing himself up to a great height and rejecting the envoy's questioning as an impertinence. Finally Maria Theresa acted and sent Count Botta as her personal envoy, to find out what was going on. Botta could guess even before he reached Berlin: he had to fight his way past immense convoys of Prussian troops blocking all the roads in the direction of Silesia. Even so, Podewils was affability itself, professing his master's desire for everlasting friendship with Vienna. Botta reached Berlin on December 1st, and did not receive audience of Frederick until five days later. But by December 6th matters could be concealed no longer. A week later, as the envoy prepared for his departure, Frederick at last declared himself. 'Sire!' exclaimed Botta, 'you are going to ruin the House of Austria and at the same time destroy yourself.' 'It depends entirely on the Queen,' said Frederick, 'whether she accepts the offers I have made her.'

It was not enough for Frederick to march without a declaration of war, thus establishing a precedent which was to end in the ruin of

Germany, though it was not until just over two centuries later that the second part of Botta's prophecy was fulfilled. He had also to pretend that he was doing nothing of the kind. His envoy, Gotter, did not reach Vienna until Frederick had already crossed the Silesian frontier. He was received in private audience not by Maria Theresa, who was heavily pregnant with the child who would one day be emperor, but by Francis Stephen, as her consort. He presented himself and his master as Austria's saviour. 'Sire,' he declared, 'I am come with safety for the House of Austria in one hand and the Imperial Crown for your Royal Highness in the other. The troops and treasure of my master are at the service of the Queen, and cannot fail of being acceptable at a time when she is in want of both and can only depend on so considerable a prince as the King of Prussia and his allies the Maritime Powers and Russia. As the King, my master, from the situation of his dominions, will be exposed to great danger from this alliance, it is hoped that, as an indemnification, the Queen of Hungary will not offer him less than the whole Duchy of Silesia.'

Gotter then went on to spoil the effect of this preposterous communication by immediately exposing the threat: 'Nobody is more firm in his resolutions than the King of Prussia; he must and will enter Silesia; once entered, he must and will proceed; and, if not secured by the immediate cession of that province, his troops and treasure will be offered to the Electors of Saxony and Bavaria.'

Frederick had, of course, already entered Silesia, and was proceeding. For what followed we have to rely on Prussian and Austrian accounts, which, not unnaturally, differ. The Prussians said, in effect, that Francis wavered, grasped at the chance to come to an agreement by making concessions, and was only stopped when Maria Theresa, who had been listening behind a door which stood partly ajar, suddenly appeared and announced that it was time for supper. The Austrians record that Francis behaved with perfect hauteur. The Queen, he said, no matter what she herself might feel, had no power to alienate even the smallest fraction of that estate which had been handed down to her, under strict entail, as an indivisible whole. Further, beset she might be, but she was not reduced to that condition in which she might be expected to treat with an enemy in the heart of her own lands. He left it to Gotter to say that it was time for him to go. 'Have your troops actually entered Silesia?' he then asked. Gotter replied that they had. 'Go then,' said Francis Stephen, 'return to your master and tell him that while he has a single man in Silesia we will rather perish than enter into any discussion.'

Whether Francis wavered or not, this was the message he finally delivered.

Gotter was surprised, as so many Germans thereafter were to be surprised when, having stamped on their neighbour's foot, they were answered back. He was also deeply put out that he had not been received by Maria Theresa, only by her consort, who, still more surprisingly, had not embraced Frederick's offer to back his claims to the imperial crown with proper gratitude. When he reported to Berlin the Prussian ministers were also surprised and embarrassed. They had, in fact, advised Frederick to proceed more subtly; but it was too late now. Though they suggested compromise and an abatement of immediate demands, Maria Theresa stood firm: so long as Prussian troops stood on Silesian soil, she would not treat.

Not that Frederick wanted to treat. He did not have to fight for Silesia. He had 40,000 beautifully trained men; in the whole of Silesia Austria had 6,000 with no commander-in-chief. The rest of what remained of her army was scattered and incapable of rapid concentration. The first Silesian campaign was not a war, it was robbery with violence.

It made everybody think again. The English were perfidious; the French deceitful; every monarch in Europe was more or less unashamedly on the make. But hitherto their shadiest activities had been concealed and to some extent inhibited by the observance of certain forms unthinkingly taken for granted as desirable and necessary unless the dynasts were to destroy their own trade union. Frederick's rape of Silesia proved that, whether desirable or not, such observances were no longer necessary. This, though shocking and unsettling, opened up new vistas. Things were never to be quite the same again. So much so that the time was to come when a Scottish sage, one of the loftiest formers of opinion at the height of the Victorian age in England, could hurl contempt at all those little men, milk-and-water moralists, who presumed to question the hero's actions, could hold up Frederick as a model of the great ruler and justify his morality in terms that even a Goebbels might have hesitated to employ:

> Opportunity, rushing hitherward, – swift, terrible, clothed with lightening like a courser of the gods; dare you catch *him* by the thunder-mane, and fling yourself upon him, and make for the Empyrean by that course rather? Be immediate about it then; the time is now, or else never! – No fair judge can blame the young man that he laid hold of flaming Opportunity in this manner, and obeyed the new omen. To seize such an opportunity, and perilously mount upon it, was the part of a young magnanimous King, less sensible to the perils, and more to other considerations, than one older would have been.

And again:

> 'Never was such dissimulation!' exclaims the Diplomatic world everywhere, being angered at it, as if it were a vice on the part of a King about to invade Silesia. Dissimulation, if that mean mendacity, is not the name of the thing; it is the art of wearing a polite cloak of darkness, and the King is little disturbed what name they call it.

This was Carlyle, preaching the doctrine that might is right. All the same, even Carlyle saw fit to omit from his account both the matter of Frederick's ultimatum to Vienna and his letter to George II of England, his uncle, assuring him that he was marching into Silesia only to prevent others getting there first and stating categorically: 'I have no other purpose than the preservation and the real benefit of the House of Austria.'

'Gentlemen,' he addressed his troops, as they set forth leaving him to follow, 'I am undertaking a war in which I have no allies but your valour and your goodwill. My cause is just; my resources are what we ourselves can do; and the issue lies in Fortune. . . . Farewell, Gentlemen! To the rendez-vous with fame, whither I shall follow you without delay!'

Allies, in the technical sense, he certainly lacked; but there were no big battalions against him and he knew that his flanks were secure. Any doubts about Russia had been conveniently set at rest by the death of the Empress ('The Empress of Russia is at death's door, God favours us and destiny is on our side'). France, in a quiescent mood, was most unlikely to attack him yet: anything that reduced Austria as a rival was welcome to her, and neither Louis nor Fleury could at that distance foresee, any more than Frederick himself, the results that were to flow from the seizure of Silesia and the arrival of Prussia as an independent power. Frederick could write to Voltaire immediately after the Emperor's death:

I believe there will be, by June next, more talk of cannon, soldiers, trenches, than of actresses and dancers for the ballet. This small event changes the entire system of Europe. It is the little stone which Nebuchadnezzar saw, in his dream, loosening itself, and rolling down on the Image made of the Four Metals, which it shivers in ruins.

He saw far. He saw farther than any contemporary European; but he saw darkly. Sadowa and Sedan and what they stood for had no part in his remotest dreams. As for England, recently embroiled in the War of Jenkins's Ear, the real overture to that vast and muddled process which was to bring Asia, America and Africa into Europe, he knew very well that George II feared far too much for Hanover to start fighting Prussia. As for Austria, he was committing a limited assault on her, and she would hit back. He thought he could hit harder, and he was right. It was as simple as that.

We thus come back to Macaulay, so different from his fellow-Scot and yet in some ways so much the same.

The selfish rapacity of the King of Prussia gave the signal to his neighbours. The whole world sprang to arms. On the head of Frederick is all the blood which was shed in every quarter of the globe. The evils produced by his wickedness were felt in lands where the name of Prussia was unknown, and in order that he might rob a neighbour whom he had promised to defend, black men fought on the coast of Coromandel and red men scalped each other by the Great Lakes of North America.

Two sorts of humbug, the one, Macaulay, seeking a scapegoat for the failure of humanity to order its ways in decency and cope with vast, incoherent, unfathomable pressures too complex for any man to grasp; the other, Carlyle, determined not to be humbugged by cant and moralising attitudes, and ending by humbugging himself. Which is worse?

Macaulay cheated too – to make a point? To make a phrase? It was not true that Frederick, or his father, had pledged themselves to defend the house of Habsburg; they had only promised to recognise the indivisibility of its estates. Nevertheless, in general Macaulay expressed well enough the situation as it should have been and as poor Maria Theresa saw it when, shocked and affronted, she saw the very foundations of her inheritance threatened by the incredible behaviour of this Hohenzollern upstart who smiled as he struck. Writing of the Pragmatic Sanction, seen as a voluntary agreement embracing the whole civilised world, Macaulay went on to declare:

> Even if no positive stipulations had existed, the arrangement was one which no good man would have been willing to disturb. It was an arrangement acceptable to the great population whose happiness was chiefly concerned. It was an arrangement which made no change in the distribution of power among the states of Christendom. It was an arrangement which could be set aside only by means of a general war. The sovereigns of Europe were therefore bound by every obligation which those who are entrusted with power over their fellow-creatures ought to hold most sacred to respect and defend the rights of the Archduchess. Her situation and her personal qualities were such as might be expected to move the mind of any generous man to pity, admiration and chivalrous tenderness.

Frederick was not alone in lacking qualities of this kind. France and Bavaria, others too, watched intently to see what would happen and which way to move. England showed herself a broken reed. Through her ambassador, Robinson, she brought heavy moral pressure to bear on Vienna to seek an accommodation with Berlin, not out of tenderness for Maria Theresa, but, rather, to damp down a continental explosion in which England herself might be involved.

But George II at least acknowledged his obligation and assured Vienna that he would indeed fulfil his engagements. Maria Theresa wanted 12,000 troops immediately: these, the English promised, would certainly be forthcoming if all attempts at mediation failed. By that time the Prussian troops were all over northern Silesia, and there they stayed.

Chapter Four

Rape of Silesia

The most striking aspect of Frederick's first Silesian campaign, the opening move in the War of the Austrian Succession, which was to drag on for seven more years, was the smallness of the means employed as the instruments of furious change. Even at Mollwitz in April 1741, one of the critical battles of the world, Frederick brought only 23,000 men and 53 guns against the Austrians' 16,000 men and 19 guns. When these forces had been shattered in head-on collision neither side found itself capable of contemplating another battle for some time to come. It all boiled down to a matter of hard cash.

On the Austrian side, to the lack of resources was added ineptitude. What army existed was hopelessly scattered. The commanding general in Silesia was Lieut.-General Maximilian von Browne, one of a line of Irish soldiers in the service of Catholic Austria, who had already distinguished himself under Prince Eugene and now found himself in acting command of an area of 16,000 square miles. He had just 3,000 troops when danger first threatened, and it was only by a tremendous exercise in self-help that he managed to scrape together from Bohemia enough men to double this force. He had no artillery at all, apart from a few museum pieces (the whole army had only forty guns); and the picturesque old fortresses on rocky pinnacles commanding the broad highways of the river valleys of the Oder and the Neisse were falling to pieces and decrepit to a degree. It was not only that Browne himself was convinced of Frederick's intentions long before the Vienna cabinet suspected them: Prussian agents were busy spreading the rumour throughout his command that Vienna was preparing to cede Silesia to Prussia.

When at last the cabinet in Vienna understood that the worst was happening, the mood of the old men was such that still no sense of urgency influenced their actions. Thus, for example, even when the invasion had begun and reinforcements were being sent, the desperately needed Hungarian hussars were held up by quarantine regulations at the frontier of the province they were racing to defend. It was in this spirit that the young Queen, soon to show herself passionate and impatient to the point of recklessness, was forced by her advisers to go to war. It is easy to understand how in later years she could write of those old men: 'If God Himself had not arranged for the death of them all I should never have come through.'

Meanwhile at least she had in Silesia a commander of initiative, quick perceptions and strong character who neither repined at the hopelessness of his position nor feared to tell the Court at Vienna the true state of affairs as he saw it:

> I must humbly beg Your Royal Highness [he wrote to Francis on 11th December] to be good enough to hasten the despatch of the considerable reinforcements we need here in order to comfort the frightened and allay the suspicions of the simple-minded. I make bold to report to Your Royal Highness that by this means we may silence the talk that stems from the belief that we have arranged to cede Silesia to the Prussians: a belief founded on the knowledge that for a month now we have known for sure of the enemy approach and their imminent invasion of our territory, and have yet taken no counter-measures.

He knew that the most he could do was to conduct an operation of harassment and manoeuvre. Coming against him up the river valleys was an army of 27,000 Prussian troops, backed by a rearguard of 12,000 — all immaculately drilled, fresh and equipped to the last button. He had to keep his own forces intact, to maintain, so far as he could without his main body being entirely cut off, footholds based on strongpoints throughout the province, command of sufficient areas for forage, all pending the time when the main army being collected in Vienna would come to his assistance across the snowy mountains and drive the Prussians out.

He did well in quite impossible circumstances. 'The whole land rejoices at our arrival and is only afraid that we shall leave,' Frederick exulted to his brother, Prince Henry. This was going too far. Browne was immensely helped, and his very survival made possible, by the friendliness of the peasants, largely of Polish stock, who might have been forgiven for welcoming the conqueror. But, while the people remained loyal, the nobility, true to form, behaved outrageously. Browne himself wrote to Francis Stephen: 'From all outward appearances we can promise ourselves nothing but good from the country people. I only wish we could be sure of the same from the whole of the nobility.'

And then there was the Breslau fiasco. 'If we hold Breslau, there is nothing more to fear, and we shall retain the mastery of the province.' But here the Prussian agents had been very active indeed. Breslau, the capital, called by Frederick the finest city in Germany, was a free city, and refused to admit the small garrison proposed by Browne, even though it was commanded by a Silesian officer, even though it would be withdrawn when the emergency was past. In due course authority arrived from Vienna: Browne could take what action he saw fit to compel the magistrates of Breslau. But it was too late. Breslau, with magniloquent deceit, had announced that it would defend itself with its own resources. These were nil. On January 3rd that city made its submission and sent out food and supplies to the invaders.

Browne at this time, and for many years afterwards, was to show himself a commander of great gifts. He did wonders at keeping his tiny army intact, retreating with extreme skill and never exposing his detachments to envelopment, though he had his work cut out to persuade some of his junior commanders to renounce immediate glory in favour of living to fight another day. But he was severely hampered by instructions from Vienna. Maria Theresa, who in years to come was to see him as a man above all others to be relied upon, now knew of him only what her senior advisers cared to tell her; and here she was badly served. She herself had the right instincts. In Marshal Khevenhüller she had one senior commander who had

shown himself not only successful in battle but also, supreme gift,
lucky. To her the obvious thing was to make him commander-in-
chief on the Silesian front and give him all the troops that could be
quickly scraped together. But she found herself up against a coalition
to which, in her inexperience, she felt compelled to bow. Prince
Kinsky, her Bohemian chancellor, the vice-regent for the war zone,
backed by her own husband, vehemently insisted that Marshal
Neipperg, just out of prison, should be placed in command; Khevenhüller could look after the Austrian forces watching the Bavarians,
so far passive.

The reasons for their insistence on Neipperg's preferment had
nothing to do with the immediate necessity of defeating Frederick.
They illuminate the essentially frivolous spirit in which the men
around the young Queen approached what to her already appeared as a
struggle for survival. Francis Stephen, who had been largely responsible for Neipperg's rehabilitation after his release from prison, gave
his backing to this most unsatisfactory soldier for purely personal
reasons: Neipperg had been his tutor when he had been brought from
Lorraine to the Vienna court, and the tutor had known how to
please the future husband of his future Queen. To this long-standing
affection was added a feeling of guilt on Francis Stephen's part. He
must have known very well that Neipperg had shown himself a
mediocre commander in the Turkish War and a disastrous negotiator
at the time of the surrender of Belgrade. He must have known that
Neipperg was eaten up with conceit (when he had gone forward to
negotiate with the Porte he had deliberately cut himself off from all
communication with his own headquarters and from Vienna) and
was one of those vain, weak men, indecisive in attack, but liable to
sudden panic actions when beset, masquerading as a bold and
resolute cutting of losses as part of a calculated plan. But he also
knew that the main blame for the Turkish campaign and its miserable outcome lay firmly on the shoulders of his father-in-law, the
Emperor, who had made Neipperg and others the scapegoats for
his own failure.

Kinsky's motives were less creditable. It is on record that he
favoured Neipperg above Khevenhüller for the Silesian campaign for
one reason only: he feared that Khevenhüller would fight too hard,

seeking battle where he could most advantageously find it, regardless of the incidental damage inflicted on the countryside – his, Kinsky's, countryside. Whereas Neipperg could be relied upon to temper his zeal, fight like a gentleman, keep his sense of proportion, and steer the fighting away from the vast estates of Kinsky and his friends. The matter was in any case decided when Khevenhüller, who was not a sycophant but a gifted professional soldier, asked for more men, and the money to pay them, than existed. Neipperg asked nothing. Like Kinsky, who had blackmailed himself into the War Council, he thought it would be an easy matter to knock out Frederick.

Once in command, he busied himself quite effectively, but with no sense of urgency, with the task of mobilising a powerful army to take the field in the following spring. To this end he required Browne to content himself with a holding action, even when his forces had been doubled and strengthened altogether disproportionately by the arrival of two regiments of Hungarian hussars, which, with what he had, gave him a very marked superiority in mobility over the more stolid Prussian forces. Neipperg saw that he did not use them. He sent out his own man, Major-General Lentulus, to keep an eye on things – a gifted but inexperienced officer of inferior character, who was one day to desert Vienna for Berlin. The Lentulus episode was to be repeated in remarkably similar circumstances over a century later, when Lieut.-Colonel Beck was sent out from Vienna to harass poor Benedek on the eve of Prussia's final victory over Austria at Königgratz, Sadowa. Lentulus was full of brilliant ideas, none of them relevant to the task in hand, some of them plain silly. 'The people who suggest such ideas,' wrote Browne, 'should also be the ones who are expected to carry them out. . . . I am confident that I myself would have been able to devise many seemingly fine projects in a short time – as long as someone else would be prepared to carry them out.'

Neipperg and Lentulus could think only of cordoning off the mountain passes and standing firm behind artificial barriers. Browne, with his splendid new cavalry eating their heads off, was sure he could cause Frederick a great deal of trouble:

The enemy quarters in Silesia are scattered to such an extent that it would not be costly to destroy them one after the other, but as my hands are so tightly bound, and General Neipperg insists so emphatically every day upon the conservation of the troops without incurring any risk, there is no possibility of gaining an advantage, and I dare undertake nothing.

The Queen was a fighter too. We can guess from her later attitudes towards dilatory generals that her heart must have bled as she sat with the War Council and listened to Neipperg and others smoothly or angrily explaining why her gallant and enterprising General Browne must be put firmly in his place. Almost the only thing that can be said in favour of Neipperg was that he did not take umbrage at the repeated complaints from his subordinate in the field. When, in March, he at last arrived at Olmütz, the great fortress on the Morava river, to assume command, he made an ungrudging demonstration of friendship and trust, and the two men immediately set about devising a plan to cut the Prussian forces in two.

It was a good plan. The Austrians descended from the hills of the watershed down the Neisse valley weeks before Frederick was expecting them, and in sufficient force and with a boldness of manoeuvre to lend desperation to his own reactions. So far he had had things so much his own way that he had come to take his own security too much for granted. He reacted well. With Schwerin he came tearing in from the west, while Neipperg, his movement terribly hampered by the bottomless mud of a sudden thaw, hesitated in front of Brieg. Neipperg's plan had been good and bold; but now once again he panicked and decided that there were big forces in front of him at Ohlau on the Breslau road. There were not. But this hesitation gave Frederick time to cut across the Neisse and come up behind him. Movement was easier now. It had frozen again, and there was much snow to confuse the Prussians in their deployment among the wooded hills to the south-east of Mollwitz. Neipperg now acted decisively and turned his whole army round to face the threat to its rear faster than Frederick could deploy his blue columns into line of battle. This brought Browne, who had been commanding the left wing, into the place of honour on the right, and he had hardly completed his manoeuvre before the Prussian artillery opened rapid fire against Romer's cavalry, who charged furiously and shattered the horse of the Prussian right. Such was the shock, such the confusion, that it looked like overwhelming victory for Austria. The Prussian cavalry fled, and with them went Frederick himself, borne away, with death in his heart, on the horse which Voltaire was later to remark had been his only friend. Twelve miles he rode, without drawing rein. At Oppeln, where he thought he would find haven, he ran instead into a detachment of Austrian hussars, who all but took him. 'Farewell my friends!' he cried to the little company riding with him, 'my horse is better than yours!' And off he rode into the night.

Meanwhile, unknown to the King, Prussian defeat was being turned into Prussian victory. The superb training of Frederick William's infantry was paying its first dividends. When the Prussian cavalry broke and fled it had all seemed over. But suddenly, uncanny in their force and symmetry, rank on rank of blue-coated infantry loomed up through the smoke of battle, unyielding, unbudging. Three times the Austrian horse hurled themselves at this phalanx, three times they were beaten off. The Prussian foot were unbreakable. They were also terrifying with the coolness and steadiness of their musketry fire. They did not, in fact, inflict many casualties. Their shooting, rapid, was also wild, they opened fire much too soon for killing effect, but they made a great noise and advanced quite steadily despite heavy casualties. It was the turn of the Austrian cavalry to break, and it fled in disorder, leaving the field to a brand-new body of troops, a new arm, which had never fought before, but which, first in dark blue, then in field grey, was to dominate the battlefields of Europe for nearly two centuries to come. Early next morning, Frederick, staggered by the news that he had won a battle, rode back from Neisse, where he had spent uneasy hours, to take his place at the head of his conquering army. He had lost his philosopher friend, the French mathematician Maupertuis who was captured, half-dressed, and borne off in triumph to Vienna, but he had won his first battle. Out of this farce, on April 10th, 1741, a new power had emerged and the balance of Europe was destroyed.

2

The shock of Mollwitz to Maria Theresa was profound; its effect on the powers galvanic. Until this moment Maria Theresa and the more sanguine of her advisers had taken it for granted that Neipperg, with his great effort, would run the Prussians out of Silesia. The bitterness in the young Queen's heart had been due not at all to fears for the loss of Silesia, once Browne had shown that he could hold the fort until Neipperg's arrival, but to Frederick's treachery and to the necessity under which he placed her of fighting a war, and paying for it, when Austria so desperately needed peace and inspired retrenchment. On the eve of Mollwitz the prospect had seemed fair. The Austrians had concluded an amicable arrangement with Turkey. They expected help from Russia. Saxony, they thought, would rally to their side, fearful and jealous of the growth of Prussia. France still spoke fair words. England, after months of delay, must surely at any moment make up her mind and honour her obligations.

It was all delusion. England, indeed, saw clearly enough what Maria Theresa's advisers should have seen — that France was making active preparations for war, that nobody could count on Russia, that the Dutch, as usual, were arguing among themselves: in a word, that a prolongation of war between Austria and Prussia would so weaken and expose Austria that France would be tempted to strike. London knew very well that Paris had worked out an elaborate plan for the effective dismemberment of Austria. Bohemia and Upper Austria were to go to the Elector of Bavaria, who would also be crowned Emperor; Moravia and Upper Silesia were to go to Augustus, Elector of Saxony, in his capital at Dresden; Lower Silesia and Glatz were to go to Prussia; the whole of Austrian Lombardy would go to Spain.

This was not a wild dream; it was a carefully considered plan. The trouble was that like all such carefully considered plans to rearrange large areas of the globe in the interests of a single power, it ignored the human element. Like all those who seek to buy allies with promises calculated to appeal to immediate self-interest, Fleury allowed himself to forget that people know why, and in whose interest, they are being bought. On the face of it, however, the plan was good enough to cause England grave concern. If the Habsburg Empire could be reduced to the rebellious kingdom of Hungary and a handful of mountain provinces, France would be supreme in Europe and a deadly threat to England and her possessions overseas. There was thus every reason for London to urge poor Sir Thomas Robinson in Vienna to make one more supreme effort to mediate between Maria Theresa and Frederick. The surrender of part of Silesia to Prussia, particularly since it would cost England nothing, was an insignificant price to pay for the preservation of the great bulk of the Habsburg inheritance and a firm alliance with Prussia.

This was the situation as England saw it on the eve of Mollwitz. After Mollwitz it was plain to everyone. It was the supreme moment for the latest French fire-eater, Marshal Belle-Isle, who had been for long engaged in ardent and tortuous intrigue to persuade Louis and Fleury that war was more glorious than peace. He could now demonstrate that it could also be more profitable. Louis XV, who had idly remarked that Frederick's invasion of Silesia was the act of a madman, and Fleury, now in his eighties, were dragged behind his chariot. Belle-Isle himself broke loose and careered across Europe to concert his plans with Frederick in his camp at Mollwitz.

Maria Theresa was now entirely alone. All those advisers who had refused to believe that Paris could betray Vienna were thrown into panic. Francis Stephen himself now urged her to give in and seek an accommodation with Frederick. Pressure from England was intense. Upon her head and hers alone rested the responsibility for decision, and she had to achieve the impossible: to see her way through one of the most complicated and threatening diplomatic operations in the history of modern Europe.

What was she to make of Frederick? She had had one taste of his perfidy. Now, determined to cling to his gains, but genuinely disturbed by the prospect of French hegemony in Europe, jealous, too, of the proposed elevation of the Bavarian elector and the aggrandisement of both Bavaria and Saxony, he appeared once more with soft offers. He turned to England. The Queen of Hungary (he called Maria Theresa the Queen of Hungary as long as he lived) must be made to understand her danger: if Vienna refused to entertain his offers of accommodation he would have no choice but to ally himself with France. In the end, desperate and bitter, Maria Theresa gave her consent in principle for negotiations. But nobody knew what Frederick was demanding, what Maria Theresa would concede. George II took it upon himself through Lord Hyndford, his ambassador in Berlin, to offer three duchies in Silesia: Glogau, Schweibus and Grünberg. Not enough, said Frederick: it might have been enough once. And, in any case, you offer only a single duchy, since Schweibus and Grunberg are really part of Glogau. Must I fight again? Then, you will see, I shall take all Lower Silesia, including Breslau. 'No, my lord. And do not talk to me of magnanimity; a prince must first consult his own interests. I am not averse to peace; but I expect to have four duchies, and I will have them.' He would not say which four duchies he meant.

Maria Theresa, oppressed by the burden of her inheritance which she alone could sustain, sickened and overwhelmed by her first steady look at the chicanery and greed upon which all empires have been founded (her own, of course, was the gift of God), finding no help in her husband and her antique ministers, rebelled. If that was how it was, she would make no cessions in Silesia. What business, anyway, had the English King to have offered even as much as Glogau? She would buy Frederick off. He could have a sum of money. He could take a part of the Austrian Netherlands. But no more talk of Silesia.

So it went on—until, on June 5th, Frederick signed his treaty with France. The news came direct to the queen from George II, then on a visit to Hanover. It came with instructions to Robinson to make the most urgent representations to Maria Theresa, to get firm proposals from her, to take these at once to Frederick before the treaty could be ratified.

She was in Pressburg, after her coronation as queen of Hungary. Sir Thomas Robinson was received in audience. The queen heard him out as he read his prepared statement. She said not a word. She was tired of Robinson, who had once assured her that nothing was farther from Frederick's mind than the invasion of Silesia – and then, when it happened, had urged her to come to terms. Here he was again, reflecting as always the split between Walpole's cabinet and the King, reflecting also the King's changing views about the safety of Hanover *vis-à-vis* Prussia. She listened; then, when he began to support his prepared statement with arguments, she broke out, interrupting him 'with exclamations and sudden starts of passion'. Robinson, who admired her profoundly (some said that he was in love with her, and he probably was in his unheroic way), was deeply moved. Under extreme pressure she at last felt compelled to show willingness to negotiate; but, in her heart, she intended to stand firm.

> Not only for political reasons, but from conscience and honour, I will not consent to part with much in Silesia. . . . No sooner is one enemy satisfied than another starts up; another, and then another must be appeased, and all at my expense. I am convinced of your good will, but I pity you. Your mission to Silesia will be as fruitless as that of Count Gotter was here; remember my words.

Chapter Five

The Queen Commands

It was in the course of this interview that Maria Theresa began to rule. She could not carry Robinson, but she carried her advisers. She was, when all was said, Queen. She had been ready, she had been anxious, to defer to the wisdom of the old men while she learnt from them. But she was not obliged to do anything of the kind. She could, and would, command. And so she did.

After her outburst to Robinson everyone round her sensed that this was so. The only hope of those who had been urging accommodation, or appeasement, was her husband, Francis. But Francis himself, when he saw her determination, felt unable to argue any more. He was still a suspect figure in Vienna; he was known to have a special tie with Frederick; when he saw that his wife would not give in, even though it meant sacrificing Frederick's much-needed support of his candidacy for the imperial crown (which she desired for him above all other things), he knew that for him to speak out now would lay him open to a charge at least of gross self-interest, at worst of treachery. Thus he made the best of a bad job and stayed silent. So, when they saw their young Queen's resolution, did Sinzendorf and all the others. A command was a command; they could not cross their Queen without in effect abandoning her and laying themselves open to the charge of desertion.

Thus, already in the early summer of 1741, Maria Theresa had taken charge. Her observation, quoted above, to the effect that had death not taken Sinzendorf, the Harrachs and Starhemberg away she would have been finished was not strictly the truth. These men still remained in office until, very soon, they died; but she had already bypassed them. Advisers, instruments, men who knew the ins and outs of European diplomacy, she still needed. But from now on she used them. To Bartenstein alone she listened, now her most devoted champion. Sinzendorf no longer counted, and when he died she showed her contempt for his tradition by appointing Count Ulfeld to succeed him as chancellor, the merest figurehead, a caretaker chancellor as we might say, whose chief distinctions were a wardrobe magnificent even for those days and an infinite capacity for getting into debt: this talent was to prove useful when, later, Maria Theresa wanted to get rid of him: she simply bought him out by paying off his debts. Prince Kinsky, Count Heberstein and Count Joseph Harrach were now her chief instruments. They gave her a difficult time between them, but she ruled them superbly. With her un-inhibited vitality, her carelessness of convention, went a charm that was clearly irresistible, a spontaneity and ease of manner unheard of in a Habsburg, a feminine appeal which she exploited to the full but which was so natural and softened by self-mockery that it was never vulgar. Her beauty and her softness she owed much to her mother, who had captivated all hearts. Her natural shrewdness and the edge to her tongue came from the long line of instinctive rulers who had always known how to deflate the pretensions of their most exalted subjects, even when these were richer than they themselves.

She had, indeed, a tongue. When Bartenstein had prostrated himself before her, on her accession, knowing that she detested him, ready to throw in his hand, she had told him to get up and said: 'You had much better stay and try to do what good you can; I shall see to it that you do no harm!' He was thenceforth her slave, dependent utterly upon her to shield him in his subordinate position from the jealousy of the ministers, his nominal superiors, focusing upon her the devouring need of an arrogant but inwardly insecure soul to identify itself with a cause, in his turn quickly winning her profound admiration for the energy, industry, ingenuity and resolution upon which he had based his astonishing career. He became in her eyes the perfect faithful steward, ugly, rough, misunderstood, worth all her elegant courtiers put together. The very qualities which made him useless, dangerous, indeed, as a diplomat and a statesman, were precisely what she needed in the struggle with Prussia, which had reduced itself so quickly to the simplest terms.

One of the most striking aspects of these early years is the way in which this young Queen, whose temper could be the sweetest in the world, surrounded herself with angry men. Kinsky, Heberstein, Bartenstein himself were all furiously bad-tempered men, liable to be thrown off course in all ordinary dealings by their jealousies and rages. But the dealings she demanded of them were not ordinary: all she required was men who would stand up not only to Frederick but also to the persuasions of all those who wanted her to yield. She found them. Kinsky was particularly notorious for his rages and his arrogance. A Bohemian landowner on a spectacular scale, he had had things his own way all his life. Nepotism had given him an early start, and for a long time it looked as though this handsome, hot-tempered, overbearing man considered the very appearance of work to be beneath him. As Austrian ambassador in London during the War of the Spanish Succession, still in his twenties – at a time, that is, when Marlborough and Eugene were working together like brothers and the Austrian court was closer to England than ever before or since – Kinsky distinguished himself by his almost total omission to keep his monarch informed about English policies and moods. Twice, at least, Eugene himself, who respected his gifts, addressed fatherly letters of stern reproach. Now, as Bohemian chancellor, he managed his vice-royalty well in the interests of Vienna, and, in spite of his determination, mentioned earlier, to keep the fighting away from his own properties, he became single-minded to the point of recklessness in his support of Maria's anti-Prussian stand. She had her hands full with him, and knew it. He showed his ill-temper not only to his subordinates: he showed it also to her. But she was sure of his loyalty and respected his independence of mind. The lightness of touch with which this inexperienced girl managed one of the rudest and most arrogant men in Europe comes out to perfection in her famous note of reproach after an unusually stormy and tiring session: 'Dear me, what mutterings and ugly faces. . . . Stop making the poor Queen wretched and help and advise her instead.' He, too, became her slave.

How she could reward and inspire the more simple-minded who only wanted to serve her is best shown in an equally famous letter of 1742 to General Khevenhüller, who had just taken Munich at the very moment when its ruler was being crowned emperor in Prague. With the letter went a portrait of herself and the infant Joseph:

Dear and faithful Khevenhüller – Here you behold the Queen who knows what it is to be forsaken by the whole world. And here also is the heir to her throne. What do you think will become of this child? To you, as a true and tried servant of the State, your most gracious lady offers this picture of herself, and therewith her whole power and resources – everything indeed that her kingdom contains and can do. You, the hero and trusted vassal, shall dispose of all things as you think fit and according as you would render account before God and the world in general. May your achievements be as renowned as those of your master, the great Eugene, who rests in God. Be fully assured that now and always you and your family will never lack the grace and favour and thanks of myself and my descendants. A world-wide fame will also be yours.

Fare well and fight well.

Maria Theresa.

She sent that letter to Khevenhüller at his headquarters in Linz by her husband's own hand. That night the general gave a banquet to Francis, who sat among his officers. Khevenhüller read the letter aloud and produced an emotional outburst of loyalty. The officers, who hardly knew their Queen, were now her slaves. Next day the portrait was shown to the troops, with no less effect. Maria Theresa had done the right thing. But it was only the right thing because sincerity and spontaneity shone through what might have been an artificial gesture. Herself moved to tears by Khevenhüller's loyalty to what must have seemed a lost cause – and it was he who had been passed over for the Silesian command at the end of 1740 – she showed him, and his officers, a glimpse of the entrancing and irresistible young woman who, a few years earlier, the grandest princess in Europe, had written to Francis himself:

Dear Sweetheart — I am under endless obligations to you for sending me news about yourself, because I was uneasy, like a little dog, about you. Love me and forgive me that I do not write more, for it is ten o'clock and the messenger is waiting. Adieu, my little mouse, I embrace you with all my heart. Take good care of yourself, Adieu sweetheart! I am your happy bride.

2

She needed all her charm and resolution. Mollwitz was the precipitant which set all Europe in motion. A more experienced ruler might have recognised the danger signs and made large concessions to Frederick with the idea of winning back later what had to be surrendered today. He would have recognised the limited nature of Prussia's ambitions and, weighing them against the totally destructive aims of Bavaria and France, the half-heartedness of England, the uselessness of the Dutch, the embarrassment of Russia (embroiled by French intrigues in a war with Sweden), the fence-sitting of so many German princes, the undying bitterness of Elizabeth Farnese, would have treated immediately with Frederick as the lesser evil. An accommodation with Prussia would have been perfectly in keeping with the ideas of the times. European wars in the eighteenth century were not moral crusades, rather they were dynastic and economic expedients. Nationalism and its consequences in the way of mass armies and unlimited wars lay in the future. In any case, there was no Austrian nation. In a sense it could be said that Maria Theresa, behind the times in her belief in honour, was in advance of her time in injecting into the War of the Austrian Succession the sort of spirit which was later to express itself in nationalism and unconditional surrender. 'The resolution of the Queen is likewise taken; and if the house of Austria must perish, it is indifferent whether it perishes by an elector of Bavaria or by an elector of Brandenburg.' It was magnificent, but was it statesmanship?

Critics have said no. They have said this because, instead of manoeuvring, Maria Theresa met her enemies head on. And, in the end, after six years of fighting and a great deal of bloodshed and destruction, she finished up all the same with the loss of Silesia to Prussia. She might just as well have recognised that loss, or a part of it, after Mollwitz, and secured in Frederick a strong ally against Bavaria and France and his vote for her husband as Emperor.

But what sort of an ally would Frederick have been? And what sort of guarantee could he, or anybody else, have given her that she and her reduced empire would be left in peace? Further, she believed that the voluntary cession of any part of her realm would release all the signatories of the Pragmatic Sanction from their bond. The Sanction itself would be null.

Nobody would pretend that this angry, desperate young woman had then developed anything faintly resembling a coherent foreign policy: so far as she knew she was following her duty and her impulse, to stand in arms against all the world rather than yield, as a woman, a fraction of her inheritance. Nobody would pretend that her mainstay in this resolve, her Bartenstein, had anything faintly resembling a clear picture of the forces at work in Europe: he was moved by personal resentments, vanities and loyalties. Nevertheless, Maria Theresa's instincts were correct and her immediate reasoning was fair enough. The diffuse and muddled conflict between 1741 and 1748 is known as the War of the Austrian Succession. But, in fact, there were three wars. There was the war for Silesia (falling into two separate parts), which at first had nothing to do with the great challenge to the succession as such; and, after Mollwitz, this war seemed far from lost. In itself, and apart from its effect on the rest of Europe, Mollwitz could not then be seen as a decisive victory, and the Austrian forces which successfully outmanoeuvred Prussia in the south were expected to win the next battle when it came. Then there was the war with Bavaria, backed by France and Spain. The challenge to the succession as such came not from Prussia but from Bavaria. And when at last Charles Albert marched on Linz and, from St Pölten, opened a direct threat to Vienna, the whole realm was at stake.

Neither Maria Theresa, nor anybody else, could see in the Silesian War the first act of the great drama of the Hohenzollern challenge to the Habsburgs which would reach a climax in 1866 with the victory of Prussia at Sadowa, Königgratz. It was enough that she saw in

Prussia an imperial province in which insolent pretensions were allied with dangerous power which it would be fatal to acknowledge by a policy of appeasement. By now, too, she at last bitterly understood that war was indivisible, that she was on her own, that England, at least for the time being, and no matter what she might promise or even perform, was not interested in Austria for herself, or even in treaty obligations, but only in Austria as a pawn in her interminable struggle with the French. The fate of the Pragmatic Sanction had shown her that her faith in treaties was a snare. There was only one way to assert her sovereignty, and that was to fight for it until by her resolution and success in arms she compelled respect and won allies from among the wavering. If God willed it, she would lose. Treaties, the Pragmatic Sanction itself, were useless as bonds; but she could not have fought as she did had she not believed that God would punish those who broke them. This was a great strength.

She had to give way, all the same. The way she did so exhibited a new strand in her character. With all her natural honesty she was also an accomplished actress: she knew how to dissemble. As we shall see, most of those close to her, ministers, family, advisers, were never to grasp this point: they took her moods, her sulks, her impetuosities, her shatteringly blunt outbursts, at their face value. This is far from saying that her emotions were not strong: indeed they were; they could be cyclonic; but she also knew how and when to project them with the most telling effect.

After Mollwitz, during the rest of April and the whole of May 1741, she allowed herself to hope. A Turkish delegation came to Vienna to ratify the Treaty of Belgrade, and the Porte, full of its own troubles and happy enough to have pushed the Austrians out of Serbia, seized the opportunity to close the account: the Queen of Hungary need expect no further violence from her eastern neighbours. This was an immense relief. Her sense of gratitude to Turkey was to endure throughout her reign, and flare up with dramatic effect thirty-two years later.

Immediately afterwards a Hungarian delegation arrived to invite her to come to Pressburg to be crowned. This seemed to augur well. Maria Theresa had not had time to think about the Hungarians, but she at once applied herself to learning what she could of their history and their complaints against Vienna. She also took riding lessons, shocking her entourage by insisting on riding astride and making her ladies do the same; all wore chamois leather breeches and boots under a long skirt. It was a fashion she was to stick to; because although she learnt to ride only so that she might be able to appear at her coronation in Pressburg in the traditional way, riding became a passion with her.

She soon learnt that the murmurings of the Hungarians were unrestrained and bitter. Ferdinand I, the brother of the great Emperor Charles V, had won the Hungarian crown through marriage in 1527; but the Turks held most of his new kingdom and for a long while he and his successors had to pay tribute to the Porte. It was then that many of the great Hungarian magnates moved themselves and their portable goods and treasure out of the east and into that small area of north-western Hungary which was under direct Austrian rule. Their great estates they abandoned, their town houses as well, so that Buda, the old capital, became a ghost city. In the east, only Transylvania remained as a Magyar stronghold. But soon one Habsburg after another sought to reduce what they held of Hungary to the level of a province. Secular oppression was reinforced by religious bigotry. Revolt flared time and time again, to be violently put down. Hungarians exploited every moment of Habsburg weakness to push home their claims to independence. Many fought enthusiastically under the banners of Kara Mustapha in his great onslaught on Vienna. When the Turks were pushed back so decisively by Eugene the backwoods squires who had clung stubbornly and often in squalid poverty (their serfs, sometimes their children, carried off as slaves) to their ancient customs under Turkish rule added their voices to the western dissidents. Soon the peasants were in arms as well, and while Austria was heavily engaged in the War of the Spanish Succession, Hungarian peasant armies penetrated deeply towards Vienna. Joseph I put an end to that. Charles VI showed imagination and sense in conciliating the Hungarians without conceding his final authority. He needed Hungarian recognition of the Pragmatic Sanction. In return he gave the Hungarians their own Diet in Pressburg (Bratislava) and put an end to religious persecution. But they were far from content and were determined, most of them, to take advantage of the confusion over the succession and the weakness of the girl-queen to press further demands.

All this Maria Theresa was soon made to understand. Here, for the first time, she was lucky in her mentor. Count John Palffy was also an old man, but he was a wise and a brave one. A Hungarian patriot, he was one of the great magnates who saw clearly that Hungary could not stand alone: she must look for support either to Vienna or Constantinople, and this support must be paid for. For him the Austrians were a much lesser evil than the Turks, so the thing to do was to make the best of them and work for Hungary through them. This he did, beginning by fighting at Eugene's side in Charles of Lorraine's great campaign, winning quick promotion and the friendship of the Emperor. Maria Theresa he knew in her childhood: she liked him and looked up to him, and he was quick to recognise her quality even before she had left the schoolroom. Now he was there to present her to his Hungarians, and to tell them that if they behaved reasonably and played their cards well great things might result.

They needed to be told. It is true that the story of Hungary is the story of incessant and often heroic striving for independence against always overwhelming odds. It is a story that continues. But there is another side to it, and one which, down to the twentieth century, was to weaken and flaw the Magyar cause: these reckless freedom fighters recognised nobody's freedom but their own; they sought to throw off oppression the better themselves to oppress. Thus, for example, for eight hundred years they had tyrannised over the Slovaks. Again, in the fifteenth century one of their hero kings had earned the undying hatred of the Czechs by siding with the Emperor of the day in the Hussite Wars. The Hungarians, never, thus, had the vision or the restraint to make common cause with their Slav neighbours against Habsburg domination; instead, they used the Habsburgs in their attempts to dominate those neighbours. And if this would appear to throw back too far into the remote past, the answer is that the Hungarians themselves found their inspiration in a past which was equally remote. If they could invoke their early kings as national heroes in the struggle against Austria and Turkey, so the Czechs could invoke King Wenceslas in their own struggle with the Magyars. The Croats, also subjugated by the Magyars, were no less entitled to dwell in dreams on their own once proudly independent dynasty.

The young Queen could not be expected to know all this; but the moderate and sensible Hungarians, like Palffy, at least understood that there was something altogether too self-centred and one-sided about the pretensions of their fellow-countrymen. It was he who smoothed the Queen's path, and he, with a strange figure, Count Grassalkovich, who guided her and sustained her through the difficult and frustrating, sometimes terrifying, months which were to end in the most dazzling achievement of her whole career.

In that early summer of 1741 the omens appeared to be good. France had not yet declared herself and Maria Theresa had by no means given up hope of reviving the Dresden Concert and bringing Russia and Saxony into an alliance with the Maritime Powers aimed at the recovery of Silesia. She was, moreover, still exalted after the birth of the longed-for son, the future Emperor Joseph II, in March—the son she had been carrying when her father died, and whose birth, had Charles lived to see it, would have allowed him to die in peace and charity. The Viennese had responded hugely to the birth of a male heir; even the Hungarians were pleased. It was an auspicious omen for the Queen who was determined to win them by kindness, generosity and charm, at the same time to show herself as ruler. Already in her father's time the Hungarians had declared that they recognised only kings of Hungary and would never be governed by a queen. Very well, she would be a king! Hence the riding lessons. In June 1741, at the very moment when the French, the Bavarians, the Spaniards meeting in the Nymphenburg Palace at Munich were plotting her destruction, she presented herself in Pressburg to be crowned.

It was the first full-dress occasion of her reign. Bankrupt, she ignored her debts and lavished money on resplendency. Down the river she proceeded, escorted by a flotilla of barges decked in the Hungarian colours, their crews in Hungarian dress. Maria Theresa, preparing herself for the ordeal to come, was installed with her husband in a sumptuous tent, or pavilion, erected in the bows of the flagship. As the sun was sinking the flotilla tied up on the Austrian side of the border. Leaving her ministers on board, Maria Theresa, with Francis, was escorted over the frontier and conducted to a meadow, trimmed, garnished and beflagged, in which two pavilions had been set up. In one were assembled deputations from the two chambers of the Diet; in the other Maria Theresa changed into a dress in the Hungarian style, picked out and embroidered with gold. Then she moved out to face her new subjects, heard herself addressed as *domina et rex noster* (our mistress and king), replied in Latin, and was then escorted to her carriage, which took her through cheering crowds, to the ringing of bells and the firing of the royal salute, through the dusk up Castle Hill, nearly 300 feet above the Danube and the ancient town, to the vast Renaissance palace raised on the site of a medieval fortress, the symbol of Magyar domination of the Slovak people since the eleventh century.

Next morning the real business began, that is to say, the ordeal. The cheering crowds seemed far away now as Maria Theresa had to face the coolness of the Hungarian magnates, the sullenness of the lower house, to announce her intentions and give into Hungarian hands the coronation oath, drafted for her in Vienna. She had gone some way to meet them, conceding for the first time the election of a native Palatine, or viceroy. Palffy was chosen, in accordance with the plan, but she ran into serious trouble when she flatly refused to accede to the Diet's request that future Palatines should be chosen by them without reference to the Crown. Now, for the first time, she saw the real size of her problem. But now, also, she found in Grassalkovich, Speaker of the Lower House, her champion. A peasant's son, as a 'beggar student' he had put himself on the path to rapid promotion by outstanding ability. After the death of his first wife he had married an heiress and made himself rich enough to be accepted by the nobles of ancient lineage as their guide and counsellor. He was not born a Magyar; his father had been a Slav. This brilliant man of affairs, who was also outwardly impressive, had quickly taken the measure of her character and saw in her (he cannot have known this earlier) a heaven-sent bastion of order, able, with good guidance, to rule, and thus to hold off the state of virtual anarchy which would inevitably arise in Hungary if the contentious factions were faced with no restraining power. If old Count Palffy knew how to pour oil on troubled waters, the parvenu Grassalkovich proved himself now the born manipulator. On the one side he kept his own people within bounds, on the other he persuaded Maria Theresa, in the teeth of her Austrian ministers, to make minor concessions in the way of changes in the Coronation Oath and to promise to negotiate further with the Diet once she was crowned.

The day was saved, and the coronation went off well, even though on the very steps of the cathedral the Austrians in their robes of the Order of the Golden Fleece and the fantastically colourful Hungarians, their tunics frogged with gold, their dolmens lined with sable, the egret feathers attached to their caps by brilliantly jewelled mounts, quarrelled and all but came to blows over precedence. The ceremony took its course. Maria Theresa was pale as she emerged from her carriage, some said she was remote and even sorrowful in her expression. It is more likely that the haggling and, in her eyes, downright offensiveness of the day before had made her angry. Anger must be concealed, but distance she could show. Her Hungarians, her stubborn Germans too, had done their best to spoil for her the enjoyment of what should have been her greatest day. Did they expect her now to smile her gratitude? There was also the small matter of dedication. She was to kneel to receive the ancient crown, the iron crown of St Stephen, heavy indeed, which symbolised with her kingship her absolute responsibility for the lives and welfare of millions. She wanted only to dedicate herself weighed down by the crown and the rich and heavy robes, a ritual scapegoat, the loneliest figure in the world. But how to speak with God through a miasma of secular ill-feeling?

She was lonely too – and here was another cause for the anger which was out of place on such a day – among all those peacock men. They had parted her from Francis, adamantly refusing to recognise him as co-regent, excluding him from any share in the ritual of the day.

But she thawed a little under the shouts of acclaim from the crowd, her people. And after her crowning the warmth of her beauty began to melt the hearts of all but the most hostile among the magnates and the squires. Now she had to ride a black charger to the top of an artificial mound built up in the cathedral square, to point her drawn sword, after an immemorial custom, to all four points of the compass in token of her role as Hungary's protector. She had learnt to ride well and she herself, flushed now, looked splendid even with the antique crown and the eight-hundred-year-old faded, tattered mantle of the first Hungarian king. The day was hers after all. And later, at the coronation banquet, with the crown laid down, her fair hair shining, she was able at last to show her natural self. Anyway, she was happier now. The day had been lived through without disaster, and at the table with her she at last had her husband. She had been deeply hurt by his exclusion, but also deeply grateful for his amiable refusal to take umbrage, his readiness to efface himself and yet remain close at hand for when she wanted him. A more spirited and assertive man could have wrecked the very difficult negotiations which had preceded the coronation and were to continue long after it.

Here again she was alone. Most of her German advisers had no faith in Hungary. The emotional excitement of the coronation soon died down, and Maria Theresa found herself deadlocked between the extravagant demands of her new subjects and the bleak and bitter rejection of her ministers. Yet something had to be done to sort out relations between Vienna and Pressburg, and that urgently. She had the dire news by now of the Nymphenburg Treaty. France and Bavaria, allied with Spain, were on her back. Frederick was preparing to strike again. In the midst of the endless wrangle with the Hungarian magnates, the English (Robinson again), this time in unison with all her ministers, to say nothing of her husband, pressed the imperative need for yielding to Prussia's demands. On July 24th Robinson arrived in Pressburg, and after violent altercation, the Queen agreed to the concessions to be made to Frederick, repeatedly altering the document with her own hand. She was playing for time. She still could not bring herself to believe in the reality of the Grand Confederacy. How was it conceivable that the French, the Bavarians, the Spaniards could, in cold blood, break their pledged word and conspire with Frederick for her destruction? What had the French to gain by breaking Austria and raising Prussia up? She had no conception at this stage of the inward nature of the long-drawn-out struggle between France and England which, if France was to win, called for French hegemony over a divided and fragmented continent. She saw the matter in personal terms. Frederick she thought she understood. Charles Albert was ambitious for himself and for

Bavaria: he had set his heart on the imperial crown, but surely he could be bought off and satisfied by a compensatory gain – for example, the Austrian Netherlands?

It was in this mood and with this incomprehension that she pretended to agree in principle to surrender a considerable part of Silesia to Frederick in exchange for hard cash and his support for her husband's candidature for the imperial crown. Robinson thought that Frederick would never agree to the conditions with which she sought to hedge round her offer. 'I wish he may reject it!' she flashed back at him. She was agreeing, not believing, as a matter of form to keep England at her side, and because even she, understanding too little, could not isolate herself completely not only from her solitary committed ally but also from her ministers – and her husband. But she was dissembling for the first time in her life. Thus, from Pressburg she wrote to Kinsky:

> I have found it necessary to deceive my ministers, but since you are the only one I trust, I do not include you, and I confide in you my true intentions. Today we shall inform Robinson of our conditions; since he has gone so far as to threaten us it is necessary to keep the door open behind us and indulge him. Perhaps by doing this we may obtain better terms from the other side. My firm resolve is never to give up any part of Silesia, still less (at least) the whole of Lower Silesia; I have meanwhile indicated to Robinson through the Chancellor that, hypothetically, I might give up Breslau in return for a payment of two million to compensate us and Saxony, if Prussia will then bring all her force against our enemies and support our claim to the Imperial crown; I will allow myself to be bargained with a little; in this way we should be able to tide Robinson over his difficulties. God preserve me from really wishing this! No, I wish only to deceive the ministers so that they will put the story round and thus keep Robinson in play until a reply comes from Bavaria. . . . Nobody but you knows anything about this idea of mine: you may discuss it with Bartenstein this evening with me; I shall be alone. . . .

This episode seems to have been the young Queen's first essay in individual diplomacy. There is no record that she confided in

Francis. It also illustrates, with its contradictions, the confusion in her own mind which, solitary, she was struggling to order.

The essay was foredoomed. No sooner had Robinson appeared to Frederick than the Prussians took Breslau. Frederick put on one of those theatrical performances which were to inspire later rulers of Germany to emulation. 'Beggarly offers!' he exclaimed to poor Robinson, who, in dutifully reminding him of his obligations under the Pragmatic Sanction, was on rather shaky ground:

> Who observes guarantees in these times? Has not France guaranteed the Pragmatic Sanction? Has not England? . . . Why do you all not fly to succour the queen? . . . I am at the head of an invincible army, already master of a country which I must have and which I will have. . . . My ancestors would rise out of their tombs to reproach me, were I to abandon the rights they have transmitted to me. . . . Return with this answer. They who want peace will give me what I desire. I am sick of ulti-matums. I will have no more of them. My part is taken. This is my final answer. I will give no other.

At which, with flashing eyes, he swept off his hat and vanished into the private compartment of his tent, leaving Robinson to find his way out.

Maria Theresa was to take the initiative once more. Back she went, from Pressburg to Vienna, leaving the Hungarians still wrangling with her ministers, to pay a private call on her aunt, the widow of Joseph I, who lived in retirement in the Salesian convent. If the French would not help her to influence the Bavarians, perhaps she could use Charles Albert's mother-in-law as an intermediary. But, offer what she might, the old lady was not sympathetic. Had not her own daughter been forced out of the succession by Charles VI, her brother-in-law? Why should she help Maria Theresa, who had profited from this, to have things all her own way.

In any case, it was too late. On July 31st Marshal Saxe headed a French army, commanded by the duc de Broglie, as it crossed the Rhine. Throughout August there was incessant diplomatic activity, but all to no avail. Even Saxony, having allied herself with Austria, changed sides to be in at the kill. The Hungarians, faced with the eternal negatives of the Queen's ministers and unable to get at Maria

Theresa herself, were in an increasingly ugly mood. Some were declaring openly that the young Queen was a fraud: she had disarmed them with false assurances and feminine charm, but her purpose was to shackle them. At the beginning of September Charles Albert swept into Upper Austria, virtually unopposed. He was moving on Linz. He would soon effect a junction with the French. Belle-Isle's great design was coming alive on the ground. Frederick, beside himself with glee, wrote to express the impatient eagerness with which he looked forward to meeting him at the gates of Vienna and embracing him at the head of his victorious troops.

'Breslau is lost, and our propositions have been rejected. This is the end.' Maria Theresa had written to Kinsky towards the end of June. Now it really looked like the end. Robinson was back again after a further vain call on Frederick, and now he had even Bartenstein on his side – not for fear of Frederick, but for rage at the French betrayal. There was no way out. Bartenstein drafted a note of surrender. The Queen would cede Lower Silesia, 'as understood by the King', together with Breslau and the Upper Silesian counties stipulated by him in return for his assistance against France and Bavaria. But she still had a shot in her locker. This time there is no letter to Kinsky to explain what her true intentions were. For the record she wrote on Bartenstein's draft: '*Placet*, as there is no other way, but with profound grief.' Even after that she wanted changes, but Sinzendorf told her it was too late. 'Very well,' she said. 'If it has to be, then let it be. The whole matter has been settled against my will. So let it take its course.'

It appeared to be total capitulation. Everybody went about on tiptoe so as not to distress or offend the young Queen, who was supposed to be broken-hearted. The great thing was that they had got their way. Their royal mistress had learnt her first lesson in the hard school of international chicanery and violence. She had bowed at last to the inevitable. They thought they had the measure of her now. Let her complain, weep, rage, blame them for her defeats, provided she listened to the wisdom of their distilled experience. She was, clearly, incomparably brave; she was cleverer than they had believed only a few months earlier; now, learning to be amenable, she would make a splendid queen. . . .

They still did not understand what sort of a person she was.

In Frederick she had no trust at all. In any case, any agreement with Prussia could be no more than an armistice. The Bavarians were moving swiftly down the Danube valley; Belle-Isle progressed with an overpoweringly brilliant retinue from court to court in Germany, insinuating, cajoling, intimidating; Saxony, Cologne and the Palatinate were joining forces with Charles Albert; de Broglie's army disguised as Bavarian auxiliaries (there was no French declaration of war) was moving up to make a junction with the Bavarians; George II, even while he was engaged in collecting troops to succour Austria, was declaring the neutrality of his beloved Hanover; Spain was preparing to attack in Italy; Sardinia seemed to be coming down on the Bourbon side of the fence. In this moment of fearful crisis Maria Theresa did not lose her nerve. With no help from anyone at all she conceived a new idea. She was determined to keep Hungary, but keeping Hungary would be worse than useless unless she could harness the Hungarians to her cause. She decided that if the stubborn Magyars could not be coerced they must be wooed. She would present herself to them as a woman in distress, appealing directly to the chivalry which was still a real element in their make-up while, at the same time, offering them a genuine partnership. She would call them to arms and throw herself on their mercy – and this in the teeth of her advisers, who insisted that to allow the Hungarians to arm would be to invite immediate bloody insurrection.

In Pressburg on September 7th she summoned to the castle the leaders of the nation, gave them a true account of the desperate position in which she found herself, told them that the safety of their own land as well as others depended for the time being on their will and strength alone. She had calculated well. These difficult, often selfish, always arrogant men were touched by the courage of this tender beauty who chose to defy a world in arms; they were impressed by the clarity with which she weighed the dangers; they were also touched in their pride. Above all they saw that their new young Queen was, unbelievably, addressing them not as their Habsburg master but rather appealing to them as rational men; she had cast aside all official advice and was taking them into her confidence. She knew a Gordian knot when she saw it, and when she saw it she knew what to do. She had decided to break the deadlock. Things could never be the same again. They for their part knew how to respond. Then and there they pledged themselves to serve her; to levy 40,000 troops and 25,000 horses to fight for her; to offer their fortunes for her cause. They could talk about taxation later; it was one thing to make a grand and ruinous gesture, another to accept in principle the right of the Crown to levy taxes. . . . More, they urged her to put herself and her infant son under their protection, to take up her residence in the fortress of Györ and leave the danger to them.

The battle was half over. Soon she must present herself to both houses of the Diet. For the moment she must leave the elders to carry her cause to the rank and file. But it looked as though she had won. She would not, she said, abandon Vienna unless and until it was immediately threatened. Indeed, it was high time she returned there briefly to prepare the defence of the city and bolster up morale. The occasion was a thanksgiving ceremony to celebrate Vienna's delivery from the Turks. Khevenhüller was in command of the defences, and she trusted him. She was in tremendous spirits. She had discovered what she could do with people if she approached them directly and paid no attention to ministerial scepticism. It came out now in her attitude to the Viennese, who had given her and her husband such a difficult time. She told Khevenhüller to remember that 'the Viennese will do anything, if talked to kindly and shown affection'.

Back in Pressburg she found that her friends among the Hungarian magnates had been doing their work well. Above all Palffy, who had given a grand banquet and made a speech explaining that all the difficulties of the summer had been due to her German advisers. She had always loved and respected Hungary; now she had broken free from those who sowed suspicion. On September 11th came the test.

Dressed in mourning she stood before the grand assembly of the two houses and made her appeal. She spoke not with her own words, brisk and direct, but in the Latin which was the official Hungarian language of state and was to remain so for more than a century to come:

The very existence of the Kingdom of Hungary, of our own person, of our children, and our crown, are now at stake. For-saken by all, we place our sole resource in the fidelity, arms, and long-tried valour of the Hungarians; exhorting you, the states and orders, to deliberate without delay in this extreme danger, on the most effectual measures for the security of our person, of our children, and of our crown, and to carry them into immediate execution. In regard to ourself, the faithful states and orders of Hungary shall experience our hearty cooperation in all things which may promote the pristine happiness of this ancient kingdom and the honours of the people.

I quote this paraphrase by that underrated historian, Archdeacon Coxe (he supplies the original Latin also) because it brings out the sobriety and matter-of-factness of the appeal. The more usual English translation has an emotive colour, more in keeping with Maria Theresa's personal pleadings, but quite absent on this occasion. Her listeners, at first puzzled, were then transported. They were transported not by rhetoric, not be a silver tongue, but by the promise of a compact. Of course they intended to turn this promise to their own best advantage; and, indeed, the haggling was later to continue: the size of the promised levy was reduced, the nobility retained their traditional exemption from taxation; the Hungarians were conceded the right to elect their own Palatines. On the other hand, Maria Theresa was quite blunt about her resolve to keep direct control of Transylvania; more important, Francis was to be recognised as co-regent.

The myth and legend which has grown up round this scene has sometimes obscured its true meaning. Nothing could be further from the truth than the picture of Maria Theresa presenting herself as a mother in distress, displaying her own stricken beauty and the helplessness of her infant son to the multitude. A few days later she did indeed show the child, but not as an appeal, rather as a pledge: Francis was to be co-regent; here, in the infant Joseph, was the promise that Hungary should one day have a real king. What Maria Theresa gained when she appeared before the Diet was not pity but admiration and respect. Here, for the first time in their history, was a Habsburg speaking to them as partners, not trying to beat them down but offering her trust. Being highly impressionable, of course they were touched by her youth and beauty; being highly demonstrative, of course they allowed that emotion to show. But, as already indicated, at least some of them, in past months, had come to regard that charm and beauty as a snare. What moved them most was something other: they were assisting at a turning-point in their own history. The Queen of Hungary had placed herself in their hands, she had called a madly proud people to arms as a nation. Things could never be the same again.

Things could never be the same again for Maria Theresa either. She had gone against all advice, and even now her ministers had no faith in her judgment. There were noisy scenes in the great hall when, to wild shouts of acclamation, she had withdrawn. 'The Queen would have done better to wish herself and hers to the devil rather than trust the Hungarians!' one of her ministers was heard to mutter. There were scuffles, shouts and countershouts. 'Long live the Queen and down with her counsellors!' 'To the gallows with all who come between the Queen and Hungary!' She knew now all about the selfishness and the volatility of the Hungarians; but she also knew about the brooding rancour of her Germans. And already she was coming to look for superior loyalty in those who had most openly defied her. It was only three days later that the French and the Bavarians, now united, occupied Linz, the capital of Upper Austria, without a struggle. At once Charles Albert proclaimed himself Archduke of Austria, and at once the Estates did homage to him. So much for the fidelity of her German lords (only a few remained loyal). How different in Pressburg! To Charles's claim to the crown of Hungary the Diet replied with incredulous scorn. What sort of people did this Bavarian upstart think they were? They had given their new Queen the roughest imaginable passage, but once they had sworn fealty to her she was theirs to protect. They could still be tough in their demands, but she herself was showing toughness in her further bargaining. That was as it should be: it was all in the family now.

Maria Theresa sensed this better than anyone. Difficult as her Hungarians were, and always were to be, she responded with warmth and gratitude for the rest of her life to their warmth and ardour. They were to keep a special place in her heart. More immediately, they had given her confidence in her own deep instincts, a confidence she was never to lose. She had been ready to defer to men old, experienced, reputedly wise. They had failed her, and, diffident at heart as she always was, there was to be no more deference. She and she alone had done the impossible and swung the Hungarians into line. She knew how to manage people. It was as simple as that. From now on, unless and until she could find men she could trust, she would use her ministers purely as technicians, as she would use her generals, to implement her commands. Francis was her co-regent, one day he would be Emperor; but she knew now, and for ever, that she had to rule alone, which meant that to her husband, no less than to her ministers, she must, on occasion, dissemble. She was above them all. She was also – she was still only twenty-four – a little above herself.

Chapter Six

The War of the Succession

The Queen had long and tedious strife ahead of her and she made a number of mistakes, not least in putting first her husband, then her brother-in-law Charles, in charge of her armies. The war was to drag on for another seven years, until the Peace of Aix-la-Chapelle was signed in October 1748. Long before then the fighting which had started with Frederick's invasion of Silesia had exploded into a European conflagration the sparks from which flew far and wide, starting new fires as far apart as the American continent and India. What had begun as Austria's fight for survival was transformed into a full-scale overture to the Seven Years War of 1756, which was to establish the new pattern of overseas empires and the maritime and mercantile preponderance of England. Long before then the origins of the conflict were largely forgotten, except by the two original antagonists, Maria Theresa and Frederick. Austria and Prussia were now only elements in the renewed struggle between England and France, the struggle which Walpole had foreseen and feared when he set Sir Thomas Robinson the unheroic task of bringing moral blackmail to bear on a young, perplexed and vulnerable queen, who might thus be induced to surrender part of her domains in order to postpone a European war involving England – that very struggle which, when it came, was, out of muddle and confusion, to exalt England herself to world supremacy.

Not that it looked like that at the time. When at last Walpole fell and Carteret briefly took office, when at last England backed up her large subsidies with a show of force, things did not go at all well. Dettingen, in 1743, was an English victory, but George II and the earl of Stair were lucky to escape annihilation at the hands of the ducs de Noailles and de Gramont. There was no formal declaration of war against France until the following year: at Dettingen the 'Pragmatic Army' under the English King had fought as an Austrian auxiliary. England had been at war with Spain since 1739, but the Spanish fleet had managed to hold its own; and the first battle with the combined fleets of Spain and France, off Hyères, would have ended in catastrophe and disgrace but for the initiative of two junior captains, one of them later to be the famous Admiral Hawke. Only the threatened bombardment of Naples redeemed the situation, forcing the Bourbon King of the Two Sicilies to recall the forces he had sent against Austria. Then, in 1745, came the new threat, the landing of Charles Edward Stuart at Moidart, under French auspices, and the subsequent Jacobite rising, which was not broken until Culloden a year later.

It was not until 1747 that England at last rose to the occasion. The scandal of Hyères had brought it home to Whitehall that the proud navy which had swept the seas in the days of Louis XIV and smashed the attempted French invasion of 1692, had been neglected and taken for granted for too long. A great spring-cleaning was called for at the Admiralty, and the need, as it sometimes does (not always, contrary to superstition), produced the man. Anson, that sailor of genius, who had lately covered himself with glory by his circumnavigation of the globe, first beat the French off Finisterre, then went to the Admiralty, where he showed himself to be a great organiser as well as a great fighting seaman. It was he who pulled out of the ruck and swiftly promoted that astonishing galaxy of brilliant officers whose exploits later in the century were to resound across the seas: Hawke, Rodney, Keppel, Hoe, Saunders and Boscawen. This, as far as England was concerned, was the meaning of the War of the Austrian Succession. The French, under their great commander, Mashal Saxe, heavily encumbered by the presence of Louis XV and his elaborate train, had overrun the Austrian Netherlands. Their famous victory at Fontenoy in 1745 against the combined English, Dutch and Hanoverian forces, broke the way to a deeper penetration of Holland than even Louis XIV had been able to achieve. They had captured Madras in 1746. But they had long been driven out of Bohemia by Austria alone. And England was master of the seas.

When Pelham decided that the time had come to make peace, every ruler in Europe was only too happy to oblige – every ruler with the single exception of Maria Theresa, who had to give way, leaving almost all Silesia in Prussia's hands. England relinquished her recent maritime conquests; France, her dream of subduing Germany to her own designs long shattered, was left with nothing to show for her very great exertions. But the state had been cleared for a still more critical confrontation, which was to end with England winning Canada and India. It was all very far removed from Vienna, which had nothing at stake in these far-ranging maritime and empire-building movements. On the face of it, indeed, Maria Theresa was the greatest loser in a war begun in her name. To her the Peace of Aix-la-Chapelle appeared as a humiliation and a betrayal. In fact it represented, without anyone realising what was happening, a great step forward. Silesia was gone. The dream, dazzling while it lasted, of winning back Lorraine, of forcing the Elector of Bavaria to surrender his south German possessions in exchange for Naples, to be won from the Spanish Bourbons, had vanished into thin air. Prussia was established as a major power, rendering null further Austrian pretensions to dominate the German states. But, with all this, the Habsburg Empire itself, eight years earlier on the verge of extinction, had miraculously survived as a concept and matured as a power. Even without Silesia it was stronger and more real than it had ever been, and, still more to the point, the upheavals of the long and agonising war had created the conditions for a complete reorganisation of government, administration, army and constitution. The Austria which had moved into the War of the Austrian Succession had been a ruin; the Austria which, in 1756, was to move into the crucible of the Seven Years War, was a modern, centralised power.

2

The story of Austria under Maria Theresa, the story of the great Queen herself, can all too easily be lost in the diplomatic and military history of Europe. Indeed, it is not too much to say that the character and impact of a very remarkable ruler have been obscured by the mass of detail, largely irrelevant, arising from her involvement in war and diplomatic scheming at the opening of her reign while she was establishing herself as a person. Moreover, if the day to day pre-occupations of the Court at Vienna and the activities of Maria Theresa's generals and statesmen are to be chronicled in detail there is room for nothing else. Further, if the course of the wars – if only the two great wars of 1740–48 and 1756–63 – is to be plotted, wars which were so extensive, which were fought on so many fronts simultaneously and by so many governments concerned with matters which affected Austria only in the most indirect way, it would be necessary to take in not only the history of eighteenth-century Europe, but also of the making of the modern world, the process which brought three continents into the European orbit and, still continuing, has already in the eyes of non-Europeans reduced Europe to its absurd place on the map – the fringe of a vast Eurasian complex in a world which includes Africa and the Americas, to say nothing of Australia and Japan. This is not our theme. We are here concerned with one small corner of the old Europe, a vitally im-portant corner of that little world which still exercises, for good or ill, an influence wholly disproportionate to its size, whose ideas, institutions and manners, whether projected by Loyola, Luther or Karl Marx, for better or for worse, set the tone of the world as a whole and will continue to do so until non-Europeans produce some new ideas of their own – or until Buddha, Confucius or Mohammed countervail.

Even in that small corner, we need not concern ourselves here with the details of the strictly Austrian campaigns except in so far as they affected the mind and purpose of Maria Theresa herself or throw light on the character of her institutions. The conduct of eighteenth-century wars is a fascinating study in its own right, and they have been well studied. All were different, all had their special features, all have much to say about human nature as exhibited, above all, in the characters and attitudes of the senior officers who fought them. They had, nevertheless, one important feature in common: their indeterminacy.

Mollwitz has been referred to earlier as a decisive battle; but it was not decisive in the usually agreed sense, in the sense, that is, of the closing of a chapter and a dramatic shift of force. Eighteenth-century rulers did not think in terms of closing chapters. It took the forces of revolution in France, when the century had almost run its course, to bring back into European politics the spirit of all or nothing which was alien to the age, except, in a special way, as exhibited in the character of Maria Theresa herself. And her own all was the *status quo*. Frederick, a dynamist if ever there was one, set himself, as we have seen, almost austerely limited objectives. He was also the last person to think in terms of decisive battles. Time and again in the years of strife to come he would say in so many words: we must pull out now; it will take (for example) three battles to achieve this or that desired objective; Prussia cannot afford to fight more than one – or sometimes two. Mollwitz was only decisive in the sense that it opened a new chapter, establishing Prussia as a force to be reckoned with in future by Europe. His great victories in the Seven Years' War, did no more than confirm what Mollwitz had already demonstrated. The successes of Khevenhüller and, later, Daun, showed only that Austrian troops, given able commanders, could still fight and manoeuvre as well as any others.

Victories were celebrated with rejoicing. Handel could compose his *Te Deum* for George II after Dettingen. But such occasions were no more than the punctuation of an agreed process of manoeuvre, long-drawn-out and costly in human suffering, whereby the governments of Europe sought to hold their own while grabbing, where they could, quite small advantages. Only the French, with their passionate romanticism, allowed themselves, as so often, to be carried away by dreams of conquest beyond their strength, not stopping to ask themselves what on earth they would do if, by some miracle, they won. They gave up quite cheerfully when they failed, and there was no inclination on the part of the victors to destroy them or even to reduce them to impotence. A strong France could be, and often was, a menace to her neighbours; but she was also a necessary part of the basic and deeply cherished *status quo*. In this general mood, all wars, even more than battles, had to be indeterminate, except for peripheral adjustments.

Thus, for example, the Habsburg armies alone in the war of 1740–48 were engaged over a vast area of Europe, from Alsace to Bohemia, from Naples to Antibes. The Italian campaigns against the Spanish forces form a major subject in themselves. There could be an enthralling chapter about a sideshow, the astonishing campaign along the Riviera coast conducted by Maximilian von Browne, already encountered in Silesia – a campaign fought through that then roadless and waterless maquis, now penetrated by the corniche roads. It took Browne's troops across the Var, as far east as the burning wilderness of the Estérel forest, as far north as Castellane (with the French coming up the dizzy Gorges de Verdon to do battle); it included the reduction of Antibes and the bombardment and storming of the great fortress and monastery on the Isles de Lérins, just off Cannes, to which half the population of the mainland had fled for refuge. Browne was supported by a small English naval force which kept in step with him and bombarded the French positions from the flank. He had to give up in the end because of the gross failure of the commander of his supply base at Genoa; and a bitter disappointment it was. But even this great and dedicated soldier, the first Austrian commander since Eugene to train and condition his troops professionally and turn them into a self-reliant and intelligent fighting-force with an understanding of what they were supposed to be doing, and how, must have known that no matter how far he and his Austrians penetrated into France, they would not stay there, and that the most his wildest success could achieve would be the bringing of a little more pressure to bear in the final peace negotiations to extract limited concessions when it came to redefining frontiers in the interests of Austria and her allies, which might very well be contradictory.

3

From 1741 Belle-Isle, with Fleury and Louis XV now helpless in his train, was certainly intent on sweeping changes. But, as already remarked, even he did not seek vast conquests for France. Austria was to be reduced, so that Vienna might never again effectively challenge French influence. The Germanic principalities, electorates, kingdoms, were to be prevented from ever again combining as a counterpoise to France. But Belle-Isle was quite content to see a greater Bavaria, a greater Saxony, bound to France by expediency and obligation, to say nothing of an aggrandised Prussia which he knew very well must always be a dangerous joker in the pack. Maria Theresa was perfectly aware of this. She was naturally furious with the French, as treaty breakers, and fearful, sometimes despairing, at the initial success of the Belle-Isle campaign. But this whole operation had no radical effect on her mind; it was no more than a perilous lesson in power politics of the kind also taught her by the self-regarding temporisings of her ally, England. She would learn to play the game too, and so she did. It was a lesson which hardened her resolution and showed her, too soon for the harmonious development of so young a woman with such potential for good, that she must be harsh and that her harshness must come from her own strength alone. It was only *vis-à-vis* Frederick that she allowed her emotions their head, and even in the great cause of reducing Prussia she allowed herself to compromise when it came to the very desperate matter of turning the French, the Bavarians and the Saxons out of Bohemia.

At the time of her appeal to the Hungarians in October 1741 her situation was indeed critical. Frederick was menacing as always; the Bavarians and the French were threatening Vienna itself, now put into a state of defence by Khevenhüller and the students, and the citizenry were manning the barricades. Then, suddenly, Charles decided to leave Vienna alone and cut straight up to Prague. Now, unless things went quickly better, all Bohemia would be lost. It was Frederick himself who came to the rescue. It was one thing for him to use Charles Albert and Belle-Isle so to weaken Austria that his hold on Silesia would be secured. It was quite another to stand by and watch the imminent aggrandisement of Saxony and Bavaria, the swallowing up of Bohemia, the triumph of France. Thus it was that Austria and Prussia came for a moment almost ludicrously together. When Frederick for his own good reasons indicated his willingness to withdraw from the fight, at a price, and leave his allies in the lurch, Maria Theresa reluctantly, but swiftly, took him up, even though the price was higher than the demand which a few months earlier she had contemptuously rejected.

Here she was abetted by Bartenstein, who had now transferred all the bitterness of his hatred from Prussia to France. France had let him, Bartenstein, down, the worst crime. Frederick must be wooed. It was a tortuous operation after Frederick's own heart, conducted through the mediation of the ever-helpful Lord Hyndford, proof against every snub. Austria was to cede Lower Silesia, including the fortress of Neisse, then under siege. Prussia would then pull out of the fight. But this exercise was to be conducted in total secrecy: the French, the Bavarians, the Saxons, were not to be allowed to suspect that Frederick was breaking his treaty engagements. Nothing was to be put into writing. Nothing was to be signed. And if Vienna let the cat out of the bag the whole agreement would be null. The siege of Neisse was to continue in form, on the understanding that the Austrians would surrender at a predetermined moment. The Prussians were to appear to persist in their advance, the Austrians were to appear to resist: but the whole affair was a trick. Shots would be fired, but there would be no more than showy skirmishing. Admittedly, men on both sides would die, innocently believing that they were laying down their lives for their king and their queen – as indeed they were, if not quite in the way they imagined.

This comedy was devised by Frederick because he needed a rest and because he did not wish his allies to be too successful. But he needed to be free to enter the game again at his own convenience, while Maria Theresa required a breathing-space at almost any cost. The agreement was reached in a castle at Kleinschnellendorf belonging to the Dietrichsteins. The Austrian negotiator in chief was Marshal Neipperg.

People have wondered why Neipperg, who had previously displayed his ineptitude as a negotiator with the Turks at Belgrade, should have been entrusted with the handling of another surrender. But who could have been more suitable? Neipperg was commander of the army facing Frederick. The surrender was no more than a cease-fire. Once she had made up her mind to buy Frederick off, for how-ever short a time, with Lower Silesia, Maria Theresa was not interested in the details; certainly nobody close to her was to be in-volved in this ignominy. And, in fairness to poor Neipperg it should be recorded that he despatched a baffled and agonised plea to Vienna to be taken off the job. 'Believe me,' he wrote to Francis, his old pupil and protector, 'I am not the man to cope with this King in this labyrinth of a treaty.' It was to no avail. Lower Silesia had to be written off, but only for the time being. Maria Theresa, having brought herself to admit it, was racing on in her mind to the next thing. And the next thing was for Francis himself, in command of a force of 60,000 troops, to intercept the enemy and destroy him before Prague. At the same time Khevenhüller was to clear Lower Austria and carry the war into Bavaria and beyond, to the Rhine, to Alsace and Lorraine.

It did not work out like that. The Silesian manoeuvre was con-ducted according to plan, but less than three weeks after Klein-schnellendorf the Bavarians and the Saxons, with their French auxiliaries, reached Prague and stormed it while, in effect, the great Austrian force trailed behind them. For Maria Theresa the dis-appointment was extreme, and especially bitter because she had allowed herself to believe that, spurred on by her, Francis would prove resolute, swift and decisive enough to rise to the occasion. He failed. Instead of inspiring progress reports, instead of news of battle, she received from her husband a constant flow of despatches stressing the rigours of the climate, the difficulty of the country, the shortcomings of supply and the sufferings of the troops (were the enemy forces untouched by such afflictions?) It was the end of two dreams. Her husband would never make an adequate commander; Khevenhüller could no longer concentrate single-mindedly on the extended advance which would take him over the Rhine and restore Lorraine to Francis Stephen, but must now give close attention to what was happening in Bohemia and be ready to detach troops to prevent the army in Bohemia from being taken by Belle-Isle in the rear. Worse, Frederick grew tired of his armistice and within a matter of weeks was threatening Vienna.

Maria Theresa's mood, and her spirit, is finally revealed in a letter to Kinsky written immediately after the fall of Prague. Francis had failed. The burden was now hers. She was a girl no longer:

So Prague is lost, and perhaps even worse will follow unless we can secure three months supplies. It is out of the question for Austria to supply them, and it is doubtful even if Hungary will be able to do so.

Here then, Kinsky, we find ourselves at the sticking point where only courage can save the country [Bohemia] and the Queen, for without the country I should indeed be a poor princess. My own resolve is taken: to stake everything, win or lose, on saving Bohemia; and it is with this in view that you should work and lay your plans. It may involve destruction and desolation which twenty years will be insufficient to restore; but I must hold the country and the soil, and for this all my armies, all the Hungarians, shall die before I surrender an inch of it. This, then, is the crisis: do not spare the country, only hold it. Do all you can to help your people and to keep the troops contented, lacking nothing: you know, better than I, the consequences of failure in this. Help my poor husband who feels so deeply for the suffering of the troops and the countryside, who urges that the troops are doing all they can, that their condition fills him with pity. . . . You will say that I am cruel; that is true. But I know that all the cruelties I commit today to hold the country I shall one day be in a position to make good a hundred-fold. And this I shall do. But for the present I close my heart to pity. I rely on you. . . .

She had pleaded, she had commanded, now she was driving, and with a singleminded ruthlessness which must have struck wonder, dismay and awe in those who were called to obey.

4

The Kleinschnellendorf convention had been sealed on October 9th. On the 26th Prague fell. Almost at once Frederick was busily at work. He had sent an envoy to discuss final peace terms in Vienna, but he himself, on November 4th, arrived at a secret agreement with Charles Albert of Bavaria who, as King of Bohemia, was to sell him the county of Glatz at a bargain price in return for Frederick's electoral vote. On December 19th Charles Albert had himself crowned in Prague, and on the same day Frederick moved into action again, without warning, and occupied Troppau. Two days after Christmas he took Olmütz, the ancient Moravian fortress and the key to Vienna.

This time Maria Theresa did not bother to repine. She was back in Vienna, having done all she could in Hungary, and she was about to set in motion the brilliant campaign which was to launch Khevenhüller across the Enns to clear the enemy out of Austria and occupy Munich, the Bavarian capital, on the very day, February 24th, that Charles Albert was crowned Emperor at Frankfurt, turning him into that rather ridiculous figure, Charles VII, an Emperor without a home. The belief was allowed to grow that Frederick was stampeded into resuming hostilities by Khevenhüller's victorious progress, which threatened to take Austria into France and raise her to a new pinnacle of power. In fact, Khevenhüller did not cross the Enns into Lower Austria until four days after Frederick's treacherous move. The great King broke his pledged word not in desperation but because he was made that way. 'Is anything to be gained by honesty, then we shall be honest,' he wrote to Podewils; 'if deceit, on the other hand, is called for, let us be knaves.' Or again, as he observed in one of his famous memoranda which he used for clarifying his own thoughts (this time when he was preparing the formal betrayal of his allies by withdrawing from the war quite openly): 'It is bad to break one's word without good reason ... one earns a reputation for unreliability.'

Maria Theresa was past indignation by now; that could be left to Frederick's allies. She showed herself for the first time a great commander as well as a courageous one by refusing to panic. Although later she was to call on Khevenhüller to release some of his best units to meet the Prussian threat, now she kept her nerve and let him proceed as planned, moving ever farther away from Vienna. She herself would hold that fort. She held it, while her main body, now under command of Charles of Lorraine, her brother-in-law (Francis had been recalled), sat helplessly under the walls of Prague, while all her advisers urged on her the folly of pursuing the Bavarian campaign when the threat to Vienna was so acute and with the enemy still in Prague. And she won through.

Frederick was prevented from achieving his main objective, releasing the French troops locked up in Bohemia. And although his cavalry penetrated as far as the suburbs of Vienna, and although in May 1742, he won a formal victory at Chotusic (the Austrian infantry did well, but their cavalry got above themselves and went roaring after loot), proving his own courage under fire, the Queen's steadfastness now told. Each side lost over 7,000 men, and Frederick could not afford another victory like that. He was also sceptical about the further fighting power of his allies. Maria Theresa believed that given half a chance her new commander, Charles of Lorraine, would be able to knock out the French. Hence the Treaty of Breslau which brought to an end the first Silesian War. 'It is with bitter feelings,' wrote Frederick to the Emperor, 'that I have to inform Your Imperial Majesty of the collapse of your cause,' but it was all the fault of the French and the Saxons, who would not pull their weight. 'You are aware,' he had the effrontery to write to Cardinal Fleury, 'that since our agreement I have done everything possible to support the designs of the King your master with inviolable fidelity.' But he could not go on any more. He had born the heat of the day, he had carried his burdens on behalf of others virtually unaided. He must resign himself to the inevitable. He did not mention that he carried under his belt nearly all Silesia and was leaving his allies to get out of trouble as best they could.

5

Enough is enough. Morley in his life of Walpole threw up his hands in despair when faced with the infinite and meaningless complexities of the eighteenth-century diplomatic game. Not even Carlyle, he exclaimed, could give sense and significance and life to the incessant manoeuvring, finessing, double-dealing conducted between the courts of Europe in that age. Walpole was out of it before the Breslau Treaty was signed; but the dreary game went on for decades to come. The cliché about war being the continuation of diplomacy by other means, generally accepted as a truism, is in fact only valid for a very short period of European history – from the Napoleonic Wars to the dawn of the atomic age, in which the presence of the hydrogen bomb and its ingenious propellants has produced an inhibiting effect on the war-makers, who now have to suffer severe limitations to their objectives and constant interference from the diplomats. In the eighteenth century, far from being a continuation of diplomacy, war, limited by problems of supply, transport, recruitment and ready cash, was no more than an arm of diplomacy, which continued unceasingly while the troops marched, sweated, shivered, starved, looted and sometimes clashed. A major battle, far from deciding things, was the signal for a renewed frenzy of diplomatic activity.

So far as Maria Theresa was concerned, hardly a week went by during all her years of armed conflict when she was not actively engaged in diplomatic exercises, confused, repetitive, and leading nowhere in particular. The great climacterics – the Treaty of Breslau which ended the first Silesian War in 1742; the Treaty of Dresden which ended the second on Christmas Day, 1745; and the Treaty of Aix-la-Chapelle which finally wound up, in 1748, the long-drawn-out struggle for the Austrian Succession – far from marking the end of an affair, at once led to further diplomatic exertions; and these continued until the close of the Seven Years War in 1763. Prussia was the constant foe, first allied with France against Austria and England, then with England against Austria, France and Russia. By his Silesian aggression in 1740 Frederick put Prussia on the map, but he had also ensured for himself a lifetime of conflict which wore him down, transformed his nature and, at one stage, over twenty years later, swept both him and his kingdom to the very edge of extinction – from which he was saved only by a miracle of a characteristically Russian kind: the accession in 1762 to the Russian throne of an imbecile, Peter III, whose one positive action in the short interval before he was murdered with the tacit approval of his wife, the great Catherine, was to take Russia out of the war against Prussia just in the nick of time to save the great Frederick, thus establishing the power pattern which was to endure until the twentieth century.

The sense of these events must be recorded. There is no escape. But we need not follow Maria Theresa through her campaigns, military and diplomatic, in close detail. With Frederick neutralised by the Breslau Treaty of June 1742 she obtained the breathing space she needed to deal with the French and the Bavarians. Operations against the Spaniards in Italy were going fairly well. Belle-Isle was locked up in Prague and Fleury tried to negotiate a peace, only to be sharply rebuffed by the young Queen, who thought she had the French at her mercy. It was a reasonable assumption, but she reckoned without the incompetence and half-heartedness of Francis and his brother Charles. Francis, in particular, flirted with the idea of an accommodation with France in return for her support as reversionary candidate for the imperial crown. His wife rebuked him in no uncertain terms and told him in effect to pull himself together and understand, and make his brother and his generals understand, that the war was serious. It was too late. In midwinter Belle-Isle, who should have been captured with his whole force, slipped out of the city with 13,000 men. Leaving his sick and wounded behind, he managed to straggle back through terrible winter conditions, and suffering appalling losses, across half Europe: an epic journey that might have been a small-scale rehearsal for the retreat from Moscow. Belle-Isle, arrogant and flamboyant as he was, turned out to be a better man than Napoleon, he stayed with his men and brought the ravaged remnant home with all their colours and their guns.

That was one great disappointment. The failure of Austrian plans for seizing Naples was another. Nevertheless, the general prospect seemed reasonably bright. In May 1743 Maria Theresa had herself crowned Queen of Bohemia. The English were at last backing up their subsidies with troops, and in June the Pragmatic Army, with George II at its head, contrived to beat the French at Dettingen. Frederick looked on with mounting unease, but did nothing until August 1744, when he decided it was time to fight again to safeguard his possession of Silesia. So he struck, and in the following month took Prague, sacked it, and overran a great part of Bohemia. It was a bitter blow. It meant, among other things, that the Queen must withdraw Prince Charles's army from across the Rhine at the very moment when it was threatening Strasburg. It also meant that there was nothing to prevent the triumphant return of the Bavarians, under Seckendorf, to their own land. Khevenhüller was dead and the most gifted senior general now was Traun, who had seen much service in Italy. Slow, excessively cautious, he was nevertheless an adept at the old war of manoeuvre, of marching and countermarching; and for once Frederick found his own technique of swift and devastating movement defeated by the old-fashioned tactics which he thought he had superseded: he was caught and entangled as in a net. But it was far from being a lethal net.

Meanwhile the French were recovering their strength and will. In January 1745 everything was thrown into confusion by the sudden and premature death of Charles Albert of Bavaria. He had been Emperor for barely three years, but, unfortunate and over-ambitious as he was, he had suffered a rough passage, never recognised by Maria Theresa, his chief opponent: he was worn out. As far as France was concerned, all the plans which had been built on Charles as Emperor were now as dust. So far as Frederick was concerned, there was once again everything to fear from Austria. But the French now were more interested in their struggle with England than in what happened in Germany. Austria was on the sidelines. And in May came Marshal Saxe's crushing victory at Fontenoy, opening up Holland to the French and exposing the Austrian Netherlands, Belgium, to an immediate threat. Almost at once came news of a new Prussian victory at Hohenfriedburg. Then, for good measure, Charles Edward Stuart set up his standard in Scotland.

It was time once again for England to put renewed pressure on Maria Theresa to make her peace with Frederick so that all energies could be devoted to the struggle with France. If Francis succeeded Charles Albert as Emperor what more could Maria Theresa want? She wanted a great deal more. She wanted Silesia, or at least some of it. Hohenfriedburg had been a defeat, by all means; but soon her troops would win a victory and put Frederick in his place and Francis would be elected Emperor anyway; and, indeed, at Frankfurt, only lately threatened by the French, who had been pushed back by Traun, the electoral process was already in train. This was the position when Robinson once more appeared before the Queen. England, he said, had 'this year provided one million seventy-eight thousand seven hundred and fifty-three pounds' to Austria alone. It could not go on. There must be a proper sense of priorities. 'The force of the enemy must be diminished, and as France cannot be detached from Prussia, Prussia must be detached from France.' Only then could Austria hope to save Belgium; only then could the Maritime Powers overcome the threat to their very existence. Where would Austria be if England fell?

Maria Theresa temporised. She was milder than she had been in the past. But her eyes were on the coronation of her husband, and she still expected to change everything by defeating Frederick in the field.

The imperial election went off successfully. Since the Golden Bull of 1346 the seven members of the Electoral College had consisted, oddly, of three archbishops – Mainz, Cologne, Treves – and four secular princes – the Elector Palatine, the duke of Saxony, the margrave of Brandenburg and the king of Bohemia. After a great deal of argument as to whether Francis was a prince of the Empire at all, and after the demonstrative withdrawal of the envoys of Brandenburg (i.e. Prussia) and the Elector Palatine, who held that the Bohemian vote, Maria Theresa's own vote, was no longer valid, all went smoothly. The coronation took place in October 1746.

To see and be close to Francis parading in his medieval splendour had been the young Queen's devouring ambition since her accession. She accompanied Francis to Frankfurt in great style, but flatly refused to share in his coronation. This, Frederick characteristically insisted, was because she regarded the imperial honour as a second-rate affair compared with the very real substance of her own regal power. Certainly she would have had to play a subsidiary part in the actual ceremony. It is possible, too, that she jibbed at being crowned without the unanimous vote, which would have included the vote of Frederick himself as margrave of Brandenburg. It is certain that she was determined that this should be Francis's day and that she knew she could afford to stand back while he, for once, stood forward. It made no difference. She had already been behaving like an empress; now, through Francis, she was Empress also in name. She had one more humiliation at Frederick's hands. Instead of the hoped-for victory, the Austrians had suffered yet another defeat, at Soor, on September 30th: her beloved brother-in-law had failed again, this time not through indecisiveness but, of all things in face of Frederick, through over-confidence. But she was still full of hope and had a plan now for joining forces with Saxony to march directly on Berlin. The Tsaritsa Elisabeth of Russia was in a mood to put a spoke in Frederick's wheel, and promised to march on Prussia should Frederick invade Saxony. But once again Frederick's physical movements were faster than other people's thought. Even as Maria Theresa's bold plans were maturing she received the dire news that Frederick had smashed a Saxon formation at Hennendorf and chased Prince Charles out of Silesia and into Bohemia, with very heavy losses. Almost at once another Prussian force had broken the rest of the Saxons and opened the way for Frederick's triumphant entry into Dresden. All this was in the first half of December 1745, and it was sympathy with the plight of her new ally, Augustus of Saxony, as much as fear of further defeat at the hands of the Prussians that drove her quickly to make an end. On Christmas Day 1745 Silesia was lost to Austria for ever by the Peace of Dresden. Frederick for his part recognised Francis as Emperor, undertook to evacuate Saxony, and removed himself from the war without a word to his French ally.

The war, without Prussia, dragged on for nearly another three years. So far as Austria was concerned it was a period of indeterminate fighting in the Netherlands and in Italy, marked by unceasing bickering and recrimination between allies: the Dutch, the Austrians said, were cowardly and infirm of purpose, the Sardinians too demanding in return for their assistance against Spain. England and Holland complained that Austria was not pulling her weight. France and England showed increasing determination to negotiate a peace and call it a day, but the Dutch were awkward, and Maria Theresa would not let go; soon she was hoping that Russia would intervene decisively on Austria's side. But to no avail. The pity of it was that her mind, the most active part of it, was already racing on to other things: above all, the radical reform of her own dominions. An earlier peace, had she been able to bring herself to make it, would have saved much misery. But, having been forced to concede Silesia to Frederick, the thought of further sacrifices, even the cession of a tiny part of Italy to provide 'an establishment' for the younger brother of Don Carlos, brought out all her stubbornness, which could be blind. In the end she had to give way, and the great Succession War ended in October 1748 in the Treaty of Aix-la-Chapelle — with a whimper, not a bang, and with all the chief contenders more or less as they were and in a state of considerable exhaustion.

Personal Interlude

Chapter Seven

The Queen's Conscience

While Maria Theresa was establishing herself, through strenuous conflict, as a ruler to be feared by the corrupt and self-seeking among her servants, respected by the honest and straightforward, she was also engaged in a secret process of self-criticism, and for this she needed help. Nobody close to her had the least understanding of the complexities of her make-up. We have seen how she appeared to the outside world; her courage verging on recklessness; her refusal to recognise the facts of power verging on perversity; her high-handedness tipping over into arrogance. Even those who did not suffer from them took her 'moods' at their face value. The man who was to develop into one of the most valued and faithful of her servants, Count Khevenhüller-Metsch (a kinsman of the famous soldier), soon to be promoted to be Lord High Chamberlain, responsible for the ordering of her court, went in awe of her rages, her *fumo*: his day-to-day journal, one of the most valuable documents of the time, is partly vitiated by his failure to grasp how the Queen's mind really worked. He faithfully reports her passages of anger and her passages of graciousness, but he did not understand the calculated purposefulness of the way she used her anger and her charm. And he never suspected the existence of a deep vein of diffidence beneath her outward assurance. Detachment he had. He knew how to criticise his revered mistress. But humour he lacked altogether. If only we could have a description by this privileged observer, who saw and knew nearly everything over decades, to compare with, for example, Sir

John Harington's report to his wife on the moment in the life of another great queen, Elizabeth of England, when he had returned with Essex after the failure of the expedition to Ireland:

In good sooth I feared her Majesty more than the rebel Tyrone, and wished I had never received my Lord Essex's honour of Knighthood. She is quite disfavoured and unattired, and these troubles waste her much. She disregardeth every costly cover that cometh to the table and taketh little but manchet and succory pottage. Every new message from the city doth disturb her, and she frowns on all the ladies. I had a sharp message from her brought by my Lord Buckhurst, namely thus, 'Go tell that witty fellow my godson, to get home; it is no season now to fool it here.' I liked this as little as she doth my knighthood, so took to my boots, and returned to the plow in bad weather. I must not say much, even by this trusty and sure messenger; but the many evil plots and designs have overcome all her Highness's sweet temper. She walks much in her privy chamber, and stamps with her feet at ill news, and thrusts her rusty sword at times into the arras in a great rage. My Lord Buckhurst is much with her, and few else since the city business; but the dangers are over, and yet she always keeps a sword by her table.

Elizabeth is there, in a single paragraph. In the whole of Kheven-hüller's seven volumes Maria Theresa is never there. We have to find her not in commentary and memoirs but in her correspondence and in her own memorials. Thus, when at last Prague had been retaken and Charles Albert deposed early in 1743, she had to go to Bohemia to be crowned. The senior traitors, who had welcomed the Bavarians, had been bundled off to their estates and a great welcome was being prepared. But Maria Theresa was going to stand no nonsense from the Estates and from the people who had so easily deserted her cause. And she had to make this clear to Kinsky, her Bohemian chancellor, who was all too ready, as she saw it, to let bygones be bygones and smooth over the past. She entered Prague resplendently on April 29th. She proposed to be crowned on May 11th, early in the morning and on a Sunday at that. Kinsky suggested that the notice was too short. She replied pretty sharply in a handwritten note:

In Pressburg the time was even shorter. The Diet in Prague is less important that the Hungarian one, where everything happened in three days. The Elector [Charles Albert] gave even less time. The banquet is of no account: I can eat fish. . . . There are plenty of churches for the people to hear Mass in. . . . I shall be in a bad temper anyway. Don't make it worse. . . . Nothing is to be changed, even by an hour.

And again: 'The crown has come. I tried it on. Heavier than the Pressburg one and looks like a fool's cap.'

These communications have sometimes been offered, with many others, as examples of natural ill-humour. Of course the Queen was angry with her Bohemians and she knew how to put them in their place by slighting their coronation arrangements. But every word was calculated and cool. She was assuming the Bohemian crown as her right, not by favour of the Bohemian people, still less of the Bohemian nobility, so many of whom, like so many of her Austrians, had betrayed her. This had to be brought home to them. It had to be brought home to Kinsky too; for although Kinsky had been loyal, he was a great deal too close to the traitors, his fellow-nobles, for her liking. On the other hand, the Hungarians, in spite of the difficult time they had given her, had in the end stood by her. This also had to be made clear. She was not giving way to ill-humour. She was carrying out a calculated act of policy. It was a revolutionary policy, the full implications of which neither she nor her nobles understood.

Maria Theresa was Queen, and she was determined to be mistress of her realm. This meant bringing the great magnates and aristocrats to heel and putting an end to the particularism which for so long had distinguished the conduct of the Empire. The true inwardness of what she was doing was concealed by the accident that the first phase of her action was directed against traitors to the Crown. It had begun in 1742 after the recovery of Linz and Upper Austria when, reproached by her closest advisers for seeking to punish those who had sworn fealty to Charles Albert, she replied: 'I am sure that enough loyal and honest men can be found to fill the positions made vacant by a purge. Many of my Silesians are out of bread because of their loyalty and have nothing to do. Don't tell me there are no able men among them!'

It was not until some years later that she, and others, began to see that she was in fact inaugurating a new system which involved breaking the power of the Estates and subordinating the interests of the nobility to the interests of the Crown. At first, largely ignorant and wholly unappreciative of the loose and unstated arrangement which had held the Empire together and had been taken quite for granted by her father – the Crown bribed the nobility with gifts of land and vast possessions in return for their support in times of crisis: the nobility ran the provinces in their own interests and provided support for the Crown on more or less their own terms – she had gone to the heart of the matter with practical, unspeculative logic. Either the Crown meant something or it did not; she was determined that it should mean something; it could mean nothing unless it was supreme. It was in this spirit that she sent a shudder of horror and outrage through her nobles when, in March 1742, she insisted on a sort of *levée en masse* in Moravia, commanding that muskets be distributed among the peasantry, still serfs. The peasants were her subjects no less than the nobility; they too could fight for her, and should. Perish the thought that they might turn their arms against their own landlords.

Soon the logic of all this was to be brought out into the open and formalised in her first great movement of reform. In the early 1740s she was acting purely from instinct. And the immediate point to be made is that she was groping forward into a future which she did not understand, using her anger because it was the only weapon she had when her charm was not enough, but very much at sea. It is only if this is appreciated that we can understand her loneliness and the nature of the persistent impulse which, at the very outset of her reign, made her feel the need, to the point of desperation, for a confidant, a man stronger, more experienced, more intelligent, wiser than her husband, to whom she could turn for advice on how to live, concealing nothing from him and expecting from him complete outspokenness.

It was a tall order. It could not be a Melbourne: there was nobody faintly resembling a Melbourne among her ministers and official counsellors: these, anyway, were to look up to her. It could not be an Albert: Francis Stephen was too soft and easy-going, born to be led rather than to lead. It could not be a priest: the young queen knew what she had to render to God, and it was a great deal; but she herself was Caesar. It could not be a woman: there was no woman in the realm whose political views she could respect. It had to be somebody who understood the problems of government and power, the demands of kingship, and, at the same time, had a feeling for life and an understanding of the moods and desperations, the desolating inadequacies, of a twenty-four-year-old girl, untrained to rule, in the isolation of her secular magnificence. It was an impossible demand: only the girl who was prepared to take on the world of men single-handed, could have made it.

The man, amazingly, was there. He was a Portuguese noble in the service of the Habsburgs, born Don Manoel Telles de Menezes e Castro, Count Tarouca, later, in 1755, created Duke of Silva. He was forty-four at the time of Maria Theresa's accession. His father, as a consequence of the Austro-Portuguese alliance, had served in the Austrian Netherlands. The young Tarouca had been a page at the Court of Charles VI and later entered the Habsburg army, serving under Eugene at Peterwardein and Temesvar in the brilliantly successful war against the Turks. Afterwards he had entered the Austrian civil service and risen to occupy a distinguished but subordinate position in the Netherlands.

When he first struck the young princess as a man in a million is not known. He was good with children, and Maria Theresa as a child had loved him. As soon as she came to the throne she lifted him out of the ruck and made him president of the Ministerial Council for the Netherlands. Very soon afterwards she began to show him especial favour. She would appreciate it, she said, if Count Tarouca would visit her each day not only to discuss the affairs of the Netherlands but also to favour her with his personal advice on the many problems she had to face. Very soon she went further. During her great ordeal at Pressburg, while on the one hand she was interminably negotiating with the Hungarians, on the other keeping the rest of the world at bay, she asked Tarouca to devote himself exclusively to her service, to act as her conscience, to advise her in all matters, to tell her the truth about all things, including herself. In her own words, Tarouca's job was 'to show me my faults and make me recognise them. . . . This being most necessary for a ruler, since there are few or none at all to be found who will do this, commonly refraining out of awe or self-interest.' Or, as she put it in her own original commission: 'From now on, without intermission, you are to tell Her where she errs, and to explain with perfect openness Her faults of character.'

It was extraordinary enough that Maria Theresa, at twenty-four, should appoint a secular conscience and listen to it. It was still more extraordinary that the friendship, unique in the history of European monarchies, should survive for thirty years, so that a little before Tarouca died, at seventy-five, Maria Theresa could write: 'How happy I was to see once again a man, a character, to whom I owe what sense and moderation I displayed in the days of my youth.'

For Tarouca himself, tiny, swarthy, very much a foreigner at the court of Vienna, wise and shrewd to a degree, moderate and sober, but with a brain like a razor – as a Dutch ambassador who had been worsted by it once ruefully exclaimed – this mark of grace and favour was at first felt as the seal of doom. What had he done to deserve this frightful destiny? He was a good servant of the Crown, a devoted admirer of his Queen; to be singled out in this unprecedented way was indeed an honour, almost unthinkable, but it was also ruin. The young Queen was married to a highly presentable prince, nine years her senior, with whom she was known to be in love; she was surrounded by established advisers who would regard the new star at best with jealousy and suspicion, at worst with deadly and dangerous enmity; her daily life was ruled by courtiers who had all the time in the world for gossip and intrigue and whose hearts were not, as a rule, bathed in the milk of human kindness. Even if, remarkably, she did not change her mind quite soon and repent her impulsive decision, she would be unable to protect him from any but the most extreme manifestations of malice and malevolence, to say nothing of perfectly reasonable suspicion. What would Francis Stephen have to say about his young bride's choice of an avuncular outsider for a confidant? How would he be able to cope with the incessant pin-pricks of the courtiers, the rumours of undue and unhealthy influence which jealous ministers would spread? Would the Queen, anyway, even as long as she still felt the need of him, be ready to accept the criticisms of her personal conduct which she was now, in all good faith, demanding? And what would happen when she no longer felt she needed him? His entirely respectable career, by which he set great store, would have been broken — for what? His enemies, and he would accumulate more of these the longer he stayed close to the Queen, would fall upon him.

All these questions, and many more besides, Tarouca asked himself, and there were no happy answers. He resisted with all his force Maria Theresa's appeals, until these, persisted in, took on the nature of a command. Then he obeyed.

Maria Theresa had chosen well. Tarouca was the first of a series of men whom she picked for herself and to whom she gave her trust. Nobody knows how she explained 'the little Portuguese' to her husband. To judge by her character she did not explain at all. She was perfectly capable of saying, 'I need Tarouca; I must have him near me,' and leaving it at that. Francis knew, if nobody else did, that though Tarouca might give her something that he could not, he himself was the exclusive object of her self-acknowledged sexual life. He was not noted for the intensity and depth of his emotions and at thirty-three, secure in the knowledge that his wife was deeply in love with him, he may very well have welcomed a certain dilution of the passionate demandingness hitherto centred on him alone. On the other hand the fact that Maria Theresa, married only five years, felt the need for an intimate counsellor whom she could respect and with whom she could be herself, reflects interestingly on Francis. There is nothing on record to suggest that Tarouca's proximity, from the beginning to the end of his life, was in any way resented.

With others, less immediately concerned, things were different. But here, too, the young Queen showed herself more capable than might have seemed possible of ignoring gossip and ensuring that it remained nothing more than gossip. There was plenty of this. In the rococo world which Maria Theresa adorned and for some years almost passionately enjoyed, it was the most natural thing in the world for people to assume that the Portuguese was the Queen's lover. The more so because at the Court of Vienna in her father's day (her father, after all, had been dead less than a year when Count Tarouca took up his new position) a peculiar convention had reigned.

Promiscuity was frowned upon, but every husband had, effectively, two wives, and every wife two husbands. Marriages were arranged with an eye to material advantage; this being secured the partners were free, were expected, to take a lover or a mistress to their hearts. There was nothing clandestine about this, there was no concealment; the paramours enjoyed all the public privileges of married couples. Indeed, they behaved like married couples and were expected not only to swear eternal fidelity but also to maintain it. This, more often than not, they did, passing hand in hand through life and moving into their declining years with their close attachment unimpaired. Visitors from lands with other morals were frequently hard put to it at first to distinguish legitimate spouses from the official lovers and mistresses, all sitting amicably together round the same dinner-table. These cosy arrangements did not, of course, preclude the carrying on of less permanent or more passionate affairs, but in these discretion of a high degree was required to be observed.

This system began to break down in the middle of the eighteenth century when the sort of morals that had long distinguished the French court — others too, not least the court at Petersburg — were picked up everywhere as the intensity of the baroque gave way to the cooler light-heartedness of the rococo. In either context it was hard for any of her contemporaries who did not know her to grasp the simple truth about Maria Theresa: she was a one-man woman, jealously and passionately so. And she remained this even though, with frequent paroxisms of indignation, she recognised that Francis Stephen was not a one-woman man. She moved freely among men; she knew how to handle them and make them her slaves. She had close women friends, but essentially she was a man's woman — what woman was there with a tenth of her vitality, drive, common sense (she was not interested in brains as such)? But whatever quasisexual needs were at least partly satisfied by her friendships with men were concealed, most successfully, from herself.

Because of this historians, guarding her reputation, have been content to follow the young Podewils, the son of Frederick's foreign minister, who was immensely struck by the charm and beauty of his master's implacable foe when he saw her for the first time. She was in her middle thirties then, and clearly at the peak of her mature beauty. Podewils would have liked to have been able to report to Frederick any scandal attaching to her name; but there was none that stood looking into. The Queen and her husband, he said, were made for bourgeois marriage.

But the conception of Maria Theresa as a good bourgeois is no less silly than the belief that she took lovers. It is based partly on her fidelity to Francis, partly on her fanatical attachment to her children, partly on the very undress way in which she and Francis led their domestic lives: they liked to sit about in dressing-gowns and slippers. Both, in fact, were aristocratic to the core in action and in feeling. Francis Stephen, who liked a home to call his own, was an easygoing grand seigneur who could not be bothered with appearances except when splendour was required by protocol; who preferred a quiet life to arguing points with his overwhelming consort; who pursued his own pleasures as the mood took him: his passion was reserved for hunting. At cards he could lose 30,000 ducats in a night with the greatest good humour — Maria Theresa played less high but with far greater intensity; he went to the theatre and the ballet to look at pretty women; and, apart from one affair of long standing with the current Countess Auersperg, his loves were easygoing too. He would have been happier as Duke of Lorraine than he was to be as Emperor; but as Duke of Lorraine he would have been no bourgeois.

Maria Theresa, as we have seen, was higher mettled. Her love for Francis Stephen was devouring. When a friend of his youth once suggested that he should insist on a separate bedroom, she was not only furious; she pursued the unfortunate with contumely for the rest of her life. She was not a Habsburg for nothing, and possessiveness had been the distinguishing mark of this family for centuries past. Silesia was hers, and so was Francis. She was, unlike many Habsburgs, emotional and volatile: she could present herself as an accomplished actress, as when she appealed to the Hungarians, or threw herself at the feet of her successful generals; but this sort of acting, at this level of accomplishment, has to be felt, and the feeling comes first. She could tease a Kinsky for making ugly scenes, but she could make violent scenes herself. She knew how to storm as well as charm. Poor Francis dreaded those scenes, which took more out of

him than they took out of her, and he went out of his way to avoid
them. Writing to her sister in October 1744, Maria Theresa showed
that she was fully aware of this fact and knew how to exploit it. The
occasion of this particular scene had not been another woman but,
less excusable, her husband's expressed wish to go off to the wars.

> I was sick with anger and pain, and I made *mon vieux* [she re-
> ferred to her husband thus, habitually] ill with my wickedness.
> I fell back on our usual refuge, caresses and tears; but they did not
> work, although he is the best husband in the world. . . . In the
> end I got into another temper, to such effect that now we are
> both ill. I can't move him at all, and at the same time I have to
> confess to myself that his reasons are plausible enough. All the
> same, if he really goes off I shall either follow him or shut my-
> self up in a convent.

In the end she got her way, as she always got her way. But goodness knows how many scenes of this kind poor Francis had to endure.
She was then twenty-seven; Francis was thirty-six. Tarouca, who
was supposed to teach her to learn her faults, was fifty-four.

Maria Theresa's belief in the sanctity of the marriage vows had
nothing bourgeois about it. It was simply out of place in the
eighteenth century. It was part and parcel of her religious faith, of
her regard for the pledged word, of her insistence on honour among
princes in an age when none of them knew the meaning of the word.
These qualities went hand in hand with her genuine concern for the
welfare of her subjects and that instinctive understanding of the need
for a centralised, healthy and reasonably just state which were to
occasion her great domestic reforms. They went with her rejection of
the eighteenth-century conception of warfare and her determination
to fight to the finish in the name of a country which, until she had
got to work on it, hardly existed as a country. Nothing could have
been farther removed from her imperious and passionate temperament, and the softer womanly arts she employed to make sure of
getting her way, than the bourgeois ideal of contrived respectability.
She was monogamous, and later, having her revenge on the sort of
woman who had caused Francis to give her such bad moments, she
came down with all her weight on marital infidelity. But she was

unshockable and habitually considered sexual practice with clinical detachment.

This was the woman who, at twenty-four, pleaded, then commanded, Tarouca to take charge of her.

In the nature of things there is no record of their conversations, which were frequent, about life in general, the duties and obligations of princes in particular, and most specifically the personal conduct of this individual monarch. Tarouca was discretion itself; Maria Theresa could preserve absolute discretion when she chose, which was by no means always. There are a few political recommendations which have come to light, not all of which she followed; there are a few written notes, a few anecdotes, which illustrate the difficulties Tarouca had in trying to curb the appetite for pleasure and excitement which was not exceeded by her appetite for work.

These fragments tell us more about Maria Theresa than about Tarouca himself. All we know about him is expressed in the soundness and wisdom of his general views and in the one supreme fact: that Maria Theresa stood by him for thirty years and at the end of them could refer to him as 'mon ami intime et ministre particulier'.

'Votre Majesté m'a honoré du plus delicat, scrupuleux employ, que jamais puisse avoir un pauvre sujet.' Thus Tarouca expressed his position at the outset of the strange arrangement. He started modestly enough, as pedagogue. The Queen must bring order into her days. Life at Court in her first year was a great muddle with work and play, tears and laughter, ministers, petitioners and family all mixed up together. This must cease. The Queen must learn to economise her time; method was half the battle. She must allow time for dressing properly, for eating properly and for retreat; only thus could she keep her end up and the world at bay. Very well then, assuming that she got up at eight o'clock she was to give herself an hour for dressing, breakfast and hearing Mass. After Mass, half an hour with her children. Then, from 9.30 to 12.30 it would be solid work: documents to read and initial, ministers to confer with, audiences to take. At 12.30 she was to stop everything, to relax before the midday meal at 12.45. Above all she must be punctual at meals, and she must eat her food before it got cold — and drink up her after-dinner coffee before *that* got cold. After the meal an hour for herself, her children, her mother the dowager Empress – 'sans rien faire de plus sérieux'. More work sharp at 4 and right through to supper at 8.30. Seven and a half scheduled hours of work each day. But no more work after supper. Now she must relax, dance, play cards – but not too much!

How different from Versailles.

Tarouca followed up with warnings about wearing herself out with dancing and riding – and here he was one with his critics. Everyone in responsible positions around the Court was on at her about her dancing and card-playing to all hours, above all her riding which for a time became a mania. She rode hard and fast whenever she could. She developed a passion for that peculiar form of mock-tournament called the carrousel, in which she and her ladies took part. Even when she was heavily pregnant in the winter of 1742–43 she insisted on concealing her condition with a heavy riding-habit and taking part in a carrousel, riding side-saddle instead of astride, thereby, according to Khevenhüller, causing much speculative comment. In that same carnival time she scandalised Khevenhüller again by the way she carried on. It was Shrove Tuesday. She lunched in style with her brother-in-law, Prince Charles of Lorraine, at his castle at Mollersdorf just outside the city.

> Then the whole afternoon they danced, until eight in the evening. Back to the Hofburg, where her Imperial Majesty supped *en petite compagnie* and went on to a masked ball, her whole party dressed as peasants. Then they slipped dominoes over their peasant dress and went out to the public dance in the Mehlgruben, where they took part in the contre-danses; then back to the ball-room and the carrousel, which continued until seven in the morning.

After that, with no sleep at all, but fresh as paint, the young Queen attended Mass and began her new day.

Khevenhüller at first was inclined to blame Tarouca for this sort of thing: he called him disparagingly the master of the Queen's pleasures. But Tarouca himself was in despair. Time and time again he would tell his charge that her pleasures were more like hard work than recreation. 'Your old nagger,' he would call himself – no doubt because she had accused him of nagging, which indeed he did. She may not have heeded him, but she was not ungrateful. Once when he reproached her for paying no attention to his warnings she retorted: 'Never mind! Go on telling me. Even if I don't always do what you tell me I should, your words come back to me later and make me think.'

It did not go on for long. Within ten years, in less than ten years, the little Portuguese was urging her, imploring her, to rest, to give herself time off, to remember her early days and the refreshment and delight her pleasures had given her. Now, far more than then, she had earned the right to relax. She was thirty-four. It was useless to talk like that, she replied: 'I am no longer what I once was, there can be no more distractions for me! Useless to think there can be, but let us at least try to live, so that the others never see what a burden all this hunting, all these pleasures now are to me! I advise you, my dear, to go back to the city as soon as you can – I would do the same, if only to hide myself the better.'

That was after eight years of war and many pregnancies. She did not always feel like that: there was an element of the manic-depressive in her make-up; but as she grew older the depressions grew deeper and longer. Ten years later Tarouca had to speak to her again, and in language which would have amazed and outraged those who still insisted on thinking of him as a flattering courtier. Francis Stephen was dead. Joseph her son and co-regent was being difficult, she was in the depths of despair and beginning to think of giving up altogether. Tarouca begged her to remember her own childhood, its happiness and serenity, the gaiety of her early years, and how much she owed to the spirit of her mother, who also went through bad times:

'Therefore, Madame, we must banish melancholy, like every other idle frittering of time; for all these faults are damaging and sinful in the eyes of God. If we kick against our duties we betray our calling and render ourselves useless to the millions of our subjects. Above all we must never forget that all Europe is watching us and will all too easily regard us with contempt.'

What, one asks, was left for the Queen's confessor to do? Tarouca once himself observed that he was listened to with a humility that was in keeping with the occupant of a convent cell more than with the occupant of a throne.

In manners he was the perfect courtier, and, since nobody knew, or could know, what he said to Maria Theresa, and she to him, about her personal conduct, he was judged as a jumped-up courtier who, alas, was also cleverer than those who would have liked to have pulled him down. The faithful, grumbling Khevenhüller, who had once liked him – in his proper place – was clearly convinced that he was a skilled political intriguer as well as a busybody, 'the sort of man who happily busies himself with everything'. Not content with his official job of overseeing the building of Maria Theresa's new palace at Schönbrunn, he had got control of all building in the city and mixed himself up with all sorts of matters outside his proper sphere. From being an 'Espèce de directeur des plaisirs de la Reine' he had managed to insinuate himself into the Queen's 'grace and friendship', so that she was beginning to consult him in the most secret affairs of state. Indeed, he could no nothing right: some said he overwhelmed the Queen with his 'too despotic maxims', some that he flattered her too much into taking bad advice. At the end of this entry Khevenhüller covered himself with the observation that it was not his place to determine how much truth there was in these allegations. He simply reported what was being said about 'this *sopra fino* Portuguese'.

Tarouca had been a good diplomat, ambitious in his career. Khevenhüller was a diplomat *manqué*: he had not been doing very brilliantly when Maria Theresa had summoned him to rule her household. He ruled it honestly and well; but that he became personally jealous of Tarouca there is no doubt. Later there were to be occasions when Tarouca tried very hard to influence his Queen in matters of high policy. For example, he stubbornly opposed the authority she vested in Haugwitz who, more than any man, was to devise and carry out the radical reforms which turned the Habsburg possessions into a viable state, fit to survive the epoch of revolution. He also frowned on the diplomatic genius of Kaunitz, above all his famous reversal of the alliances which, for the first time, made Austria an ally of her hereditary enemy, France, and put her in opposition to England allied with Prussia. On these occasions, as on other lesser ones, Maria Theresa showed that no matter how much she valued Tarouca's friendship and private counsels it was she and she alone who decided the great questions of state. She went ahead with her plans, paying no attention to Tarouca, for good or ill.

His true role was to teach her how to think, how to organise her days, how to manage her ministers, to give her self-confidence and smooth out her moods as they oscillated between elation and despair. For a lifetime he was the man she could turn to when clouded by uncertainty and doubt; in the early years of her reign he was her rock.

PART TWO

Reflections of the Age

Chapter Eight

❦

Imperial Splendour

The Vienna of Maria Theresa's youth was a bewildering mixture of the huddled and the grand; the grand was new and shining.

In 1717, the year of her birth, Eugene had taken Belgrade in the teeth of the largest army in Europe, 200,000 men. It was only then that the Turkish menace was known to be broken for ever. Until then, in spite of Eugene's earlier exploits, notably at Zenta in 1697, the Turks had appeared as a threat in being liable to coalesce with little warning and launch themselves across the Danube plain. That threat had in fact been finally broken fourteen years earlier in 1683, with the destruction of the Grand Vizier's army at the gates of Vienna following a sixty-day siege, and at the eleventh hour. From then on, with certain setbacks, it was to be only a question of pushing the Ottoman Empire back, ever farther. But it did not look like that at the time. Then 200,000 men had encamped themselves under the city walls and set about its deliberate reduction. Commanded by Kara Mustapha, renowned even in Turkey for his cruelty, his greed, his insatiable appetites (he had 1,500 concubines and 700 black eunuchs to guard them), he gave Austria its first real taste of the meaning of Ottoman culture and of what happened to infidels caught beneath the holy standard of Mohammed. There is no God but God.

It had been happening all over the Balkans and Hungary, for century after century, fair lands laid desolate by this remarkable race for which — such are the mysterious ways of God — the English were for so long to entertain a romantic regard. 'The scourge of mankind,' as Kara Mustapha was called, had, as usual, given his armies full licence for looting and burning and rape. At Perchtoldsdorf, a village just outside Vienna, now a suburb, the pattern was first displayed. The Turks set fire to the village, and the villagers, men, women and children took refuge in their church. After a great deal of bargaining they were allowed to ransom themselves, and when the money had been paid over the villagers emerged fearfully into the open, preceded by a young girl who carried a crown and a flag. There were over 4,000 of them, and no sooner was this great crowd clear of the church door than the Turks surrounded them and massacred them all. This was only one example. It is frequently assumed that Kara Mustapha's hordes, having ravaged all Austria west of the Leitha, were brought to a standstill under the walls of Vienna. Far from it. While the city was invested Turkish troops outflanked it and pene-trated deeply into Lower Austria, looting, sacking, burning every-where. In all the country east of the river Enns only a handful of fortified monasteries were able to hold out, notably the great Bene-dictine Abbey of Melk which had stood on the sheer Danube cliff since 1089, long before the advent of the Habsburgs; in 1700 it was to be rebuilt to form Prandauer's stupendous masterpiece of baroque which towers above the river to this day. The Ottoman forces, in a word, occupied, ravaged, devastated all that part of Austria which was to form the Soviet zone of occupation over two and a half centuries later.

The encampment outside Vienna was a cross between an army headquarters, a travelling circus and a mobile city. While the engineers sapped and mined and dug their parallels, breaching the walls on the very day that succour came, heavily armed detachments swarmed over the countryside with murder in their hearts, swarmed back with loot, and Mustapha held court at the heart of a complex of silken tents of vast size. 'I find it quite impossible,' wrote Sobieski to his wife immediately after the battle, 'to convey to you the exquisite luxury of the Vizier's tents: there are baths, small gardens, fountains, rabbits and even a parrot.' The tents were lighted by silver lamps and chandeliers, hung with carpets worked in silver and gold, stacked with chests of precious stones and furs. As for the stores of this vast array, the people of Vienna, issuing on the heels of their deliverers, seized 20,000 buffaloes, bullocks, camels and mules; 10,000 sheep; 100,000 quarters of corn; storehouses crammed with sugar, flour, oil and coffee – the coffee, unknown until then in Vienna, with which an enterprising merchant was to start the first coffee-house in Europe.

All this was in the time of Maria Theresa's grandfather, Leopold II, Carlyle's 'little black Herr in red stockings', who had fled the city, with the whole of his court, leaving it to be defended by the Star-hemberg of the day and to be relieved by distant allies, the King of Poland and the Duke of Lorraine, the grandfather of Francis Stephen. Leopold was to display one of the more unpleasant aspects of the Habsburg character, an aspect notably absent in his granddaughter: ingratitude. He could not bring himself to receive the victorious Sobieski, to whom he owed his city, perhaps his throne, in the Hofburg. Sobieski, when all was said, was no more than a general of the imperial army. He must be treated as such. The proper place to thank him was on the battlefield, not at home. So Leopold rode out to Sobieski's camp, duly thanked him and congratulated him, and rode home again.

It was in the course of this battle for Vienna that the young Eugene won his golden spurs at the hands of the duke of Lorraine. And his first impressions of Ottoman barbarity were themselves to spur his determination not to rest until the Turks had been pushed far enough back, and weakened into the bargain, so they could never again threaten Vienna. His distrust and dislike of France, in whose service he would have fought had Louis XIV not taken a dislike to him because of his rather lurid family history as well as his own un-prepossessing appearance, was sharpened by the knowledge that Louis himself had been active in his help and encouragement of the barbarians in their last almost overwhelming onslaught on the Habs-burgs. In 1717 he was to take Belgrade. He lived, an old man out of favour with Maria Theresa's father (who was jealous of his genius and his repute), to see it lost in 1739. But there were to be no more Turkish invasions after that.

Until 1683 Vienna had been a fortified outpost of the western culture, first of the Roman Empire, then, as Europe emerged from the Dark Ages, under the Christian Babenbergs, for a short time under the Bohemian king, finally, from the thirteenth century, under the Habsburgs. These, until the seventeenth century, made more of Graz in Styria, Innsbruck in Tirol, well off the main track of the invaders from the East and protected by high mountains, than of Vienna. Until 1683 Vienna was still confined within its medieval walls. With the constant threat of barbaric hordes moving easily and quickly across the great Danube plain it had little time to think of the graces of life and was left behind by the rest of Europe, by Prague and Cracow even, as a centre of culture and civilised living. The flowering when it came was spectacular and swift, a forced flowering. It expressed itself above all in a fantastic building boom, and the spirit behind this boom was Teutonic baroque, a fusing of post-Renaissance Italian fantastification stiffened by northern strength and intensity of purpose.

The pattern had been established outside Vienna long before the siege. Thus, for example, at Salzburg the new cathedral by Solari, built in 1652–55, was entirely Italianate in style, while hundreds of churches all over the Austrian lands, as well as in Bavaria, assisted in the development of a truly Austrian style, an infusion of gothic tradition into Italian baroque, executed by thousands of Italian architects and workmen. This great burst of church building, indeed, was started off by the triumph of the Counter-Reformation and the consequent reassertion of the Catholic spirit. It gave a physical unity to the Habsburg lands, from the high Alps into Bohemia. Everywhere the infinitely various landscape was punctuated by the white stuccoed churches with square twin towers surmounted by bulbous cupolas. Inside were the retables and reredoses brilliant with a dazzle of gilding, with sunbursts of the Trinity and life-size golden saints. Only from the shape and structure of the columns and the arches could one tell whether the painted vaultings and the veneers of coloured marble belonged to a new building or concealed the fabric of medieval gothic.

Thus when the great building boom struck Vienna, and, at the same time, the great religious orders with their huge monasteries all to be rebuilt, the solution was ready-made. Early Italian baroque had been transformed by constant practice and amendment into what amounted to a new style. And the great architects were there and ready to exploit and celebrate it: Prandauer, Hildebrandt, the Fischers, father and son.

The building began in the crowded inner city within the walls; but it soon spread to the level ground and the small hills beyond the glacis, which had to be kept clear. Maria Theresa grew up in a Vienna that had already been transformed. By the time she was born all the grand families had their new palaces, some of them two: the summer palaces outside the walls, the winter palaces within. With the exception of Eugene's summer palace, the Belvedere, they were not overwhelmingly pretentious. The splendour was indoors, where broad and imaginative staircases opened out into state rooms. Façades were cool and Renaissance-classical, with sometimes an efflorescence of statuary along the skyline, more often an elaborately conceived and executed baroque portico with sunbursts or swags of trophies seeming to grow out of the stone. The greatest of all the Viennese baroque architects, Bernard Fischer, known later as Fischer von Erlach, received his inspiration direct from Rome, which he visited as a young man, above all from the work of Bernini, the architect of the great colonnade of St Peters. One of his first commissions was to assist the Italian Burnacini in designing the great Plague Column in the Graben, the prototype of many such columns to be raised to the glory of God for deliverance from the plague. The Graben column expresses perfectly the spirit which drove the baroque architects, sculptors and painters: the total conquest of nature by the human vision. In the vast formal gardens of the eighteenth century nature is defied and driven out. The vistas, the parterres, the flights of steps, the formal pools, the fountains, the grottoes, the teeming statuary were arranged to express grand geometrical designs; trees, shrubs, flowers and grass were never displayed for their own sakes, they were seen simply as living materials to be clipped, dwarfed, shaven, trained into artificial shapes as part of the design. So in the Graben column the only thing that mattered to the designer was his own conception of heaven and earth and the universe. The steepsided pyramidal mass exhibits a realisation in stone of the Trinity, the Father, Son and Holy Ghost, floating on a billow of clouds.

Maria Theresa inherited this glory. Most of the palaces were completed before her birth, though still very new and white; but three very important buildings, two masterpieces of Fischer von Erlach and Hildebrandt's supreme monument, Prince Eugene's Belvedere Palace, were still going up. The Belvedere, then incomparably the city's most splendid palace, planted on its hill outside the walls, its long formal gardens descending in steep terraces, was completed when she was six. She saw the trees grow to maturity. This palace was far grander than her father's own summer palace, the Favorita, which it overlooked. From the Hofburg itself, then a large, rambling, but unpretentious complex of buildings in the huddle of the city centre, she could watch the building of Fischer's superb Court Library which brought together, working as a team, a brilliant galaxy of talent, painters, sculptors, wood-carvers, workers in marble and metal, to produce one of the richest and most stately halls in Europe.

Fischer was dead, but his designs were carried out by his son, who was also building, again to his father's designs, the great Karlskirche with its soaring dome, in the open fields beside the little river Wien, now no more than a conduit, largely built over. This church, still the greatest in Vienna after the romanesque and gothic cathedral of St Stephen, was her father's special pride. It was dedicated by him in 1713 to St Charles Borromeo in thanksgiving for the ending of the plague. Scenes from the plague were cut in relief in the tympanum of the great Corinthian portico, and the portico itself, with its six columns, was flanked by two free-standing pillars, imitations of Trajan's column in Rome, with spiral reliefs showing scenes from the life of St Charles. This was the final flowering of Viennese baroque. Started two years before Maria Theresa was born, it was finished and solemnly inaugurated by her father in her twenty-first year, two years before her accession. The saplings planted to break the great empty spaces round the church grew up with her, and as a child she must have watched the heavy drays, or tumbrils, bringing up the dressed stone from the Danube wharves to which it had been floated down on rafts from quarries deep in the mountainous interior, or from Italy across the Brenner Pass.

But even while the Karlskirche was building, the impulse which had sustained the baroque had died. Fischer's genius belonged to an earlier age. We have no record of the young queen's attitude towards the strange and sometimes oppressive mixture of brilliance and solemnity, aspiration and secular pomposity which marked the epoch of her father and her grandfather. All we know is that she did not continue the style. It is clear that her personal taste was for the cool, unforced, glancing extravagances of the rococo which was wholly and wholeheartedly of this world. Cheerfully excluding all intensity of feeling, concerned only with extracting the utmost possible elegance out of any given situation, no longer flatly denying nature, but seeking to harmonise with it, it thus indirectly, and with the emphasis on elegance, begins to exalt the human sensibility, reflecting a changing mood.

2

Elegance was not at all the dominating impression given to visitors to Vienna in the early eighteenth century. These were first aware of darkness and huddle. The tall cathedral with its soaring spire, itself dark, gloomy, dirty, damp and hung densely with dusty, tattered regimental colours, dominated a labyrinth of walled in, bastioned lanes, lined with crammed apartment houses as lofty as the palaces squeezed in among them, blankly shining. 'This town,' wrote Lady Mary Wortley Montagu, 'which has the honour of being the Emperor's residence, did not at all answer my ideas of it, being very much less than I expected to find it; the streets are very close, and so narrow, one cannot observe the fine fronts of the palaces.' Over fifty years later, towards the close of Maria Theresa's reign, Dr Burney echoed her: 'The streets are rendered doubly dark and dirty by their narrowness, and by the extreme height of the houses.' The city has been opened up since then, but many of those old streets follow their old lines, and it is still impossible, for example, to take in properly Fischer's long façade for Eugene's winter palace in the Himmelpfortgasse. From the outside there is nothing to suggest the splendour within: the superb staircase hall opening from a hidden courtyard itself entered through the main gateway, barred by blank doors; Chiarini's brilliant painted ceiling in the Blue Room; the carved and gilded ceiling of the golden cabinet. In the interior decoration of nearly all the baroque palaces of Vienna the transition to Austrian rococo is effortless and often imperceptible. Wheres in other countries the rococo marked a clearcut break with the baroque, in Austria it appears more as a softening and humanising influence, more than anything else gently emphasising the intrusion of personal taste and, as it were, the human touch into the impersonal and formal grandeur of the true baroque.

In a very real sense Austrian rococo was a manifestation of the functional in architecture: an easy background of lucid and unexacting elegance was required for a high society which was beginning to set store by the light of reason. But only in a timid and tentative manner. It was a Catholic society apparently untouched by the philosophical and scientific revolution of Locke and Newton in England and the later iconoclasms of the Encyclopaedists and Voltaire. Maria Theresa herself was a devout and totally committed believer, contemplating with horror the heresies of the Protestant north; with contempt, coloured by alarm, the devilish atheism of her great antagonist, Frederick; with disgust the moral nihilism of Louis XV and his court. But even she was coloured by the spirit of the times; her religion was utilitarian – functional again, one might say – rather than doctrinaire, and with a faint tincture of Erastianism. God was supreme. She obeyed him and expected her subjects to do the same. She treated her priests and confessors with proper submission and respect: they were God's servants, or liaison officers. But her relations with the Almighty were strictly personal and concerned exclusively with the state of her soul, with particular reference to the after life. She would attend to her priests on this subject, but on no other. Problems of heaven and hell they understood. But they had no more understanding than the next man, probably less, when it came to problems of government, administration and secular education. This was true, indeed of the Pope himself. The Queen, the Empress, would prostrate herself before him with perfect humility as the vicar of God, but his vicarate was established for the care of souls. This was quite enough for any one man, and provided she, the Empress, strove to keep her own soul in proper shape and prayed earnestly for the souls of others, the management of her secular affairs, her inheritance, her empire, was to be conducted in accordance with the light of reason – her reason, and the reason of advisers determined by her.

Thus, too, her subjects, those who set the moral tone, although for the most part not at all intellectual – rather, indeed, anti-intellectual, inheriting as they did the mood of the Counter-Reformation and basing their authority, which was immense, on the possession of vast estates worked by serf labour; although, too, they tended to be interested in alchemy rather than in science if they had speculative minds – were coloured in their attitudes by the spirit of reasonableness, if not reason, and empirical common sense rather than passion and dogma. And into this mood the Austrian rococo fitted to perfection. Of course there were show-pieces. Thus many of the rooms at Schönbrunn, for example, had no functional purpose whatsoever: they were fantasies, elegant toys, a nobleman's whim, no less than a Fabergé Easter-egg. And yet, at the same time, they reflected the deep eighteenth-century spirit which became ever stronger as the epoch reached its halfway mark. That is to say, they were not assertions of arbitrary fancy, rather reflections of the strong and muddled passion which saw the whole purpose of art in the imitation of nature. What imitation meant, what nature meant, and how this preoccupation with both led insensibly into the flowering of the romantic movement we shall have to consider when we come to contemplate the musicians of the Theresian epoch.

It is enough for the moment to record that Theresian rococo was rarely in tune with, for example, the consciously breathtaking fantasy of the Amalienburg in Munich. Indeed, the functionalism of Austrian rococo was not a sudden development. This functionalism may be seen beautifully illustrated in the Winter Riding School attached to the stables of the Hofburg and built at the very end of the baroque period by the younger Fischer for Maria Theresa's father. This wonderful arena, used now for the Spanish Riding School, all white, with its colonnaded gallery, is, with all its elegance and glorious proportions, a stunningly simple realisation of a perfectly straightforward purpose: to produce a covered hall fit for an emperor to ride in. And this directness of purpose is echoed time and time again fifty years later, not only by large parts of the palace at Schönbrunn and the state apartments fitted out by Maria Theresa in the Leopold wing of the Hofburg but also in quite small details – as for example the neoclassical porcelain stoves which still stand in the anterooms of the state ballroom, or *Redoutensaal*, exquisite in their absolute simplicity, relying for ornamentation only on the delicate gilding which emphasises rather than conceals the utilitarian form.

3

With all this went, of course, the lavish display of the very rich, which is always with us. The great palaces of the ancient nobility stood by themselves, and some of them might have belonged to kings. Thus in one small corner of the city, the Kinsky, Schönborn and Harrach Palaces stood almost touching, each a world in itself, each no more than the town houses of families who lorded it over immense tracts of countryside, living to themselves like monarchs: the Kinskys at Kamnitz in Bohemia, the Schönborns near Korneuburg, across the river from Vienna on the way to Prague; the Harrachs in the Leitha valley, which used to divide Austria from Hungary. There were many more of these families, some of them ancient in their splendour, others aggrandised after the battle of the White Mountain, when Catholic families were settled in Bohemia after the expulsion of the Protestant nobility: Lobkowitz, Schwarzenberg, Starhemberg, Windischgraetz, Liechtenstein, Dietrichstein, and the rest. Their wealth was in their timber, their mines, their quarries, their corn, above all their serfs. Thus the Harrachs built up their dazzling collection of pictures and housed them in style on the labours of innumerable serfs, who included the ancestors and the immediate family of the composer Josef Haydn; the Kinskys owed their splendour to the skilled management of tens of thousands, including the family of Christian Willibald Gluck.

These were the grandees. Only the richest of them, however, could compare with the stupendous wealth of the great Hungarian magnates, who preferred as a rule to remain on their own estates, even those who most actively supported the crown. Thus, the most showy of them all, the Esterházys, who sometimes entered the service of the Crown as soldiers or diplomats when the mood took them, who were responsible among others for swinging their compatriots to the support of Maria Theresa, who were later to be offered the Hungarian crown by Napoleon Bonaparte, lived very much to themselves in a splendour and with an ostentation exceeding that of the royal and imperial family itself.

The original seat of the Esterházy family was a medieval castle perched on a wooded, dolomitic crag at Forchtenstein not far from Wiener Neustadt, since 1918 part of the Burgenland province of Austria, until then part of Hungary. One of a line of antique barons, Paul Esterházy was made a prince of the Holy Roman Empire in the seventeenth century in recognition of his services in securing the kingship of Hungary for the Habsburgs. He was also the first Esterházy to patronise the arts on a large scale, building a superb picture gallery at Forchtenstein and rebuilding in the baroque style his palace at Eisenstadt near the Neusiedlersee, where he established a resident orchestra. His descendants went on from there. In 1918, when the dynasty fell, the Esterházys owned twenty-one castles, sixty market towns and over four hundred villages in Hungary, as well as a number of castles and lordships in Austria and a considerable slice, a whole county, of Bavaria. The last Esterházy to achieve international renown was imperial minister for Foreign Affairs under Francis Joseph at the time of the Austro-Prussian war, a gentle, elegant, sceptical, questioning man with a keen intellect and far too much sensibility. He could charm anybody into accepting his lead, argue anybody into accepting his view; but he was so conscious of the deep complexities of life that he did not want to lead and could never for long sustain a view: he was enchanted by all views. In the end he went melancholy-mad and died in an asylum. In the end, too, this autocratic and acquisitive family which amassed as much wealth as any family outside Asia in the days before the discovery of mineral oil, is remembered for one thing: its patronage of Josef Haydn, born a serf on the neighbouring Harrach estate. Francis Joseph's Count Esterházy would have found this pleasantly amusing, but his ancestors, Paul and Nikolaus the Magnificent, would not have seen the joke.

It was Paul who rebuilt the palace at Eisenstadt, a rather hideous building on the hill above the town, looking away to the mysterious Neusiedlersee and the infinite horizon of the Hungarian *puszta* beyond. Carleone's baroque is heavy and clumsy and the domed towers at the four corners of the monstrous block do nothing to diminish the institutional appearance. Inside, of course, all is splendour, with 200 guest-rooms, a frescoed hall, a picture gallery, a library, a chapel, all the amenities, in short, of a nobleman's residence. The park on the slopes running down to the Leitha was superb.

Although Prince Paul had a small orchestra and liked to compose, it was his son, Paul Anton, who was a passionate musician. After playing an active and valuable part in the War of the Austrian Succession (taking with him his own regiment of hussars, equipped down to the last button at his expense), he settled at Eisenstadt, determined to make it famous for music, and it was he, in 1761, who engaged the young Haydn as assistant director to Gregorius Joseph Werner, who was old and hidebound. Within a year he was dead, and for the next thirty years the reigning Esterházy was Nikolaus, known as the Magnificent. It was this Nikolaus who, bored with the Eisenstadt palace and dissatisfied with its dullness, took it into his head to build a new Versailles in a swamp a few miles away.

It was a fantastic undertaking, and the difficulties of the site were part of the challenge: Nikolaus could perfectly well have built on dry land. The Neusiedlersee, today covering an area of 130 square miles – it is twenty miles long and between four and eight miles wide – is one of the largest lakes in Europe, but it is slightly salt and never more than ten feet deep, usually a good deal less. Lying just below the Leitha hills, on the eastern side the land is perfectly flat as far as the eye can see. There it still is, fringed with reed-beds half a mile wide, a paradise for water-birds: the giant reeds are noisy with the violent, harsh, hectoring chatter of the great reed-warbler; bearded tits and smaller warblers keep up an incessant and mellifluous chatter: bitterns boom; egrets and white heron flop silently out of the reeds and back again, disappearing without trace; black storks beat low to reach their nests on the chimney-tops of the little town of Rust. So it must always have been. And in Maria Theresa's day the whole place was malarial.

On the southern side there was no division between lake and *puszta*. Between the dry land, where the great bustards roamed in droves, and the lake itself, there was swamp. And in this swamp the Esterházys had a little shooting lodge for wild-fowling. It was here that Nikolaus Esterházy, having done his duty as a soldier, having dazzled Europe on his special missions with his famous coat covered with diamonds, decided to build his Versailles. The swamp was drained; deep canals were cut; dams raised. The whole operation from the draining of the swamp to the building of the palace, called Esterháza now, no longer Sutor, was completed in four years, costing over ten million florins, or nearly two million pounds. That was in 1762–66, at a time when Maria Theresa was desperately trying to stabilise Austria's finances during and after the Seven Years War. There was an opera house, with elaborate machinery and superb decoration, which was Haydn's domain. It stood in a grove of chestnuts apart from the main building. It seated 400 people, with side-boxes and ante-rooms 'furnished most luxuriously with fire-places, divans, mirrors and clocks'. In addition to the opera house was a separate puppet theatre, also large. The whole stood in an elaborate park in the French style. The castle was guarded by the prince's private company of grenadiers, 150 of them, six-footers all, and beautifully trained, in their blue and scarlet uniforms, their white waistcoats and trousers, their black bearskins with yellow visors.

The palace itself had 126 guest-rooms, all show-pieces, and two state ballrooms, the white parade hall and the *sala terrana*, packed with artistic treasures and used for special performances when the prince wanted to be alone with his guests. Both the opera house and the marionette theatre were open to chance visitors; but in that watery waste there were not many of these. The palace was supplied by immense kitchen gardens in the French style, hothouses filled with exotic fruit and flowers, orangeries too. The game preserves were limitless and teeming. In season, partridges and bustards, venison and wild boar, an infinity of wild-fowl, hecatombs of hares, supplemented with farm-produce which had to be delivered as part of their dues by the peasant serfs. Huge ice-houses held meat to feed a regiment; game larders were stuffed full; the cellars held vast stocks of the excellent local wine from the Esterházy vineyards, supplemented by exotic imports. The whole massive territory was completely self-supporting and, in addition to the field labour force, the Esterházys had on their pay-roll craftsmen of every kind. There was nothing that could not be manufactured on the estate.

The Esterházys were only an extreme example. Their annual income was some 700,000 gulden, but the Batthyany's had 450,000, and some of the great Bohemians had more. All the greater and lesser aristocracy lived like this to a greater or less degree. These were the great houses on whom the Queen depended, all too precariously, for her support. Some, like the Kinskys, the Starhembergs, the Khevenhüllers of Carinthia, on a lower level the Dauns, provided her with ministers, ambassadors and generals; some were generous with their treasure – a Prince Liechtenstein, for example, expended nearly two million pounds on the reorganised artillery arm which he commanded successfully in some of the great battles of the Seven Years War. But all were agreed on one thing: any contributions they made to the Crown were to be *ex gratia*. There was to be no curtailment of privilege; no interference with local princely autonomy; no regular system of taxation. When, at the close of the second Silesian War, Maria Theresa set to work on her first great reforms, which were to bring some sort of centralised rule to the Austrian lands and to Bohemia and Moravia, she succeeded in some measure, in face of bitter resentment, in subduing the great landowners; but the Hungarians she had to leave alone. They were untouchable.

Towards the end of her reign, with most of her good work behind her, she paid a state visit to Esterháza and was entertained in great style. Nothing had changed in that feudal domain. There is no record of what she thought as she crossed into the territory of a subject prince so much richer than she herself had ever been, a prince who never had to think of money, whose way of life was serenely untouched by the great changes she had pushed through in other parts of her empire, absolute in his feudal state, and irresponsible. But when the second Prince Nikolaus waved aside her praise of his brand-new Chinese pavilion, crammed with treasures that cost the earth, dismissing it as an elegant trifle, 'a mere bagatelle', she must have been hard put to it not to raise her eyebrows: some of that money she could have used herself.

4

Not that Maria Theresa was incapable of extravagance. When she thought she could afford it she spent lavishly. During the very period when she was most deeply engaged in putting the imperial finances in order and building up a new army and a new bureaucracy to defend and administer her lands, she was building hard and very expensively at Schönbrunn. The subsidies she received from England were spent more or less as they should have been spent, on keeping her fighting forces in the field; but when she had a breathing-space it did not occur to her that it might be better to go on living in the Favorita Palace, which was no longer so secluded as it had been in her father's day – the Wieden suburb was being built up quickly – and, in any case, was insufficiently grand for an imperial summer residence. Nikolaus Esterházy was not the only man in Europe to be excited by Versailles. That had been going since 1661. Blenheim went up at the turn of the century, Marlborough's equivalent of Eugene's Belvedere. The Russian autocrats were building on a fabulous scale at Petersburg. Frederick, harder up than the Queen of Hungary herself, and always having to break off campaigns for lack of cash, set to work on Sans Souci at Potsdam immediately after the peace of Aix-la-Chapelle. Every German elector was building in the grandest manner possible. At Caserta outside Naples, the Bourbon king completed in four years the largest and most luxurious palace in the world after Versailles, a colossal monument to miniscule glory, imposed on a starving countryside. In the context of the times Schönbrunn, for all its splendour, was a modest concept.

Anyway, Schönbrunn was built. It had started, like so many great palaces of the seventeenth and eighteenth centuries, as a modest hunting-lodge a few miles from the heart of the city in a delightful setting at the foot of the Wienerwald. Charles VI decided to rebuild in the grand manner, and Fischer von Erlach, as part of his duties, drew up the plans for what would be a baroque colossus. Nothing happened, because Charles ran out of cash. But in 1744 Maria Theresa decided to make a new start. She found the Erlach designs too grandiose, and, anyway, as we have seen, the baroque impulse had died out. She wanted something lighter. And so the Italian architect Pacassi was given the job of adapting Fischer's plans to modern requirements. The result was the palace we know today.

Fischer's first project was stupendous. The building was still called an imperial hunting-lodge, but it was a palace on a fabulous scale. The grand entrance from the city side was flanked by twin pylons with spiral reliefs, surmounted by imperial eagles. These broke the low line of the two-storied guard-houses, which enclosed a vast space for carrousels and other equestrian delights. Elaborate twin fountains with large circular basins gave relief to this immensity, which was bounded by a still larger, curvilinear basin spouting more fountains and backed by rocky cascades. On each side of this basin were walled gardens, and the whole divided the parade, or carrousel, ground, from the approaches to the palace itself. Making use of the gentle hillside for further terracing, the next level was approached by two ramps overlooked by colonnaded retaining walls bristling with life-size statues. The ramps led to each side of an imposing parterre, with more basins and fountains and flower-beds. And this parterre served as a sort of pediment for the palace itself, approached now by two more ramps, this time centring on a great circular space broken by the largest basin of all, which was encircled by the carriageway passing before the main entrance, a classical portico on a powerful scale, with wings curving forward to form a semicircle half enclosing the carriageway, and then thrown out on each side to make the great façade. The whole was pierced by 150 windows on two floors, and the skyline was broken by statues surmounting each vertical piercing. Two large pavilions, domed and cruciform, flanked the main façade.

Erlach's second project was less grandiose. The terracing was reduced, and the main building brought forward to front the vast courtyard. The great semicircular re-entrant was done away with, and the wings came forward in stepped blocks to embrace a less ambitious portico, which, nevertheless, was still distinguished by the circular basin, smaller, and enclosed by terraced lawns.

Even this design was too heavy for Maria Theresa, who was clearly antipathetic to the monumental, the grand Roman style of Fischer. The Italian Pacassi, nevertheless, owed much to Fischer's second plan. The entrance, the flanking officers' quarters and stables, were preserved. The courtyard was reduced still further and the palace brought forward to stand at ground level. The approach stairs and ramps and the circular basin were thus done away with, and carriages drove straight through the pierced façade into the inner courtyard. But the ground plan, with the stepped wings, of Fischer's second design, was kept, the elevation carried a floor higher. Behind on the garden side the hill rose up, and this was later landscaped and crowned with the famous Gloriette, where Fischer's original palace should have stood, an operation supervised by Prince Kaunitz, who took time off from his virtuoso diplomacy to help transform the Schönbrunn gardens into one of the most enchanting artificial landscapes in the world.

The building of the palace itself started in 1744 and continued through the second Silesian War and on into the peace. In those days Maria Theresa, based on the Hofburg, where she had the Leopold *Trakt* completely redecorated to her own taste, spent as much time as she could at Laxenburg, ten miles from Vienna, an old castle in the heart of the flat country of the Danube plain, rebuilt by Leopold after its destruction by the Turks in 1683. Even when she built the new castle, which was started in 1752, the whole complex was unpretentious to a degree, low and plain and unexacting, though containing some charming rooms. The great park with its lake, which was to become a sanctuary of the unhappy Empress Elizabeth, before she took to endless travelling, was not laid out until a year or two after Maria Theresa's death. But even in her time the Laxenburg countryside, for centuries a favourite hunting-ground of the archdukes of Austria, was well timbered, and it must have been a rather wild paradise, teeming with game, and alive with the singing of nightingales and golden orioles. Even when she had taken Schönbrunn to her heart, the Queen liked to go to Laxenburg so long as her husband, with his love of shooting, was alive. Quite a number of grandees had small houses there, including Prince Kaunitz, who did a good deal of entertaining.

Laxenburg today, its buildings fallen into disrepair (but now being slowly restored), stands just off the main road to the Hungarian border. It is reached in twenty minutes by car from the city – no longer the dusty journey on a rutted track with the heavy coaches lurching and swaying on creaking leather springs. But there are still plenty of roe deer, and on a June evening I have seen a strange pinkish, purple shimmer in the slanting rays of the setting sun on the fresh, light green of the fields of young corn: the shimmer turned out to be an effect of the almost horizontal sun shining through the raised ears of innumerable hares, sitting up and taking notice on the approach of dusk after lying snug in their forms through the heat and glare of the day. It was here that the Queen, on her accession, told her stewards to destroy the game which was eating up the substance of the starving peasantry.

But much as she loved the simplicities of Laxenburg, she loved Schönbrunn still better, spending long hours watching the building work, moving into her own apartments as soon as they were completed, and after her husband's death in 1765, settling in for good. Behind the great façade, all 656 feet of it, there are nearly 1,500 rooms, and she herself had a good deal to say about the fitting out of her own apartments, the guest apartments, and the great state rooms. For years it must have been pandemonium. The Great Gallery, nearly 150 feet long, all white and gold, was still full of scaffolding while Gugliemi and his assistants painted the ceiling in 1761. Other painters were hard at work on the Rose Room and the Mirror Room, even while the Queen was holding her privy councils in the fantastic circular Chinese Room. The theatre, by J. F. Hohenberg, was not built until 1763. And although the great park, nearly 500 acres, was started in 1753 by the Dutch landscape gardener Steckhoven, working with Hohenberg – its long walks and vistas, its tall clipped hedges, its symmetry of ponds and grottoes, representing to this day one of the finest examples of garden-making in the French style, but contained in a setting of great timber – the Gloriette, also by Hohenberg, standing 150 feet above the parterres, an enchanting colonnade 300 feet long and 63 feet high, was not complete until 1775. While the botanical and zoological gardens, begun in 1752 and 1753 were still being laid out when Maria Theresa died in 1780. In her last years when, beaten down by the self-willed radicalism of her son, the Emperor Joseph II, she used to sit on every sunny day under the arcading giving on to the great gardens, a little wooden box containing state papers, strapped to her chest, she must still have been constantly disturbed by the incessant constructional activity. It was in 1745 that the young Haydn, then a member of the choir-school of St Stephen's Cathedral, distinguished himself by climbing the scaffolding at Schönbrunn, expressly forbidden by the Queen, who saw him and told the choir conductor to get that young oaf with the fair hair down and punish him. Thirty years later, when the young Mozart and his sister played to her, the Gloriette was still building, though the palace itself was long finished and stood as it stands today.

As already remarked, the little Portuguese, Sylva Tarouca, was at first responsible for supervising the works at Schönbrunn; but Francis had a good deal to do with it too, particularly with the outdoor arrangements. His influence on certain broadly cultural aspects of life in Vienna has been underrated. He had next to nothing to do with his wife's administrative and educational reforms – though his financial talents helped to make these possible, besides building up the Empress's private fortune – but he acted as a useful leaven for the less obviously utilitarian sciences. When he abandoned Lorraine he did not desert his old friends, but brought with him, first to Tuscany for that brief stay, then to Vienna, practically the whole of his court from Nancy, including many scholars and artists. He was the founder of the Schönbrunn zoological and botanical gardens. He had his own laboratory, where he conducted genuine experiments in chemistry, a cut above the usual alchemistic fantasy that was fashionable among the born Austrians. And he established the natural history museum, which is one of the city's prides to this day.

One of his favourites was the architect Nicolas Jadot, Baron de Ville-Issay, who built the old Burg Theatre on the Michaelerplatz and the Aula of the University. Jadot did much work too in the gardens at Schönbrunn and drew up plans for a new Hofburg, which were never used. The theatre, such as it was, owed a great deal to Francis Stephen's discreet patronage. He liked to take his mistresses to the little Burgtheater and would sit with them in the depths of the imperial box, largely hidden by curtains partly drawn. But everyone knew when he was there because he had a nervous cough which would invariably give him away. After the first flush of her youth Maria Theresa was too busy to spend much time at the theatre, which she had much loved. But she liked to have it going on, though under fairly strict control; and she had no objection to others frequenting it: she was after all the mother of her country, tolerant and wise, benignly smiling on the frivolities of her children (an attitude she seems to have perfected in her early thirties.) And when in 1768 Leopold, archduke of Tuscany, her second son, had his first child, her first grandson, who was one day to be the Emperor Francis II, she in person hurried excitedly down the corridors of the Hofburg and into the imperial box to interrupt a performance with the triumphant cry: 'My Poldy's got a boy!'

Chapter Nine

The Court at Vienna

The Court at this time was a highly idiosyncratic mixture of glittering ceremonial and informality. We have seen how Tarouca's first task was to persuade the young Queen to organise her life, to leave enough time for eating and dressing, to take the trouble to look her best, to moderate the enthusiasm with which she threw herself into the pleasures of dancing and cards, to go to bed earlier. The running of her Court was soon taken over by Khevenhüller-Metsch. This Khevenhüller was born with a silver spoon in his mouth. He was also a natural courtier, though he resisted his vocation with some vehemence, hoping to make a career in diplomacy, at which he was not in fact very good. He was sent off on a number of special missions and failed in all of them, perhaps because he was too honest and straightforward. He objected strongly to being turned into a courtier, but in no time at all he had developed an unsuspected talent for organisation and administration, and he had made himself the ruling genius even before his swift promotion to High Chamberlain. He had a difficult task. Privately he was intolerant of convention and capable of the most easy relationships; but on duty it was quite otherwise. It was the job of the chamberlain to organise the Court and to protect his mistress from all inconvenience, tiresomeness and embarrassment – while seeing that she played the queen. The Court had to be run on preordained lines: all from the Empress downwards must submit themselves to its disciplines for the greater glory of the dynasty. In the young Maria Theresa he found he had a handful.

We know a great deal about him from his detailed day-to-day diary, already mentioned. The Austrian aristocracy were not great memoir writers or diarists, and Khevenhüller's diary is thus of exceptional value, not only as a window into a far away society but also as a source for much detail about the Queen's activities which would otherwise never have been known. It is a very revealing diary. For decade after decade it recalls the events of the day inside the Hofburg, or Schönbrunn: wherever Her Imperial Majesty found herself there Khevenhüller was too, surrounding her en route or in strange houses with the people and things she knew, always gently grumbling. Nothing was ever quite right; the times were invariably a little out of joint; the Queen's advisers were never to be trusted; the Queen always needed to be protected from herself. But always everything worked. Long-faced, a little solemn, inclined to pedantry, rather easy to ruffle, but with a dry sense of humour, the keenest powers of observation, remarkable honesty, and a passionate (though far from blind) devotion to his empress-queen, this admirable old stick (he was an old stick even when young), kept superb order until Maria Theresa herself, all too soon, subdued the heedless girl in her and came down on the side of order too.

At first she was in head-on conflict with the demands of court etiquette and the traditional Spanish ceremonial. Indeed, she abolished this last for ever except for the most outward show. But from the beginning she knew perfectly well how she was expected to behave, and in all her dealings with her mother, the dowager Empress, she deferred to these requirements. In the very early days when Tarouca was called in to help her form her character and mind, Khevenhüller could and should have worked with the Portuguese; but, as we have seen, he was jealous. So he grumbled alone and wove his web, which Maria Theresa would one day accept. The wildness which Tarouca, no less than Khevenhüller, deplored, did not last long. Even then, the sort of extravagances which he recorded at length in his diary – as the high-spirited excesses of Shrove Tuesday, 1744, and the famous carrousel in the winter of 1742–3 – were intermittent in the extreme. It was only at carnival time, *Fasching*, that the young Queen really let herself go; and there were not many *Faschings* before sobriety set in.

There were, however, plenty of grand occasions, and until her husband's death in 1765 Maria Theresa enjoyed them. There were visits, almost state visits, to the domains of court favourites. One of the most famous of these, which Khevenhüller, whose diary entry suggests a faint disapproval, omitted to describe because he remarks, it has all been set down elsewhere. It was the custom in those days for those honoured by a visit from royalty to compose, or have composed for them, an elaborate account of the amenities and the entertainments, to be exquisitely printed and bound and circulated privately for the edification of their less fortunate rivals. This was the entertainment provided by Prince von Sachsen-Hildburghausen at his palace, Schlosshof, which had been built by Prince Eugene on the Hungarian border, very close to the Harrach and Esterházy estates. The visit took place in September 1754, and it is a date to be remembered, because as a result of that visit the composer Gluck, who had been 'discovered' by the prince in Naples, was invited to Vienna to be the court Kapellmeister. As far as the grandees were concerned, Gluck's offering, a little opéra called *Le Cinesi*, was a detail in a positive orgy of showing-off.

Their imperial majesties – Maria Theresa was thirty-seven, Francis forty-six – proceeded from the Emperor's favourite hunting lodge at Hollitsch, accompanied by the Archduke Charles and the two Archduchesses Marianne and Christina, then still in the schoolroom. They were received at the gates by the prince and his chamberlain and conducted to a meal. Having refreshed themselves they all drove off in procession to a subsidiary palace, Niederweiden, which had a famous garden and a theatre with a distant view of the hills round Pressburg. Here they were treated to an entertainment with words, as always, by Metastasio and music by Bonno, called *Il vero Omaggio*. The principal singers (Tesi-Tramontini and Theresia Heinisch) were first-class, and the high moment came when, after the final duet, there arose an echo, and out of the woods appeared a mixed choir repeating the final words of the drama: '*Tutt' in omaggio il cour!*' All this took place on the first afternoon. In the evening, when darkness had fallen and the gardens were illuminated, the Niederweiden theatre was the scene of another entertainment, a play by Metastasio called *L'Isola disabita* – to be used, many years later, by Joseph Haydn for his opera of that title.

And so to bed. Next day was Francis Stephen's benefit. There was
an elaborate shoot on the Danube marshes. A special building, two
stories high, had been erected on piles across the river. In the stream
itself shooting stands were built, camouflaged with foliage and flags.
All were connected by a temporary bridge. The river was crowded
with small boats, and the imperial family were conducted to a barge,
exquisitely fitted out and decorated, which carried them to the first
stand. Then the drive began. Hundreds of beaters stationed in the
woodland on the hillside manoeuvred in a great semicircle to drive
everything that lived towards the building and through the great
arches on which it rested, down to the river bank. But this was an
exhibition. The first two drives, which included many deer as well as
wild boar and smaller game, were allowed to pour through the arches
to freedom as they fanned out along the river banks, or swam for it.
Some 600 beasts went by in this way. The slaughter was confined to
the smaller game, 1,000 hares, 136 foxes, 60 wild boars.

It was after this excitement that Gluck made his imperial debut.
That evening Tramontini and Heinish were joined by Starzer and
the tenor, Fribert, in *Le Cinesi*, and the theatre was got up to match,
all in the Chinese style, with brilliant illuminations. Those who had
laboured all day, and all the night before, while the imperial family
slept and shot, were lucky. The weather was perfect; the performance
was perfect; and afterwards they supped and danced in the open air
in the main palace courtyard, its illuminations multiplied by mirrors.

Next morning more shooting for those who liked it: this time
hares and partridges on dry land; in the afternoon a grand regatta or
'Water Carrousel' in the immense fish-pond made for Prince Eugene.
The audience sat in leafy bowers put up on the banks. On a special
construction in the middle of the lake a choir and instrumentalists
discoursed sweet music — but music with a difference; for the apprehensive musicians were surrounded by chained animals and birds —
bears, wolves and owls, which made a wild and furious uproar, as
they tore at their chains, bellowed, roared and screamed. The
'carrousel' itself was a contest between two teams of four boats,
commanded by knights and rowed by serfs, all got up as pierrots and
harlequins. In case this was not enough to amuse the guests, partridges and pheasants were loosed from the boats to fly off with a

scurry of wings, while foxes and hares, let out of cages, jumped into the water to swim for the shore. With the livestock out of the way, the boat crews fought a spirited action with powerful hoses. When the uproar had died down and tranquillity been restored, it was time for the great set-piece. This was nothing less than a floating island, laid out with an enchanting garden and decked with allegorical groups. Flanked by more boats, the magic island was mysteriously steered across the lake towards the imperial arbour. A regiment of gardeners stepped ashore and with deep obeisances invited majesties and serenities to take a stroll round the mobile garden. Then boys and girls dressed as fishermen stepped forward with rods and nets to offer the guests a little fishing.

That evening the grounds were thrown open to the public. Thousands had been camping out on the neighbouring hills, and they all trooped down to admire the decorations, the artificial fruit trees and flower borders, all brilliantly illumined. The shooting-box on the river bank was the scene of target shooting. Every time someone hit a bullseye there was a sudden upward rush of rockets and other fireworks which exploded into elaborate pictures and inscriptions floating high overhead.

For the last day there was the Feast of Bacchus. In a procession led by heroes, warriors, shield bearers and trumpeters, two wagons loaded with great hogsheads and drawn by white oxen with gilded horns and wreathed with green leaves, Bacchus and Silenus swayed drunkenly followed by nymphs and by musicians arrayed as satyrs. Next came a great sailing ship on wheels, the crew more musicians. The ship's sides were hung with cheeses, loaves and game. Three hundred and fifty masked peasants capered along behind. While the distinguished company stood looking out through the windows of the palace, the procession approached and moved lumbering past. Mock fights and knockabout comedy scenes preceded a formal ballet. It was. at last, the end. The imperial family then said their farewells and drove off home to Schönbrunn to arrive at dusk after three hectic days.

During all this time the Empress attended to affairs of state. She had her boxes brought to her from Schönbrunn, read her papers, added her remarks, signed. But it is clear that she was delighted by the whole entertainment. And indeed even when she herself had out-grown such simple pleasures, she was child of her time enough never to object to others enjoying themselves in this way: she would enjoin her children to be gay while they could. This particular autumn and winter of 1754 was perhaps the climax of her worldly happiness. The country was at peace, its finances restored, it army in good heart, the great reforms in full swing. There were still nearly two years to go before the Seven Years War. She was close to Francis. Musicians have wondered what she saw in Gluck's *Le Cinesi* at Schlosshof to make her decide to bring the composer to Vienna. It was not a very good opera. But anything was better than Bonni, and she needed a new Kapellmeister. She was out to do anything that would give pleasure to Francis. The capturing of Gluck may have been part of this. Later that winter she conceived her last and sixteenth child. She was thinking a great deal about Schlosshof, to some effect. Before the year was out she had bought it as a present for her husband, whose favourite resort it became. The child conceived in this gay and tender mood, expressing itself in an explosion of rococo extravagance, was christened Maria Antonia, later to be known as Marie An-toinette.

2

The society of Vienna around and below the Court took its tone from the high aristocracy, which was, nevertheless, separate from it. The lesser nobility, while excluded from such fantastic junketings, nevertheless lived extremely well. Only the very great families had their palaces to themselves, and even some of these were not above letting off apartments to lesser luminaries. The rest inhabited fairly plain-looking apartment buildings, still white and shining, which con-cealed scenes of the utmost splendour on the mezzanine and the first floor, and garret life above. The Wortley Montagu descriptions of how these people lived cannot have been entirely accurate, but it is the best we have, and they fit in with glimpses obtained from other sources. Thus:

The apartments of the greatest ladies and even of ministers of state, are divided but by a partition from that of a tailor or a shoemaker; and I know nobody that has above two floors in any house, one for their own use, and one higher for their servants. Those that have houses of their own, let out the rest of them to whoever will take them; thus the great stairs (which are all of stone) are as common and dirty as the street.

But, once inside,

nothing can be more surprisingly magnificent. . . . They are commonly a *suite* of eight or ten large rooms, all inlaid, the doors and windows richly carved and gilt, and the furniture such as is seldom seen in the palaces of sovereign princes in other countries — the hangings of the finest tapestry of Brussels, prodigious large looking-glasses in silver frames, fine Japan tables, beds, chairs, canopies and window curtains of the richest Genoa damask or velvet, almost covered with gold lace or embroidery. The whole made gay by pictures, and vast jars of Japan china, and almost in every room large lustres of rock crystal.

They ate and drank well too:

I must do them the justice to say, the good taste and magnificence of their tables very well answers to that of their furniture. I have been more than once entertained with fifty dishes of meat, all served in silver, and well dressed; the dessert proportionable, served in the finest china. But the variety and richness of their wines is what appears the most surprising. The constant way is, to lay a list of their names upon the plates of the guests, along with the napkins; and I have counted several times to the number of eighteen different sorts, all exquisite in their kinds.

Always apart from the great palaces, this communal housing was universal, so cramped was the space within the walls; the houses had to be tall and crammed together, towering above narrow lanes full of filth and mud. The rich moved about by sedan chair when it was not worth getting out the carriages. What the Lady Mary Wortley Montagu did not know was that by imperial decree each householder was compelled to surrender his ground floor for the billeting of servants of the Court, who overflowed in all directions. There were practically no shops in the inner city: space was so cramped that retailing was forbidden: tailors, shoemakers, dressmakers, craftsmen of various kinds, worked in their attic homes. But all selling was done door to door by street vendors, who brought their produce in from the suburbs or traded in the great markets just outside the walls. The street-sellers of eighteenth-century Vienna were famous for their number and variety and for their quasimusical cries.

Lady Mary was writing of the year before Maria Theresa's birth, but things were much the same in her last years towards the end of the century. The population had doubled in her lifetime, to some 200,000, but the way of life remained unchanged except from a marked growth in the importance of the bourgeois element. Dr Burney writing in 1772 commented on the division of the houses just as Lady Mary Wortley Montagu had done half a century earlier, and he went on about the shops:

The inhabitants do not, as elsewhere, go to the shops to make purchases; but the shops are brought to them; there was literally a fair, at the inn where I lodged, every day. The trades-people seem to sell nothing at home, but, like hawkers and pedlars, carry their goods from house to house. A stranger is teased to death by these chapmen, who offer for sale wretched goods, ill-manufactured and ill-fashioned. In old England, it is true, things are very dear, but if their goodness be compared with these, they are cheap as dirt.

Obviously what was offered for sale to travellers, or tourists, at an inn, would not compare at all with what could be obtained to order by those who could afford it. The tapestries and velvets and damasks, the rich furniture, which excited Lady Mary's envy, were products not only of local and Bohemian craftsmen but also of the imperial possessions in the Netherlands (hence the tapestries) and Italy. Vienna itself at that time had a flourishing silk manufactury, based on Lombardy, and soon much of the fine china came from the porcelain factory founded by the Dutchman, Claudius du Pacquier in 1718.

3

The importance of chronology is relative. We are dealing with a block of time which occupied sixty years of the eighteenth century. Intellectually and artistically this was a period of far greater change than is generally agreed, as I shall try to show when it is time to consider its crowning glory, its music. Politically there were great changes too, largely concealed by the extraordinary instinct of Maria Theresa herself, who, by her reforms, largely inarticulate and not understood by her, but deeply felt, saved her inheritance from destruction by the revolutionary spirit which was to destroy her youngest daughter. Materially there was little change: the machine age was not born, and so long as transport was harnessed to the horse there could be little change in the tempo of life.

It is worth considering for a moment how people, including the all highest, got about. Maria Theresa was a great visitor. She was constantly, especially in her younger days, in transit from one palace to another, but never travelled as far, even to visit her own dominions, as Brussels or Milan. She would go to Prague to be crowned Queen of Bohemia, to Frankfurt to watch the coronation of her husband when he was elected emperor, but no farther. A glance at the movement order for her journey to Prague tells us why.

The royal procession was led by a solitary postillion (1 horse) to show the way. Behind him followed:

A landau containing four gentlemen of the bedchamber and servants (4 horses)
Another postillion with a spare horse (2 horses)
Two postillion trumpeters (2 horses)
A posting officer and a courier (2 horses)
A stable-master in charge of posting (1 horse)
A landau containing masters of the stables, posting, Court and kitchens (6 horses)
The body carriage containing the Queen, the Archduke and the chief lady in waiting (6 horses)
Two pages, two members of the imperial body-guard, and a postillion (5 horses)

A coach with 4 ladies in waiting (6 horses)
A coach with ladies' maids (6 horses)
Two coaches with servants (12 horses)
A landau containing the father confessor and the court chaplain (6 horses)
Another coach with servants (6 horses)
A chaise (apothecary of the body) (6 horses)
A half-covered caleche containing courier and gentlemen at arms (6 horses)
Another containing couriers (6 horses)
4 baggage wagons for the courtiers' luggage (24 horses)
A wagon for the chief steward (6 horses)
A shafted coach for the master of the plate and the pastrycook (6 horses)
A royal coach for the cellarer (6 horses)
A shafted coach for the plate and more pastrycooks (6 horses)
A large caleche for the master of the table linen (6 horses)
A half-covered caleche for the purchasing official and boy assistants (6 horses)
Four kitchen coaches (cooks travelling in advance) (24 horses)
A lady's coach in reserve, to serve as the body coach in an emergency (6 horses)
A landau in reserve (6 horses)
A shafted coach in reserve (6 horses)
Four posting masters, or couriers, of whom three will ride ahead to arrange the changing of horses and the fourth will bring up the rear and see to necessary payments (4 horses)
2 inspectors of coaches and a blacksmith (3 horses)
Draft horses in reserve (20)
The coach of the Bohemian Chancellor (6 horses)
A wagon for the Court post office and baggage (6 horses)
A baggage wagon (6 horses)

This unwieldy procession, which featured twenty bridle horses and 212 coach horses, lumbered along at a very smart twelve miles an hour when the going was reasonable. Maria Theresa liked to travel fast and long over terrible roads to get the journey over quickly. She would demand an early start and often drive for ten hours at a stretch, stopping only for the horses to be changed, which happened three or four times a day, with stages of between thirty and forty miles. She preferred to push on without a proper midday halt. Journeys of this kind obviously called for the most detailed and elaborate planning, and the victualling had to be worked out with special reference to feast- and fast-days, which abounded and complicated planning hopelessly. Immense quantities of food and drink were taken along, and large quantities were bought off the country all the way. The peasants liked these progresses: they received good prices for the food they sold by the wayside. But in the towns the sudden influx of hungry mouths sent up the prices, so that the citizens would grumble.

Not all Maria Theresa's journeys were on that scale. Not all ended in a coronation with a royal banquet. But no matter where she went, an elaborate entourage went with her. Informal as she might be and was in her personal life, she always did things in style in public, and very soon the days when she took no trouble with her dress were over. Some of her ladies must have sighed for those days. We have records of two of them, each of whom at different times acted as her private secretary and reader; Elisabeth von Friz and Charlotte Hieronymus. The first was a young woman of good family who was taken on by the young Queen at the beginning of her reign, in those heedless days when anything would do. The official secretary was a Freiherr Ignaz von Koch, but Maria Theresa so liked the Friz that she became, within certain limits, a confidante. One of her main tasks was reading aloud to the Queen – in German, Italian, French, Latin – often late into the night with Maria Theresa in bed.

The existence of all the Queen's favoured ladies was fairly strenuous and circumscribed. They were treated as what they were, as servants, that is to say, no matter how privileged. Both Elisabeth von Friz at the beginning of the reign and Charlotte Hieronymus towards the end of it, had the greatest difficulty in breaking away to get married. The Queen had no scruples in forbidding them to do any such thing, unless at her own pleasure. The ban was imposed very lightly and gracefully, but none the less absolutely for that: 'Don't do anything silly!' she admonished poor von Friz. 'I'm not giving you the day off for your Herr von Petrasch. He can wait a little. It does men good. Mine also had to wait!' Nevertheless, in due course the queen relented and behaved generously, giving Fraülein von Friz a wedding present of 12,000 gulden, promoting her husband, and keeping them both close to the Court.

Charlotte Hieronymus was on a different footing. The daughter of a junior army officer of no particular distinction, orphaned as a child, she was taken into the Court as an act of impulsive kindness when the Queen was told of her sad fate by one of her ladies-in-waiting happening to hear of this child who was being looked after, parentless, in the officer's mess of a hussar regiment. Although she was brought up with the young princesses she was marked out for service, and at thirteen showed herself so clever with her hands that she was brought in to help with Maria Theresa's own toilet, soon to become a full lady's maid and the Queen's secretary and reader. It is from her, via her own daughter, Caroline Pichler, that we learn how far Maria Theresa had moved in regality since the early carefree days. She was up at five in the morning and had to be waited on by the duty lady, fully dressed and in her right mind. And now that the first flush of her youthful looks had gone she took infinite care with her dressing, her coiffure, her powdering. There were long, long sessions, when nothing would go right, and the Queen would rumple up her hair, pushing it this way and that, demanding another touch here, another touch there – until, as often as not, the whole elaborate dressing had to be taken to pieces, the hair combed out, recurled, redressed: it might take hours of gathering tension and short temper. But although they were driven, the lady's maids of the Queen's maturity led a surprisingly free existence. They were paid poorly, but were fed and housed in style; they were able to dress brilliantly in the Queen's cast-offs, and presents of all kinds were showered on them. They were still not allowed into the city except in a royal carriage – drawn now, in these days of economy, by two horses instead of six. But, provided the queen knew where they were, they could go anywhere. More surprisingly, they were allowed to entertain in their own rooms, men friends as well as women, provided again that the Queen knew who and when, and the man's reputation and antecedents were above-board. Charlotte had to plead long and persistently before she was allowed to marry; what seemed to have won the day for her was the death of Francis in 1765. From that moment on Maria Theresa went into perpetual mourning, cared nothing for her appearance, so long as it was neat and elegant, and pushed to one side the whole business of presenting a brilliant face to the world – and with it the ladies responsible for that face.

4

This did not mean that her Court was allowed to dwindle away. Far from it. The palace and central governmental apparatus was immense. In a sense it could be said that the whole of Vienna was the Court, since most of its inhabitants were, in one way or another, sustaining, serving, or battening on the imperial family. The Court itself was less extravagant than it had been in her father's day, when it had included some 40,000 people. In spite of the great increase in the population of Vienna, the Court servants were fewer. But she still employed, for example, 1,500 Court chamberlains, nominally responsible for overseeing the various aspects of the economy of the palaces, as well as the Court entertainments and the innumerable musicians, painters, craftsmen of all kinds on the payroll. Somebody had to be responsible for importing snow for the children's sledges when there was no snow in the city; somebody else had to ensure the safe transport of the imperial glass of milk which was brought every day to the Hofburg from the dairy at Schönbrunn. More often than not, the aspiring paid in cash for the privilege of holding such office; but it seems likely that most of these managed to make a profit on the side. And, of course, such officials formed only the lower ranks of a dizzy hierarchy dominated by the great nobles, who kept what amounted to their own courts within the all-embracing magnificence of the Hofburg and Schönbrunn.

In addition to the aristocratic landowners who were the mainstay of the Court and the masters of the countryside there was another source of splendour and extravagance which seems to have gone almost unremarked throughout Maria Theresa's reign. This was the

Church: its monuments were monasteries. The great period of secular baroque, the palace building period, had virtually come to an end under Maria Theresa's father. But while the rococo flowered in Vienna, in the Church the baroque persisted, and while the Queen was fighting her desperate battles and making agonised calls for money, the religious orders continued to pour out treasure on innumerable great foundations, many of them started under Charles VI, but continuing deep into the new reign. Thus, Prandauer's tremendous Benedictine pile at Melk, started in 1702, was still building until 1749. St Florian, also overlooking the Danube, was not finished until 1751. Gottweig, a masterpiece of Lukas von Hildenbrandt, the architect of the Belvedere Palace, was under construction from 1719 to 1755; Hayberger's Admont from 1734 to 1776. Altenburg, by Munkenast and Wisgrill, with its magnificent library and dream-like stucco ceilings, was finished at the height of the first war for Silesia.

These are only some of the most outstanding of the innumerable buildings which grew out of the inordinate wealth of the Church in Austria, a wealth in which even the mendicant orders shared. Maria Theresa herself had no idea of its scale, and when, after her death, Joseph, who had long been wanting to lay hands on it, set about dissolving a great many of the monasteries, he himself was surprised by it. At the close of Maria Theresa's reign there were over 2,000 monasteries representing an estimated value of no less than 300 million gulden (Joseph was to confiscate only a fifth part of this, devoting the income from it to schools, charities and the support of indigent parish priests). The Church held three-eighths of all the land in Austria. As far as the economy of the monarchy as a whole was concerned, this immense wealth was virtually frozen and could hardly be touched when Maria Theresa, after the War of the Succession, set to work to rationalise the economy and establish a reasonable system of taxation.

Some idea of the meaning of these riches may be obtained by comparing the total wealth of the fantastically rich landowners of Bohemia which, at about the same time, amounted to some 580 million gulden, 465 million of this sum held by fifty-one princely families. The total tax yield from the whole monarchy came to

32½ million gulden at the time of Maria Theresa's death, but the great landowners made considerable contributions in other ways. Thus, when considering the extravagance of the Court and the riches of the great landowners, it is important to remember that a very considerable proportion of the total wealth of the realm was, as it were, out of play. And so it was to continue. The monasteries with their 60,000 monks, to say nothing of their sisters in the convents, formed a virtually closed society of land- and property-owners on a vast scale who, although they provided much employment, took by any reckoning far more than they gave.

Chapter Ten

Glimpses of the Other Half

At the other extreme were the peasants, most of them still serfs in the sense that they formed the matrix of a feudal society and were bound to provide services in work and kind to their landlords, but not chattels to be bought and sold as, under Catherine II, they came to be in Russia. For centuries their lives had been virtually unchanged. On the face of it the mountain peasants had the hardest lives, toiling always dourly, in bad years with desperation, to win a wretched existence from inhospitable soil, cooped up, cut off, inbred in their high mountain valleys, fighting without cease against the elements, the winter blizzards and killing frosts, the floods and mudslides and avalanches of summer: hunger because of drought, hunger because of summer storms and floods. But harsh as were the terms of life for these remote mountain people, at least they were bred to be hard, and, as a rule, they escaped the most fearful hazards which periodically afflicted their softer brothers of the fertile plains. Avalanches, floods, droughts, unseasonable frosts were acts of God. The peasants of the great plains suffered from acts of men, their smiling acres laid waste, their farmsteads burnt to the ground, their livestock slaughtered and their very existences laid in ruins by the march and countermarch of armies, spreading desolation.

In the nature of things the short and simple annals of the poor are infrequently recorded. As a rule it is only when a boy from a peasant home emerges as a genius or a major talent fit to be celebrated with a formal biography that anyone thinks it worth while to delve among parish registers, household accounts, and the collective memories of villagers — thus, incidentally, furnishing insights into the way of life of the obscure family from which he sprang, a way shared by innumerable unknowns. The early lives of Gluck and Haydn open two such windows into the human unknown of the Theresian Empire.

The Glucks were a cut above the peasantry. They were foresters and gamekeepers on princely estates. Christoph Willibald was born in 1714 three years before Maria Theresa herself. His grandfather, his father and two of his uncles all lived their lives in this way. His father, Alexander, was a bit of a wanderer who moved where the spirit took him and was clearly first-class at his job, able to turn his hand to all activities connected with forestry, shooting, hunting and the conservation of game, and sought after by the most illustrious masters. Thus, when the composer was born, his father was gun-bearer to Prince Eugene, no less. A few years later, as the great soldier, in declining health, gave up shooting and settled down in the Belvedere to die, Alexander Gluck entered the service of Count Kinsky as master of the forest on the vast Kamnitz estates. He remained there only two years and then went off to do the same job for an even greater Bohemian landowner, Prince Lobkowitz. One might think that a man filling such responsible positions in the service of the greatest noblemen would have lived fairly soft. But not a bit of it. Not for Alexander Gluck the remote seclusion of the estate office. He was out and about all day, a rather grim, hard, charmless man, striding in all weathers through the endless forests of his domain, compelling the two boys to trot along after him, borne down with the burden of papa's equipment — axes, powder flasks, snares, guns. Even in the depths of winter, through deep snow, they went hatless and barefoot. The composer in mature years brought to the rococo drawing-rooms of his royal and noble patrons a directness and stubbornness which was clearly inherited from his father, and a physique and exasperating robustness of health which sometimes struck awe. He had been trained in a hard school.

As for education, at ten he went to the village school on the Lobkowitz estate at Eisenberg — when his father cared to spare him. But at twelve he was put out to the Jesuits and lodged for six years at their seminary at Kommotau. This was interesting. When he packed his son off to the Jesuits, Alexander Gluck was unquestioningly determined to make him a forester like himself, but yet was prepared to give him some years away from the roughness of his own life for the sake of a decent education. And it was at Kommotau that Christoph learned first to sing, then to play the violin, the 'cello and the organ. So marked was his gift that his father allowed him to stay on, having the sense to realise quite soon that, big and strong and tough as this unexpected offspring still very much was, following in his own footsteps was not the right future for him. Instead of calling him in to start life on the Lobkowitz estates, he sent him to Prague at eighteen to obtain further musical instruction. But he had to work. Alexander Gluck could spare only a tiny allowance, and Christoph Willibald, living rough, had to pay most of his way by teaching singing, the violin and the 'cello, and himself playing in various churches. Whenever he could he would get out into the country and play dance tunes to the villagers. These paid him with eggs, their only currency; and the eggs he would sell in the first small town he came to. Soon he was playing in the small towns – now for cash. And in 1736 he made his way to Vienna, where, at twenty-two, his character formed, he called on the Lobkowitz at their new town palace. Prince Lobkowitz, pleased and gratified by the gifts displayed by the son of his old forester, was kindness itself. He introduced the young Gluck to the court musicians, among them Fux and Caldara. Almost at once he was taken up by the Italian Count Melzi, possessor of great palaces in Milan and on Lake Como, who put him to study under the world-famous musician Sammartini in Milan. The young peasant was launched.

Haydn's origins were humbler. His family lived at Rohrau on the Leitha, the flat, marshy country which then formed the borderland between Austria and Hungary. Rohrau was situated on the Harrach estates, not far on the one side from Schlosshof, the place of the Sachsen-Hildenburghausens (where Maria Theresa was fêted with the grand entertainment at which for the first time she encountered Gluck) and, on the other, the Esterházy estates, where the mature Haydn was to spend the greater part of his life. The endless arguments whether the Haydn family came of German, Magyar or Croat stock, which have engrossed partisan biographers for many decades, do not in the least concern us. Haydn was a European musician born into a specifically Austrian culture in a region which was a melting pot of Slav, Teuton and Magyar. His ancestors, going back as far as his great-grandfathers, were peasants of the most self-respecting kind, some of them superior. They included, beside arable and stock-rearing farmers, wheelwrights, winegrowers and millers. They all worked with their hands. They started from humble beginnings as day-labourers and achieved dignity and position in their tiny communities. They did this at a time when wars raged almost continuously, and at a place which stood in the line of march. The nearest town of any size, Hainburg, was sacked and destroyed by the Turks, on their march to the walls of Vienna in 1683, and one of Haydn's great-grandfathers, a wagon-maker, was killed together with his wife. Within seven years their elder son, Thomas, had rebuilt the family house on the charred ruins of the old. In 1704 Haydn's maternal grandfather lost his own house and everything he possessed, when the anti-Habsburg Hungarian peasant army burnt down Rohrau. He rebuilt — and in 1706 it was burnt down again. Seven years later he was appointed *Markrichter*, or village magistrate, responsible for keeping peace and order in the village. His duties included the discouragement of adultery and heavy gambling, seeing that nobody shirked his church-going, detailing the villagers to do their bond labour on the Harrach estates, keeping the local roads in good repair — all this on top of making wheels, repairing wagons, painting houses for Count Harrach and running his own little farm on the side. Joseph Haydn's father took over this job from him. His mother was born in 1707 when the peasant army was making a third onslaught on the village. Barely in her teens, and an orphan, she entered the kitchens of the Harrach family — there were nine in the kitchens altogether, and they had to deal with elaborate banquets and exotic foods. But at twenty-one she tore herself away from the periphery of glory and married Matthias Haydn, another wagon-maker. She had twelve children, some of whom died in infancy. She was a perfect housekeeper and never stopped working, but she found time to be kind and tender to her children. She lived for the day when her son would enter the church and was sad when he turned to music — as far as she knew a life of irresponsible vagrancy. She died, worn out, at forty-seven, and thus did not live to see her Joseph installed in the Esterházy household.

This came about in the following way. Matthias Haydn was the extremely proud possessor of a harp, which he had obtained on his early travels through Germany as a journeyman wheelwright. When he finally settled down at Rohrau and married he would sing in the evenings, folk-songs, to his own accompaniment, although he could not read a note of music. The infant Haydn began to join in at a very early age, astonishing first his parents, then the whole neighbour-hood, by the beauty of his childish voice and the exactness of his intonation. One day a cousin come from Hainburg to visit the Haydns was struck by the child's talent. The cousin was the head-master of the little school at Hainburg as well as the precentor of the church of St Philip and St James. Partly to help the boy, partly with an eye to a little extra income from a boarder, he persuaded Haydn's parents to let him take the boy home with him to further his education and his musical instruction. Joseph was still not quite six. His mother was reluctant: she had dreamed of having him trained for the priesthood. But she soon saw that the Hainburg adventure might help him even in this, and let him go. So the child moved from a household which was wholly taken up with village and agricultural affairs into a world of school work and church music. His health, his appearance, his clothing was neglected; he lived rough and worked impossible hours; but he came through until he was picked up by a talent scout from the capital and taken, in his eighth year, to be a chorister at St Stephen's cathedral in Vienna.

Here, under the Court composer and cathedral choirmaster, Karl Georg Reutter, he was not only worked to the bone but three-quarters starved as well. The trouble was that Reutter had neither the time nor the inclination to encourage the true musical education of this remarkable child, whom he saw simply as an asset to his choir. But he had his high moments. While his master concentrated more and more on securing for himself new posts and sinecures to consolidate his position at Court, even the famous choir was left increasingly to look after itself, and started to go off badly – to the extent that the city council gave a formal reprimand to Reutter, declaring that 'the church music was becoming worse all the time, thus leading to inattention and even disgust instead of Christian edification'. This had not the least effect on Reutter's position at Court, and on special occasions he knew how to put on a first-class performance. This was when the Empress herself was present. For the rest, good or bad, the young Haydn had a first-class induction into the world of contemporary composers, and enjoyed to the full the cere-monial occasions and the sort of outings which took him to Schön-brunn, or to sing on gala saints' days on an illuminated boat moored in the Danube canal.

When in 1745 his voice broke, he was thrown out into the world with nothing at all but three ragged shirts, a worn-out coat and no recommendation from his master. He was a peasant boy who knew about music, and nothing else besides. He might have been lost and sunk without trace in the stony city (he was only seventeen and had nowhere to sleep) but for one of those extraordinary strokes of luck which make one speculate about destiny. In the depths of misery, hungry and cold in mid-November, he bumped into a man called Michael Spangler, a singer in the church of St Michael, opposite the Hofburg, who gave private lessons to keep body and soul together. The two hardly knew each other, but as soon as Spangler heard of young Haydn's destitution, he took him along to share a tiny garret with his wife and his nine-months-old baby for as long as he liked, provided he found his own food. With a roof of sorts over his head, the youth began to earn his food, playing at dances, teaching for tiny fees, making arrangements of other people's compositions, above all exploiting the contemporary Viennese custom of serenading in the streets. This was all the rage, among the well-to-do as well as the poor. Quite serious performances were put on by trios or quartets at all hours of the summer nights, and paid for, especially to celebrate the name-day of an adored young woman. It was now that Haydn became intimately acquainted with the Austrian folk-music and dance tunes, echoes of his infant days singing with his father to the harp, which were to play so important a part in his mature music, as in the music of Mozart, Beethoven and Schubert after him.

Joseph Haydn was a genius, and it is because he was a genius that we know about his parents and his grandparents and the harshness of his early life at the very gates of the Hofburg; you could come into the orbit of the imperial Court and still go hungry and cold. But in that particular society a peasant child did not have to be a potential genius to escape from the village and enter a realm of sophistication, touching the periphery of luxury.

Joseph had a younger brother, Michael, about whom nothing would be known but for Joseph's fame. Michael also had a voice, which had a very remarkable range, and he too was brought to the choir of St Stephen's at the age of eight. Soon he had overtaken Joseph in brilliance, address and apparent gifts. At the festival of St Leopold in the superb monastery of Klosterneuburg, just outside Vienna, Michael sang a *Salve Regina* so beautifully that Maria Theresa and Francis sent for him and rewarded him with twenty-four golden ducats. By the time he was twenty he had been taken on as Kapellmeister to the Bishop of Grosswardein in Hungary, and proceeded to develop a useful and on the whole rewarding career; another country boy making good.

These illustrations are given not as sidelights on the careers of great musicians, but solely for the light they throw on the way the peasantry lived, with particular reference to the fact that, given decent and reasonable parents, prepared to forego the loss of a strong pair of arms and to make sacrifices to help a clever child to realise his potential, it was not difficult for a gifted peasant boy, provided he had courage and tenacity and determination, to make good. Given, also, a decent and enlightened landowner, like the Lobkowitzes who encouraged the young Gluck, the Harrachs who encouraged the young Haydn. Other boys became priests, lawyers, doctors of medicine, clerks. And most of these owed their elevation to the elaborate feudal complex into which they were born.

Half a generation later, Dr Burney was deeply struck by the musical education (this was after Maria Theresa's educational reforms) of the village and small town children, above all in Bohemia. This rich country then, nearly a decade after the end of the Seven Years War, was still desolate. 'The dearness and scarcity of provisions of all kinds, on this road, were now excessive; and the half-starved people, just recovered from malignant fevers, little less contagious than the plague, occasioned by bad food, and by no food at all, offered to view the most melancholy spectacle I have ever beheld.' But everywhere he went, himself subsisting frequently on a diet of bread and water, an occasional expensive glass of milk, or, luxuriously, 'a pigeon and half a pint of miserable sour wine', he found schools crowded with little children learning reading and writing and *music*. One school he visited was

> full of little children of both sexes, from six to ten or eleven years old, who were reading, writing, playing violins, hautbois, bassoons, and other instruments. The organist, one of the two schoolmasters, had in a small room of his house four clavichords, with little boys practising on them all. . . .
>
> It has been said by travellers, that the Bohemian nobility keep musicians in their houses; but in keeping servants, it is impossible to be otherwise, as all the children of the peasants and trades-people, in every town and village throughout the kingdom of Bohemia, are taught music at the common reading schools, except in Prague.

2

Turning from the countryside, if we continue to follow Joseph Haydn we may glimpse the living conditions of the urban poor in the tall apartment buildings which were an especial feature of the cramped and crowded city. He could not stay for ever sharing Spangler's garret and earning his bread by playing in the streets. When another baby arrived, he had to go out and fend for himself, and after a short spell in the choir at the famous pilgrimage church of Mariazell in the foothills of the Alps, whither he had journeyed on foot with a party of pilgrims, he returned to Vienna, rested and well fed, and walked straight into another stroke of luck. A prominent tradesman in Vienna (also a *Markrichter*, like Matthias Haydn) was so impressed by the young man's talent that he lent him unconditionally 150 florins to enable him to study in peace. It was soon repaid, and the composer left the tradesman's daughter 100 florins in his will as a memorial to her father's generosity.

Now he could afford a room of his own, and he found a garret in one of the more famous apartment buildings, the Michaelerhaus, next to St Michael's church, across the road from the Hofburg. His immediate neighbours under the roof were a cook, a footman, a journeyman printer and a furnaceman, who went out to work in a rich man's house. Young Haydn was six floors up, and his garret had neither window nor stove. Water for washing and drinking had to be fetched from the yard and carried up many stairs. But it did not matter, Haydn could work. And it was here that he toiled away at theory, working at the celebrated *Gradus ad Parnassum* of Johann Joseph Fux, the composer of the opera which had enchanted Lady Mary Wortley Montagu thirty years earlier, who still lived, covered with glory, a favourite of the Court, not far away.

What was more to the point, another favourite of the Court, perhaps the supreme favourite of Maria Theresa, more so even than the composer Hasse, Pietro Metastasio, the celebrated poet, lived in the Michaelerhaus itself, but in comfort and some luxury on the third floor. Here is a living example of the remarkable mingling, under the same roof, using the same stairs, of rich and poor, commented on by all travellers to Vienna in the eighteenth century. Metastasio, whose real name was Trapassi, a Neapolitan so thoroughly at home in Vienna that he was thought of as an Austrian, had been the chief Court poet since 1730. He was the supreme champion of the Italian School, which, until the coming of Gluck, dominated Vienna in poetry as in music. He was the greatest opera librettist of the age: no ceremonial or festive imperial occasion was complete without a new opera by Metastasio, set to music by Fux, Hasse, Caldara, Bonno, or one or other of the favoured musicians of the day. In his poetry his thoughts were easy, if not banal, his line limpid and clear. His collected works fill eleven volumes. He was a very great swell. He was also good and kind. When Dr Burney visited him twenty years later, he was overwhelmed:

He does not seem more than fifty years of age, though he is at least seventy-two; and for that time of life, he is the handsomest man I ever beheld. There are painted on his countenance all the genius, goodness, propriety, benevolence, and rectitude, which constantly characterise his writings. I could not keep my eyes off his face, it was so pleasing and worthy of contemplation. His conversation was of a piece with his appearance: polite, easy and lively.

How much more brilliant a figure he must have appeared when he inhabited the third floor of the Michaelerhaus in his early fifties at the summit of his career. Haydn, in his early twenties, poorly dressed, undersized, awkward, perched high up under the roof, freezing in winter, sweltering in summer, belonged to another world. But somehow the great man found him out, called him down to his rich apartment, talked to him, was impressed by his gifts, and engaged him on the spot to teach the clavier to his ten-year-old daughter Marianne, motherless, whom he adored and for whom he lived.

For three years this went on, the swiftly developing genius passing each day, via three flights of dirty stone stairs, from one world to another, learning much, not only because he had to articulate his instinctive feelings for the benefit of Marianne, but also directly from the conversation and example of her father. Above all, he met other musicians. The celebrated Italian singing teacher and composer, Niccolo Porpora, was giving singing lessons to Marianne, and Haydn had to accompany her during these lessons. Soon he was taken on by the surly old man as his regular accompanist, and travelled with him, meeting new patrons all the time. He was launched, via the attic in the Michaelerhaus.

3

In this way an aristocratic society could draw on the resources of the common people, encouraging and patronising native talent of all kinds, but always regarding even the most gifted of the newcomers as belonging to the servant class, however much admired, however much esteemed. There was a large and swiftly growing population to exploit. It doubled itself under Maria Theresa, amounting to nearly twenty million at the end of her reign. In addition to the Germans, Slavs and Magyars, other smaller peoples too, of the central *bloc*, in addition to the Italians of Lombardy and the two million Belgians, who formed a rich, dense population utterly remote in feeling and tradition from the peoples of Bohemia and the Danube basin, the imperial capital was a magnet for gifted men from all the German states, as well as from other lands. They came to make careers in the service of the Empress and were invaluable in the growing bureaucracy, in finance, in industry, in trade. Thus Bartenstein was a Saxon, Tarouca a Portuguese, van Swieten, the founder of the Viennese Medical School, a Dutchman. The architect Jadot came from Lorraine; the financial genius, Johann Fries, who was to make the Maria Theresa silver *Thaler* a universal coin (still minted for use in Arabia and Abyssinia), was a Swiss. The list could run on.

Even so, though lucky individuals of exceptional talent could rise from the anonymous mass from which they came, and though Maria Theresa herself and her great nobles could frequently congratulate themselves on their perspicacity in raising them up; though industry was growing fast (in Bohemia some 400,000 were employed in manufacture of one kind and another), and life in the towns and the great cities (above all in Vienna, of course, which was almost entirely centred on the needs of the vast Court, and in Prague, which in some ways surpassed Vienna as a cultural centre) was on the whole steady and secure, the great body of the people existed on a level much lower than that of the Haydns and the Glucks. Over vast areas they lived in nothing more than mud hovels, tilling the land with wooden ploughs, seasonally hungry almost every year, in bad years often starving, attached to their landlords in widely varying degrees of servitude, illiterate and often brutish, liable for conscription on a quota basis, and, until Maria Theresa's first reforms, bearing the whole weight of taxation. The attitude of too many of the landowners was summed up in the saying: the peasants should be cut down like grass, they spring up the stronger for it. And it was this attitude that Maria Theresa set herself to change, at first for purely economic reasons (the system was too wasteful of potentially first-class human material), increasingly, as she grew older, from humanitarian motives too.

Chapter Eleven

Music and the Individual Voice

In 1772, in a much quoted letter to her daughter-in-law, Marie Beatrix, the wife of the Archduke Ferdinand, Maria Theresa, writing nostalgically about the church music of her old master, Reutter, went on to say:

> But for the theatre I confess that I prefer the least of the Italians to all our composers, whether Gassmann, Salieri, Gluck, or anyone else. Now and then these produce a good piece, but when it comes to the ensemble, then I always prefer the Italians. For instrumental music there is a certain Haydn, who has some peculiar ideas, but he is only just beginning.

Haydn, then, was just forty. Maria Theresa was fifty-five. Mozart was only sixteen. He had charmed the Empress as an infant prodigy, but as a serious composer he did not exist for her.

A great deal of nonsense had been written about Maria Theresa as patron of the arts. She was, rather, a patron of entertainers. The fact that Gluck, between Paris and Vienna, was engaged in conducting, partly under her protection, a revolution in opera, had nothing to do with her. She knew nothing at all about it and cared less. She liked the surface of some of Gluck's music and rewarded him, just as she rewarded the tiny Mozart and his sister for prettily entertaining her family at Schönbrunn. She liked fireworks and fancy-dress balls as well. The fact that she could sing, liked to sing, and had appeared in operas, did not make her a profound musician. She liked the elegance of her Italians and their imitators, as she liked the elegance of her chinoiseries at Schönbrunn. Both formed an obbligato to gracious living – as did the limpid, polished elegance of the poetry of dear old Metastasio, for whom she had the warmest of corners in her heart. When she smiled on the infant Mozart embracing Marie Antoinette on the parquet of Schönbrunn, she was not smiling on a genius; she was smiling on a clever little fellow with a cocked hat and a tiny sword. Indeed, her attitude to the arts is summed up once and for all in that most revealing note to her second son, Ferdinand, who, recently married and setting up his establishment as governor of Milan, had been carried away by the young composer's brilliance and wrote to his mother (the letter alas, is lost) saying that he was considering taking Mozart into his service:

> You ask me about taking into your service the young Salzburger. I can't think what as, for I do not believe you have any need for a composer or of useless persons. But if it would give you pleasure, I shall not prevent you. What I say is do not burden yourself with useless persons, and the claims of such persons on your service . . . and he has, furthermore, a large family.

That was in December 1771, when Mozart was fifteen and had just most successfully fulfilled a commission for the Archduke's wedding, the Pastoral Serenade *Ascanio in Alba*, with its astonishing promise of Cherubino's *Non so piu* in *Figaro*. It was too late now to expect that Maria Theresa herself would give employment to the fifteen-year-old Mozart. But by encouraging Ferdinand to back the young composer as an adornment to his court at Milan his mother would have secured for herself an exalted place in the history of the arts and for Mozart a future free from the deadening frustrations of menial service under the archbishop of Salzburg. Maria Theresa had no conception of the magnitude of her blindness. She did not know she was blind at all. She never realised that she had been brushed by genius. She did not know what genius was. Had she known, she would not have approved of it.

2

On the face of it, indeed, nothing could have been more unfavourable to the development of the profound and introspective awareness of universal mystery, as exemplified in Gluck, in Haydn, in Mozart, than the highly developed but superficial and self-satisfied musical culture of rococo Vienna. It was a culture untouched by the spiritual splendours of Bach and of Handel. Bach died, an obscure but venerated Saxon organist, regarded by his sons as hopelessly old-fashioned, when Maria Theresa was thirty-three, and was virtually unknown outside Leipzig and Potsdam; Handel, at the height of his London fame, when she was forty-two. Neither had visited Vienna, and their works were not played there. It was not until 1781, the year after Maria Theresa's death, that Mozart, then twenty-five, who had already heard Handel's music in London, became acquainted with the music of Bach; and this acquaintanceship he owed to the son of Gerhard van Swieten, the new baron, himself President of the Commission for Education, who had discovered the music of Bach and Handel in Berlin. The young van Swieten was a passionate music-lover who gave Sunday morning musical parties which Mozart regularly attended. Another member of this circle was the son of Nicholas Jacquin, whom the old van Swieten had brought to Vienna as Professor of Chemistry and Botany and to develop the botanical gardens at Schönbrunn, under Francis. It was in this circle that Mozart revelled in the breath of the Enlightenment and developed the sort of ideas that coloured on the one hand *The Magic Flute*, on the other *Figaro*. And it was the young van Swieten who wound up Mozart's affairs and arranged the notorious funeral, the burial in the unmarked grave.

Maria Theresa was thus behind her own times when it came to music; but not very far behind. The conflict which appeared to her as a conflict between the Italian and the German, between lightness and heaviness, was not really a conflict at all: the composers of her time were rediscovering the power of music to express emotion and mystery, and even some of Maria Theresa's favourite Italians were imbued with the new mood – so much so, indeed, that poor Jomelli, returning to Naples after a long sojourn in the north, was derided for his new ideas and died of a broken heart. Similarly, another Italian, Algarotti, in 1763 published a book on the opera which foreshadowed the ideas developed by Gluck. On the other hand, good Germans like Johann Christian Bach, the music-master of the Queen of England, were highly Italianate in manner and approach. The German blacksmith's son, Quantz, who presided over the music at the Court of Prussia, composed nearly 300 flute concertos for Frederick the Great to perform. He might have been an Italian. Handel himself composed in the Italian manner, which his genius transfigured. The young Mozart was deeply influenced by J. C. Bach, who was very kind to him, still more importantly by his brother Karl Phillip Emmanuel, who, though *galant* in style, had much to do with the development of sonata form, which was to be the great vehicle for dramatic expression in instrumental music. So although, until the advent of Gluck, in Maria Theresa's Vienna, all that was understood by art and culture meant Italy – in a lesser degree France – this was not a unique phenomenon.

In her letter to Maria Beatrix, Maria Theresa was being a little unkind to some of her Bohemian and German composers, who composed in the Italian manner. In fact she was being careless. She forgot her devotion to one of her old masters, Wagenseil. She even forgot her favourite of favourites, the Saxon Johann Adolph Hasse, whom she had personally recommended to Maria Beatrix with all possible warmth only a year before. She also forgot that Salieri was himself an Italian – but an Italian influenced by the new spirit from the north. What Maria Theresa meant by Italian music was neither this nor the music of Monteverdi and Cavalli, who were completely forgotten, so that the German Gluck, without knowing anything of their existence, had to conduct their revolution of feeling all over again. It was the Italy of the flowing, florid, unemphatic line, elegant and cool, sprung with ingenuities, sometimes tortuous, always mild. Opera, whether *buffa* or *seria*, was conventionalised to a degree, and the composer played second fiddle to the librettist. The voice had everything. And just as Noverre was the supreme exponent of dancing, so the castrato Farinelli was the supreme exponent of singing. Dr Burney on Hasse put the position very well: 'Always regarding the voice, as the first object of attention in a theatre, he never suffocates it, by the learned jargon of a multiplicity of instruments and subjects; but is as careful of preserving its importance as a painter, of throwing the strongest light upon the capital figure of his piece.' But recitative was no less important than the arias, and the librettist, Metastasio, was held in greater honour than any composer of the age. There was only one Metastasio. There were a number of Hasses.

By the early 1760s Gluck's revolution was in full swing. *Orfeo* was produced at the Court Theatre in 1762. But to understand the period it is important that this revolution should not be over-dramatised, except, perhaps, in one particular. For Maria Theresa and all but a handful of her courtiers, for the philistines that is, the break was very great. The composers saw things differently. They were artists. And although they might intrigue against each other, they were closer in understanding. Thus, for example, we find Hasse, with his splendid melodic gifts, a man who had known the heights of fame and fashion only to be ruined when everything he owned was destroyed in the bombardment of Dresden by Frederick, writing at the age of seventy to introduce Leopold Mozart and his children to the Abbé Ortes in Bologna as though the twelve-year-old Wolfgang were his own son:

> I have tested him in various ways and he has done things which for such an age are somewhat incomprehensible and would be remarkable in an adult. . . . The boy is, in addition, beautiful, lively, charming and behaves in such a way that one absolutely cannot help loving him. On thing is certain: if his development keeps pace with his age something wonderful will come of him.

Thus a whole century was bridged, as an Italianised German born in 1699 gave his generous blessing to the Austrian genius who, at first strongly influenced by the Italian manner, was to emerge on the eve of the French Revolution as the supreme exemplar of the liberated human spirit.

Music, of course, was the immortal achievement of Theresian Austria. As the century wore on the great architectural impulse declined. There were some interesting painters, but the finest of them, Maulbertsch, was but a reflection of Tiepolo. The theatre was undistinguished: there was a native tradition of boisterous farce, sometimes remarkably outspoken, acting as a safety-valve in an age ruled by the censor. But the fashion was for French or Italian in the theatre, and not a great deal of that. It was not until Joseph turned the little Burg Theatre into a German theatre that things began to look up. Earlier in the century the Saxon Gottsched, who sought to establish a classical German and set about reforming the German theatre on French lines, had great hopes of establishing an Academy of Science in Vienna, but Maria Theresa, then engaged in actively reforming her university and higher schools through van Swieten, would have nothing to do with art for the sake of art or knowledge for the sake of knowledge. Later the great critic and dramatist, Lessing, another Saxon, had the same idea; but although he was received at Court with honour and some of his plays were performed, he too was sent away.

But music was everywhere, not only in Vienna but also all over central Europe, a sort of international language which took in Paris and London in the north, Rome and Naples in the south. Gluck journeyed endlessly from capital to capital, thinking nothing of posting across a Europe torn and made dangerous by the Seven Years War. At Mannheim in Baden there flourished the great orchestra which inspired composers from far and wide. Dresden, before it was ruined by the Prussian troops, was alive with musical culture. Germans and Italians moved between Hamburg, Potsdam, Leipzig and as far as St Petersburg. While Prague, of no account at all in the eyes of the statesmen except as a strategical and political vantage-point, was perhaps the most intensive forcing-ground for musical talent in the whole of Europe. Towards the end of the century Mozart valued his invitations to Prague, where *Don Giovanni* had its first performance, more than any others. Long before that, the devoted and obscure Franz Xavier Richter composed innumerable symphonies and also the first string quartets, for which, until the other day, Haydn received the credit. But Haydn is great enough to surrender that crown with perfect grace.

3

There is no convincing explanation of this stupendous efflorescence of musical genius, which was to carry itself through the reign of Joseph then, through the revolutionary years, broaden into an ever-widening stream receiving tributaries from all over Germany until the final collapse of the monarchy. The wind bloweth where it listeth, and all attempts to correlate the history of the arts with the development of human society have been vain. The whole point about genius in any shape or form is that it stands outside society. It represents not a development but a mutation, and such mutations may come singly, or in constellations. There appears to be no rhyme or reason in it; the mutations simply occur. Far from owing anything to the general development of society they themselves, by adding new dimensions to the human consciousness, affect the development of society – even though all but a handful of the millions who make up a given society may never have heard of them. There used to be an argument, perhaps there still is, which held that the Austrians excelled at music because strict censorship prevented the verbal articulation of ideas: no free expression, no literature. But the musicians could express themselves freely. This is nonsense whichever way you look at it. Voltaire and the Encyclopaedists were irrepressible. Under nineteenth-century Russian absolutism the great novelists exploded into new spheres of consciousness, expressed in words, while their composer colleagues, Glinka, Borodin, Mussorgsky, Tchaikovsky kept pace with them in music. There was nothing in Maria Theresa's Austria, or indeed, later, in Metternich's, to prevent a flowering of lyrical poetry, or Augustinian for that matter, or, indeed, of the novel of the heart or of character – nothing except the lack of genius.

As a rule, as in eighteenth-century Austrian music, sixteenth-century English drama, fifteenth-century Italian painting, the towering genius benefits from the preparatory work of a strong supporting cast. Musicians, indeed, need this more than any other sort of artist since they depend very much on the pre-existence of trained orchestras and soloists. (It was the superb Mannheim orchestra that gave the Stamitz family and others the suggestive stimulus which launched

a new form to bring drama into the symphony.) But even this de-
pendence will not deter them from composing music which is beyond
the range of contemporary singers, conductors, instrumentalists.
Given pen and ink the writer can write, given canvas and pigments
the painter can paint. The musician can compose with pen and ink,
but he needs a more elaborate apparatus before his compositions can
be presented to the world. In this he is closer to the scientific genius.
We are too much accustomed today to thinking of, for example, the
great physicist as a product of technological advance, forgetting that
technological advance sprang from the naked minds of earlier
scientists. The Newtons and the Einsteins are mutations no less than
the greatest artists. No one knows whence they come, no one knows
when they will come again, or where, or if at all.

The main point about Gluck's revolution is that it was a revolution
in the attitude of the artist as well as a revolution in musical expres-
siveness. The composer is becoming self-conscious: he is on the way
to seeing himself as a prophet. Thus, towards the end of his brilliant
career, the forester's son who had been first the entertainer, then the
companion, then the mentor of princes, was laying down the law
very much in the manner of a Beethoven or a Wagner. The court
composer of 1754, the music master of the infant Marie Antoinette
was, in 1776, with Maria Theresa still alive, writing about the projected production in Paris of *Armide*:

When I come to Paris I must have at least two months in which
to train my actors and actresses; and I must be at liberty to call
as many rehearsals as I consider necessary; no part shall be
doubled; another opera must be in readiness, in case any actor or
actress shall fall sick. These are my conditions, without which I
shall keep *Armide* for my own pleasure. I have written the music
of it in such a way that it will not soon grow old. You say in
your letter, my friend, that none of my works will ever compare
with *Alceste*. This prophecy I cannot agree with. *Alceste* is a perfect tragedy, and I do not think that it often fails of its full
perfection. But you cannot imagine how many shades and
manners music is capable of, and what varied paths it can follow.
Armide is so different from *Alceste*, that one would hardly believe
that they were by the same composer. . . .

With it I think to close my career as an artist. The public, indeed, will take as long to understand *Armide* as they did to understand *Alceste*.

Here is a new tone of voice. The modern age is dawning. Five years before, Maria Theresa had warned her son against taking the young Mozart and 'useless persons' generally into his household. Even while Gluck was stating his terms for the Paris production of *Armide* and announcing, in effect, that he was a genius (though with a conventional apology: 'I must end, or you might think me either a charlatan or a lunatic. Nothing sits so badly on a man as praise of himself . . .') Mozart was employed as a menial by the new Archbishop of Salzburg. While, not far from Vienna, on the shores of the Neusiedlersee, Haydn was still serving the Esterházy family, still accepting the terms of his original engagement of 1761, which read in part like this:

2. The said Joseph Heyden shall be considered and treated as a member of the household. Therefore His Serene Highness is graciously pleased to place confidence in his conducting himself as becomes an honourable official of a princely house. He must be temperate, not showing himself overbearing towards his musicians, but mild and lenient, straightforward and composed. It is especially to be observed that when the orchestra shall be summoned to perform before company, the Vice-Kapellmeister and all the musicians shall appear in uniform, and the said Joseph Heyden shall take care that he and all the members of his orchestra follow the instructions given, and appear in white stockings, white linen, powdered, and with either a queue or a tie-wig. . . .
4. The said Vice-Kapellmeister shall be under obligation to compose such music as His Serene Highness may command, and neither to communicate such compositions to any other person, nor to allow them to be copied, but he shall retain them for the absolute use of His Highness, and not compose for any other person without the knowledge and permission of His Highness.
5. The said Joseph Heyden shall appear daily in the antechamber before and after midday, and enquire whether His

Highness be pleased to order a performance of the orchestra. On receipt of his orders he shall communicate them to the other musicians, and take care to be punctual at the appointed time, making a note of those who arrive late or absent themselves altogether.

6. Should any dispute or cause for complaint arise, the Vice-Kapellmeister shall endeavour to settle it so that His Serene Highness may not be discommoded with trifling disputes; but should any more serious difficulty occur, which the said Joseph Heyden is unable to set right, His Serene Highness must then be respectfully called upon to decide the matter. . . .

And so on through fourteen paragraphs. Haydn is referred to as the vice-Kapellmeister throughout because he had been engaged to supersede the old Kapellmeister, Gregorius Werner, who had given such faithful service that his master was determined not to dismiss him from his office, even though Haydn was to be in effective charge. The Esterházys were good masters, but they were masters. Haydn stayed with them for nearly thirty years, and having a serene, humorous and reasonable temperament, rarely questioned their authority. Nevertheless, when Nikolaus Esterházy died in 1790, ten years after Maria Theresa herself, Haydn accepted an invitation to London, where his success was so great that he returned again. A new world opened before his eyes, a world in which the artist was respected as creator (a very small world, then, of course, as now), the role which Gluck, twenty-five years before, had assumed for himself. He did not exploit his 'electrifying' (Burney's word) London success. He enjoyed being fêted, but soon had enough of it. He wrote some of his best symphonies in England. He made a good deal of money, which he was pleased to have. But it never occurred to him to let his head be turned by the Queen's offer of an apartment in Windsor Castle, which he modestly refused. He was still the self-contained artist he had always been, who, while setting out to please his master, was also absorbed in the sensitive exploration of his perceptions, which deepened steadily until he died, proud of his independence and the esteem in which he was held, but still the inward-looking artist.

There was a new Nikolaus Esterházy now, and Haydn quite

naturally went back to Esterháza. He could have lived in London under royal patronage; he could have lived in Paris or in Petersburg. All three capitals honoured him with medals and awards; only Vienna did not. Maria Theresa had failed to honour him in her lifetime; Joseph did not honour him in spite of his world fame; it was only after his death that the Emperor Francis II conferred upon him the Leopold Medal. It was a curious situation. In his old age his oratorios, *The Seasons* and *The Creation* had attracted immense audiences and moved all but the All Highest to tears. But there was no recognition from successive All Highests, even when, inspired by the effect of the national anthem on London audiences, he decided, in the middle of the Napoleonic Wars, to compose a national hymn for Austria – that wonderful tune set to the words *Gott erhalte unser Kaiser* which was appropriated in 1848 by German nationalist idealists to accompany the words of *Deutschland über Alles* and thus, ironically, became the national anthem not only of Austria but also of Imperial Germany under the Hohenzollern Emperor who broke Habsburg power in Germany.

But even though Haydn went back to Esterháza, he was no longer a fulltime servant of the house. And with all his modesty, he, too, before he died, had become conscious, as Gluck was before him, of his special position as a great artist. Gluck had needed his papal title of chevalier as part of display, and used it always. Haydn had no title. Mozart was also a papal chevalier, but he never thought of using his title; his genius was enough for him. There was an interesting progression here. There was another in the manner in which Haydn sought to use his own dignity and name: to promote not himself but the young Mozart, whom he recognised as the greatest genius of the age, one of the greatest geniuses of all time. Asked to compose an opera for Prague, he replied that all his work of this kind had been written for a special theatre, to receive performance in a particular ambience, to employ specific performers: he was not used to the big, impersonal stage; young Mozart could do much better, and Prague should cling to him, honour him, reward him. Mozart, in his turn, expressed an infinite debt to Haydn, who was for him supreme, and dedicated to him six of his finest quartets. He did not know that Haydn, so gentle and serene as a rule, had exploded in his letter to Prague: 'It enrages me to think that the unparalleled Mozart has not yet been engaged by some imperial or royal court. Do forgive this outburst – but I love that man too much.'

That was in 1787, when Haydn was fifty-five years old, only seven years after the death of Maria Theresa. Mozart was to die, at thirty-five, only four years later. Haydn himself lived on into the next century, to die in 1809 with Napoleon in Schönbrunn and a French guard of honour mounted at his door. He had received every honour save one, formal recognition by the Austrian court. But for a long time this had not mattered. The times were changing. Artists no longer bowed to princes: they spoke to each other and knew, even though the price of such knowledge might be material privation and the contempt of the philistine, that they and they alone were the creators. Mozart died in misery, Haydn in glory; but it was Mozart's *Requiem*, written for the dark stranger, which was played at Haydn's funeral.

And so it has gone on. This was the real revolution inaugurated by Gluck, the gamekeeper's son, born in 1714 on Prince Eugene's estate in the Upper Palatinate, spending his childhood on the Kaunitz estate at Neuschloss and the Kinsky estate at Kamnitz, the Lobkowitz estate at Eisenberg – the Bohemian lands which were to be fought over by Frederick the Great, by Wilhelm I with Bismarck at his elbow, torn from Austria to make the shining new Republic of Czechoslovakia, overrun by Hitler, then by Stalin, then again by Stalin's heirs. Through all this time Gluck and his successors alone have triumphed, with them artists of all kinds, and shown themselves to be the only men capable of transcending human experience and adding to it. Experience as distinct from knowledge, which is the province of the scholar and the scientist. In many societies the artist had been priest. More rarely, more or less unconsciously, he was prophet. In eighteenth-century Vienna, with Gluck, he became consciously prophet. This transformation was to lead, with the development of the romantic movement, to some strange results. For example, not content with crying alone in the wilderness, the artist sought to institutionalise his mystery and turn himself, regressively, into priest once more – but priest now of a private and exclusive religion. This leads us far from our period. It is enough to say that, with Gluck, the musician became self-conscious for the first time in modern European history. He began the century as servant; he ended it as master.

Thus the preface to *Alceste* meant far more than Gluck thought it meant.

When I undertook to set the opera of *Alceste* to music, the object I had in view was to avoid all those abuses which the misapplied vanity of singers and the excessive complaisance of composers had introduced into the Italian opera, and which had converted one of the finest and most imposing spectacles into one of the most wearisome and ridiculous. I sought to reduce music to its true function, that of supporting the poetry, in order to strengthen the expression of the sentiments and the interest of the situations, without interrupting the action or disfiguring it with superfluous ornament. I imagined that the music should be to the poetry just what the vivacity of colour and the happy combination of light and shade are to be correct and well-composed design, serving to animate the figures without altering their contours.

So I have avoided interrupting an actor in the warmth of dialogue, to make him wait for a wearisome *ritornello*, or stopping him in the midst of this discourse, in order that on some suitable vowel he may exhibit the agility of his fine voice in a long passage, or that the orchestra may give him time to take breath again. . . .

I have thought that the overture should prepare the spectators for the character of the coming action, and give them an indication of its subject; that the instruments should only be employed in proportion to the degree of interest and passion involved, and that there should not be too great a disparity between the air and the recitative, in order not to spoil the flow of the period, to interrupt the movement inopportunely, or to dissipate the warmth of the scene.

I have thought, again, that my main task should be to seek a noble simplicity, and I have avoided parading difficulties at the expense of clarity; the discovery of any novelty has seemed to me precious only in so far as it was naturally called forth by the situation, and in harmony with the expression; lastly, there is no rule I have not thought it my duty to sacrifice willingly in order to make sure of an effect.

The preface to *Alceste* was in the form of a dedication to Leopold, Grand Duke of Tuscany, the most sympathetic of all the children of Maria Theresa, whose twenty-five-year rule in Florence was the steadiest and most enlightened of the century. Had he been the eldest son, instead of his brother Joseph, the course of Austrian history would have run differently, but he became Emperor for only two years after his brother's death in 1790 and had time to do nothing but mend a few fences. The preface was published in 1769, and in the same year Sir Joshua Reynolds gave the first of his Discourses to the new Royal Academy in London. The ideas expressed by Gluck were thus very much in the air, Diderot had poured scorn on the conventional operatic manners of the time, and as already observed the Italian, Algarotti, had published in 1763 his book on the opera, which Gluck may, indeed, have read. Those ideas, moreover, were very much in tune with the times: the arts were rational and preoccupied above all, as suggested earlier, with the imitation of nature. What was meant by nature nobody seriously asked. What Gluck meant in the context of his genius was the exhibition of human emotion and sensibility in all its ideal simplicity – joy, hope, anguish, anger, misery, despair – and rendered in the most direct and economical manner possible, the means completely subordinated to the end.

It was because of this that in 1769 Gluck could believe that it was his duty to subordinate himself to the librettist, enhancing, intensifying, *colouring* the sense of the words. It was a return to the idea of 1600 which had become perverted by worship of the singer and the vocal line of the set arias (but it should be remembered that the singers were often superb), so that ladies and gentlemen ate and drank and played draughts in their boxes during the recitative passages, paying no attention to the unfolding of the drama. For Gluck the drama must be all. He had not the least idea that what in fact he was doing was liberating the music so that it could sustain the whole burden and create its own poetry which would live long after the librettist was forgotten and be sung with effect to audiences who could not understand a word of Italian or French. Certainly he was lucky in his librettist Calzabigi whose poems (in which Gluck immersed himself sometimes for months before beginning to compose)

dealing with the so familiar Greek myths had a breadth and simplicity which lifted them far above the innumerable concoctions,
even Metastasio's, on identical themes. But it was Gluck's music, not
Calzabigi's poem, which made his *Iphigenia* alive and able to survive
when at least a dozen lesser Iphigenias crumbled into dust.

In a sense it is easier to see Gluck in perspective today than it was
half a century ago when everything that was written about him, even
by critics of such superb intelligence as Ernest Newman, was
coloured by the assumption that Gluck's music marked a stage in
musical progress, a continuing process of improvement and refine-
ment of an art which, like all other arts, was moving swiftly towards
ever higher things, like the human race itself. Provided one forgot
about Monteverdi, underrated Johan Sebastian Bach, was insensitive
to Mozart, ignored Berlioz, missed the point of Schubert, it was
indeed possible at the turn of the last century to nourish the illusion
of progress of this kind, with Wagner as the highest summit then
attained. Possible, but odd. Possible, too, only if one confused the
technical development of the orchestra and the keyboard with the
spiritual development of music. Even so, one asks why these musical
believers in the inevitability of progress did not look round at some
of the other arts and ask themselves questions. In another sense it is
more difficult, since today it is clear that it is only genius that
matters, and geniuses of the highest degree may be born into any
society and under any sort of régime. It is also clearer now that the
peculiar attribute of the eighteenth century, in music as in everything, was its accepted code or framework of ideas. Today — at least
until a very few years ago — we are on the look-out for genius. It is
hard to think oneself into a time when what was required of the
artist, musician, painter, poet, was a pleasing embroidery on an
accepted theme performed in an accepted manner.

This is certainly all that Maria Theresa expected of her artists, and
yet she herself was actively engaged in a transformation of her own
society which was breaking up the accepted frame. Herself, she preferred Hasse to Gluck to the end of her days; but she was by her own
reforming acts cutting the ground from under Hasse's feet.

It should not be thought, however, that the personal tastes of
either the Empress or the Emperor held by any means absolute sway

in the cultural life of the time. The Burg Theatre itself was leased to a man of business, an impresario, who operated quite in the modern manner, though obviously susceptible to influence from on high. Thus at the time when the young Mozart was composing his first opera, *La Finta Semplice*, in 1768, the lessee was a certain Guiseppe Affligio, who did a great deal of good work, but finished up in the galleys for forgery. Affligio himself commissioned the work from Mozart, twelve years old and the wonder of the age; then he had second thoughts, induced by the sort of intrigues inseparable from the theatre in all ages, and finally told Leopold Mozart bluntly that if he insisted on the fulfilment of the agreement he would put the opera on but would see to it that it was hissed off the stage. Leopold put in a formal complaint to the new Emperor, Joseph II, who had succeeded on the death of his father, Francis, in 1765, and who took a special interest in the theatre. But it led to nothing, and the Mozart family retired hurt to Salzburg. The next commission came almost at once. It came neither from the Court nor from an aristocratic patron. It came from, of all people, the celebrated Dr Mesmer, the inventor of the theory of animal magnetism, who had built a small theatre in his garden; and it was there that Mozart first saw one of his own operas performed, *Bastien und Bastienne*. Years later poor Mesmer's theories were to be hilariously guyed in *Cosi fan Tutte*, the divine product of a world as far removed from the imperial and royal as it is possible to imagine, but a world which owed much of its relative security to the Empress then ten years dead.

PART THREE

The Reins of
Government

Chapter Twelve

Unification and Reform

For the first eight years of her reign the young Queen had stood alone against the world, overriding all those advisers, including Francis himself, who, as she saw it, lacked courage. She had fought off the Bavarians and the French, the Spanish Bourbons too, in the person of Don Carlos, King of the Two Sicilies. She had manoeuvred the English into fighting some of her battles for her; she had stood up to the man who had come to be regarded as the military genius of the age, the detested Frederick. It is true that she had in the end to yield to Prussia all but the rump of those Silesian possessions she had sworn never to relinquish. Parma and Piacenza went back to Spain. But with all this she was in an infinitely stronger position than she had been when she came to the throne. The chit of a girl who had presented herself to all the predators of Europe as a natural victim was, at thirty-two, one of the most formidable of rulers, still a beauty, still full of grace and humour and, on occasion, gaiety, but now also a power in the world not on any account to be trifled with, and unequivocally mistress in her own house.

Her territorial losses in no way diminished her in the eyes of the outside world. To her the loss of Silesia was a profound humiliation, but in the eyes of the English, the French, the Russians, it was no more than an accident of war; and the one man, Frederick, who understood the true meaning of Silesia, to Maria Theresa no less than to himself, was in no mood to crow. He might seek to denigrate his sworn foe by referring to her slightingly as the Queen of Hungary, but he knew he had been lucky in his conquest; further, he believed that Maria Theresa would not rest for long before she tried again to take it from him.

Now, for a further period of eight years, she was to wrestle with an even harder task. At peace for the first time, she set about putting her own house in order; and in this civil campaign she was to find herself even more alone than she had been during her wars. Then, at least, she had compelled the admiration of the world and had been able to rally round her the most gifted and resolute of her feudal nobles. The course she now entered held no facile glory. There were no galas, no fireworks, no Te Deums to mark her victories. Her defeats also were her own. And she had ranged against her the very men, the great landowners, the grandees, of her realm, who now saw their wealth, their privileges, their power, threatened by the Crown they were sworn to defend.

Just as in the armed fight against all-comers the Queen had depended above all on a devoted but unloved civil servant, Bartenstein, now she picked another man out of comparative obscurity and made him into her instrument for forging a centralised state out of a hotchpotch of feudal lands: Wilhelm, Count Haugwitz.

The driving impulse behind Maria Theresa's action was the need for more money and for a regular standing army. The two needs went together. The reforms she called upon Haugwitz to make in order to satisfy these needs were to lead to a radical reorganisation of the realm in the direction of a unified state. But Maria Theresa herself soon saw the logic of events and was then quite ruthless in forwarding this logic. Looked at from any angle, it was a remarkable performance. Apart from Haugwitz and the new men he collected round him, strange to her, she was sometimes utterly alone. Her great nobles resisted dourly, sometimes bitterly. They got at her husband. Even her trusted and beloved Tarouca was full of doubts. The faithful Khevenhüller, who obeyed her decisions with absolute loyalty once they had been taken, spoke out bluntly against Haugwitz's policies in the Sovereign Council and in private.

Intrigues against Haugwitz's personal position grew to monstrous proportions. It was not as though the Queen was an autocrat of arrogant and hasty temper, determined to break the power and pretensions of her nobility because these threatened the Crown directly. It was not as though she had an army at her back to enforce the sub-mission of the rich and haughty potentates of the Austrian and Bohemian Estates. She liked to be on good terms with her nobles; her own life, almost in its entirety, was bound up with theirs. She had no power except her own character and will and personality, reposing on the mystique of the Crown. She set herself the task of persuading these grandees, who were constantly in and around her Court, from among whom she chose her ministers, to allow Count Haugwitz to divest them of their independence and many of their privileges, to tax them, to take away from them their regiments and their centuries' old authority over the inhabitants of their own lands, to rusticate some, to turn others into civil servants, bureaucrats under the Crown. Maria Theresa did not retire to a high place and issue decrees. She went on behaving as though nothing of moment was happening. Anyone in her presence could say what he liked, could declare flatly against her reforms. She would listen to him, smile graciously and proceed with her plans. It is a common characteristic of great men to surround themselves with yes-men: they lack the patience to argue about a predetermined course; they also, more often than not, need bolstering up. Maria Theresa contrived to sail through life surrounded by no-men; picking their brains; paying attention to what they said; sometimes, when she saw fit, modifying her own views to accord with evidence supplied by them; more often overriding them; but always retaining their devotion.

The carrying out of the mid-century reforms was made all the harder because Haugwitz, in spirit an eighteenth-century Keynes, was just about as unprepossessing a person as it is possible to imagine. Perhaps it takes a woman to work successfully through the sort of man who would be blackballed by any exclusive male club – Bartenstein, already described; Haugwitz now emerging; van Swieten, the Dutch physician soon to be encountered; Kaunitz, the diplomat of genius whose personal habits were atrocious – all four of Maria Theresa's great civilian advisers and ministers would have been regarded with great reserve, to say the least, by any normal king. Maria Theresa gave them her trust absolutely, backed them against assaults from all sides, liked them, was amused by them, used them, respected their wisdom and drive – and never took them seriously as men: she did not have to.

Haugwitz's chief handicap was a tic. He blinked his eyes incessantly. It was no doubt this affliction which made so many of his contemporaries declare that this wise man looked like a fool. Contemporary painters, who could capture his countenance in repose, between blinks, witness otherwise. He had good eyes behind the blink, and his features were steady and strong, with a humorous line to his mouth. Steady and strong he needed to be, stubborn too, and had he lacked humour the obstruction of his opponents would have worn him down.

He was the son of a Protestant general who had been in the service of the King of Saxony. In 1725, himself the same age as the century, he entered the Silesian civil service, after going over to Rome, and distinguished himself by turning a sinecure into a career, a career which seemed to be finished with Frederick's invasion of Silesia. Forty-one years old, 'poor and with no prospects', he turned up in Vienna – to find, to his surprise, that Francis, with his interest in finance and administration, knew all about him; others, too, including Tarouca, and Maria Theresa's secretary of cabinet, Ignaz von Koch. Maria Theresa liked him on sight, and sent him off to the rump of Silesia to be her representative there. He had to make an economic and political unity of the remnant of this richest province, and he found himself at once up against the apparently overwhelming alliance of the landed gentry and the Church. He set himself to break it, and, in so doing, he made a close examination of the Prussian system as it was being applied to Frederick's part of Silesia. Thus it was that he was the first to have a clear view of what was required to give the Queen's possessions as a whole coherence and unified direction, backed by a centrally controlled army and the revenue to pay for it.

Maria Theresa herself looked at things from another angle. She saw that her age-old inheritance had been shamefully abased by the upstart king of a small German state for a long time indistinguishable from other principalities of the Empire. It had been humiliated because it had no cohesion and because, in peace and war alike, the provincial Estates, dominated by the landowning nobility, were intent only on their own interests and made no proper contribution to the central government. Indeed, there was no central government. There was a queen and a chancellor and a sovereign council who made foreign policy and conducted wars, but were dependent, in effect, on the voluntary contributions of the Estates, dominated by an aristocracy who paid no taxes. This situation was tolerable so long as the Empire meant something. Then the Emperor – Archduke of Austria, King of Bohemia, King of Hungary and all the rest – could count, as emperor, on the support of all the principalities. Prussia had threatened this system by setting herself up successfully against the imperial pretensions of the Habsburgs, who, from now on, would depend for their strength on their own hereditary lands and the support they could attract (no longer morally compel) from the imperial realms. The hereditary lands must be pulled together and organised in the interest of the dynasty.

So far as Maria Theresa was concerned there was little political philosophy behind the actions she prepared herself to take. She had not the least desire to curtail the privileges of the Estates more than was absolutely necessary to ensure that they pulled their weight. And there was a certain irony in the fact that it was the rise of Prussia which caused her to put her own house in order, to such effect that it was able to resist the Prussian challenge very successfully indeed for more than a century to come.

What Haugwitz did, with her approval and energetic support, was to create a centralised bureaucracy, a centralised standing army, a centralised treasury. In the process of bringing the Estates to heel he also separated the judiciary from the administration. Maria Theresa did not in the least intend a revolution, but she made one.

The army came first. The Haugwitz plan called for a standing army of 108,000 men with a budget of 14 million gulden (out of a total revenue of 40 million). These were to be assured by a ten-year recess, or agreement, to which all the Estates must subscribe. And the burden must fall equally on all Estates and Lands. It was to be a cash burden: the central government alone would be responsible for recruiting and equipping the army.

The system of taxation was to be clearly laid down. It was to be based on the value of each individual's immovable property, land and fixtures and rents, determined by commissions of experts. Income was calculated at 5 per cent of the relevant capital sum, and on this income the landowning nobility had to pay one-hundredth part, the peasants one-fiftieth. The uproar was tremendous. For centuries it had been understood that peasants and burghers paid taxes, their masters did not. Neither did the clergy. The thinking behind this view was not so eccentric as it seems today. The Crown depended on the nobility, who, in effect, ran the country on the Crown's behalf and provided for its defence in war. The peasants on the land, the tradesmen in the towns, owed their peaceful existence to the smooth functioning of this feudal apparatus of Estates. It was proper that they should contribute to the upkeep of this apparatus of security. It was unheard of that the protectors themselves should pay: they paid with their services and their arms; many of them disbursed large sums on the upkeep of more or less private regiments. If there were to be regular fixed levies at all, these must be self-imposed by the separate Estates.

But although there was uproar, there was surprisingly little organised resistance. The individual who spoke out most loudly was Count Friedrich Harrach, Kinsky's successor as Bohemian chancellor, whose family had long stood among the dynasty's most loyal supporters. He insisted that taxation must, and could only, be a matter for the Estates, and he opposed flatly the proposal to tax nobility and clergy. He made a direct and formal appeal to Maria Theresa, who stood firm. Though many agreed with him, none would effectively support him. So he resigned his office, suffered an apoplectic seizure and very soon died. Haugwitz went ahead with his plans. It was in no way a steam-rollering operation. The case was argued with each individual estate. Those closest to the Prussian threat submitted soonest: Bohemia and Moravia. Styria, Carniola, Gorizia and Gradisca agreed only to a three year recess; Tirol to one year only. Carinthia, the stamping ground of the Khevenhüllers, isolated behind a barrier of snowy mountains, refused to agree at all, and in due course had to be compelled. The Hungarians in the Diet at Pressburg argued for two years. They were allowed to find their own money in their own way, but, even so, they finally agreed to pay only 700,000 gulden a year as their military contribution instead of the

1,200,000 demanded: it was not until well into the nineteenth century that the Hungarian magnates paid any taxes at all.

Hand in hand with the financing of the new army went a great movement of rationalisation. It was high time. 'Who would believe,' the Empress was to write in one of her memorials, 'that there was not the slightest attempt to achieve uniformity among my troops! Every regiment had its own separate drill on the march, on manoeuvres, on deployment. One fired in quick time, another in slow time; the same terms and words of command meant different things to different regiments. No wonder the Emperor was beaten all the time during the ten years before my accession, no wonder the state in which I found the army was indescribable.'

All this had to be changed. Permanent encampments, or cantonments, were set up, and Maria Theresa was able to strengthen the romantic bond between her, the *mater castrorum*, and her troops by visiting them to watch exercises and manoeuvres. The Imperial White was already the recognised colour of the uniforms, but now the cut was streamlined and every deviation from the strictly laid down cut and trimmings punished. Count Leopold Daun first made his name as the compiler of new manuals of drill and tactics which were binding for the whole army. Prince Liechtenstein, who had already made a great personal contribution to the artillery, was now, as chief of all the gunners, busily engaged in developing light and manoeuvrable field-pieces which soon, just in time for the Seven Years War, were to be the admiration of Europe. His three-pounder regimental piece could give aimed fire more rapidly than the contemporary musket. By 1755 he had 2,000 master-gunners ready for battle and many more in training. No less important was the foundation by the Empress herself of the soon to be famous Military Academy in the old fortress town of Wiener Neustadt, housed in the rebuilt castle of the twelfth-century Duke Leopold and until 1918 the headquarters of Austrian military thought. She established also an academy of military engineering, and she gave the Favorita Palace, her childhood home, to be an academy for the education of future civil servants, the Theresianum. Out of all this movement and thought the Imperial General Staff was born. There were no longer to be individual commands. Though regimental colonels, the 'colonel proprietors' still had absolute control of promotion within their regiments, they themselves were now part of a machine, and the new academies soon began to bring forward an equally new school of intelligent and highly trained officers. Thus it was that after his first encounter with the imperial troops in the opening stages of the Seven Years War, Frederick could exclaim with feeling: 'These are no longer the same old Austrians.'

Meanwhile, as part of the general upheaval aimed primarily at the financing and reorganisation of the army, Haugwitz began to put in train far-reaching administrative reforms. Hitherto the administration of Bohemia on the one hand and the Austrian lands on the other had been separate, each controlled by its own chancellory, responsible only to Maria Theresa. Not unnaturally, instead of working together for the greater good of the whole the Bohemian and the Austrian chancellories had been at each other's throats, each seeking its own advantage at the other's expense. In May 1749, after Harrach's resignation as Bohemian chancellor, Maria Theresa abolished both chancellories and merged the two administrations into a single body, a directorate *in politicis et camerilibus*, which was to conduct the administration and domestic policy of what was henceforward to be a unified Austrian state, from which Hungary was excepted – as it was always in future to be excepted, save for a brief and deeply resented period between the smashing of the Hungarian uprising in 1848 and the formal recognition of dualism in 1867. By then Galicia had been included in the Austrian unitary state, and the Netherlands and Lombardy had been surrendered. In 1749, under the Haugwitz reforms, Hungary had to contribute 24,000 men, the Netherlands 30,000 and Lombardy 30,000, bringing up the grand total of the imperial army to close on 200,000 men.

From the point of view of establishing an empire which could live into the nineteenth century and beyond, the most significant of all the Haugwitz innovations was the formal separation of administration and judiciary. This was very closely bound up with the problems of centralisation and the reduction of the powers of the Estates. Although in England the separation had been effected a century earlier, on the Continent it was still a dream. Montesquieu's *L'Esprit des Lois* had appeared in Geneva only in 1748, but for some years it was banned in Vienna and was not allowed to circulate until the Queen herself intervened in a dispute between the Jesuits and the champions of the French philosopher. There was little philosophy behind this great reform, promulgated in a personal Rescript signed by Maria Theresa in May 1749. The drive behind it came, as with the other reforms, from the need to build up a unified apparatus of state. But its consequences were far-reaching. And it was this particular reform which filled the loyal old conservatives with the deepest foreboding. Khevenhüller, after grumbling in his diary about the merging of the administration of Bohemia and the Austrian lands, was carried away: 'Maybe the Empress has not been moved by ill intention. The lady has been overwhelmed by so many complaints about miscarriages and delays in justice, and especially that these have mostly been due to conflict between the so numerous courts, that in the end she had the idea of separating the powers.'

'Confusion,' he declared, so everyone said, 'was worse confounded.' What else could one expect when 'interested persons for their own glory' had persuaded her to overturn and totally recast a tried form of government which has lasted 'for many centuries and from the very beginning of the ruling House', employing to carry out this operation 'pen-pushers quite unqualified to engage in an undertaking of this kind'.

The reform of 1749 was the signal for the drawing up of new codes of laws. It began in 1752, and the work went on until, in 1766, the *Codex Theresianus* defining civil rights was issued, and two years later, the *Constitutio Criminalis*, which laid the foundation for the model code of 1811.

The revenue doubled itself from 20 to 40 million gulden between 1745 and 1754. Taxation was heavy, and, as was to be expected, there were loud lamentations about ruin and expropriation. They deceived even that shrewd observer, the Venetian ambassador, Andrea Tron, who wrote in 1751:

There are many who assert that these burdens are altogether too oppressive and beyond the capacity of the population. Within a few years, they say, the landowners in Austria, Bohemia and Moravia, nobility and peasantry alike, will be forced to stand by and watch their fields falling into decay; while the labourers will be driven off the land in hordes to seek sustenance elsewhere.

This did not happen. The Haugwitz reforms, coinciding with eight years of peace, did so much to improve the economy in the longish run that Maria Theresa was able to face Frederick, when once again he attacked in 1756, not only with a greatly improved army but also with all the panoply of a relatively prosperous state.

It might have been more prosperous still had the economists of the day understood political economy. Maria Theresa, once again on her own initiative, was seized with the importance of trade. Even before Haugwitz was summoned to her side she had written to her chancellor, Ulfeld (in 1743, when she was twenty-six): 'The longer I look at it the clearer I see that no proper care is being taken of commerce and manufacture in any of the Lands; and yet these are the sole means of bringing prosperity to the Lands and attracting foreign gold. Therefore, I command that the existing Commercial Commissions in each of the Lands be forthwith renewed.'

And so she continued nagging, in the intervals of fighting the Prussians, the French, the Bavarians, the Spaniards and the Sardinians, until Haugwitz came along and seven years later caused to be broadcast far and wide the first treatise on political economy by an individual called Johann Heinrich Gottlieb Justi, who had been brought from Eisenach, the Esterházy reserve, to teach in the new *Theresianum*. Alas, Justi was a mercantilist of the deepest dye, and Haugwitz, though an administrator of genius, was unable to perceive the fallacy of mercantilism. He was in good company. Another twenty-six years were to go by before Adam Smith published in Glasgow his *Wealth of Nations*.

Perhaps, halfway through the twentieth century, we can sympathise a little better with Justi, Haugwitz and Maria Theresa, than our fathers and grandfathers. To the slightly dazed and wondering laymen today, fashionable emphasis on what might be termed unrequited exports has an uncanny look of neomercantilism and a strong smell of the eighteenth century in which so many countries, striving towards economic autarchy as the ultimate goal, thought that all they had to do to prosper was to increase exports and diminish imports. Be that as it may, mercantilism was the mainstay of Habsburg economic policy, and although it led to a dead end, at least in the short term it enabled Maria Theresa to build up a number of industries, above all the textile industries in Bohemia, and silk from the newly planted mulberries of Lombardy, glass, again in Bohemia, and porcelain in Vienna. It also led to the development of Trieste as a great port, at first mainly occupied with the export of Hungarian wine and agricultural products of all kinds.

There was one more field for the Empress to conquer: education. And here again we see her extraordinary talent for picking good men and supporting them. Here again, too, we see the empirical cast of her mind. As far as conscious philosophy was concerned she did not merely resist the ideas of the times: she was oblivious of them. Locke and Newton were a hundred years dead; for Maria Theresa they might never have existed. They had inspired the astonishing fructification of the French Enlightenment. Voltaire, Diderot, Montesquieu, were feverishly occupied in preparing the fearful explosion of 1789. They fascinated a Russian empress and a Prussian king. 'An opinion launched in Paris was like a battering ram launched by thirty millions of men,' exclaimed Joseph de Maistre. The battering ram failed to carry as far as Vienna. It was not until Joseph, the heir to the realm, came of age, that the ideas and general principles of the Enlightenment were consciously brought into play, and then Maria Theresa resisted them stubbornly, bitterly sometimes, sometimes despairingly. All the same, led by nothing but the light of her own nature, and with the strength and therefore the prosperity of her realm as her ruling idea, she herself was to embody much of the logic of the new ideas in her reforms.

Justi had written: 'The State can do everything, if only it has the will.' Maria Theresa, who saw herself not at all as the state but only as the universal mother of her peoples, had the will. She needed high officials for her unified bureaucracy: the *Theresianum* was founded to educate and train to this end the children of the nobility from an early age. If the state was to prosper, its citizens had to be better educated: the more prosperous they were the more taxes they would pay. So she inaugurated her reforms of the universities and high schools – much later, in her declining years, the still more famous reforms of elementary education – all designed to turn out good citizens. She founded technical colleges and an academy for 'oriental' languages designed expressly to train future diplomats and merchants to open up the Middle East to Austrian trade. But she drew the line at learning for learning's sake, and refused to sanction an early project for a German Academy advocated by the Leipzig critic and pedagogue, Gottsched, who was under the spell of French ideas. Much later, writing to her youngest son, Maximilian, at a time when her eldest son, Joseph, was causing her much pain with his reforming zeal, she could say:

Nothing is more pleasant, nothing more flattering to our self-esteem, than wholly unrestricted liberty. Liberty is the word which has supplanted the word religion in our enlightened century when every one thinks and acts in the light of his own convictions or calculations. . . . They condemn the past for its ignorance and prejudice, while knowing nothing at all about the past and not much more about the present. Should I ever see that these so-called wise men and philosophers were happier in their undertakings and more content in their private lives, then I should be guilty of bias, pride, prejudice and obstinacy if I did not follow their example. Unfortunately, however, the experience of every day convinces me to the contrary. Nobody is weaker, nobody more cowardly than these strong spirits; nobody more servile, nobody more cast down by the least unpleasantness than they. They are bad fathers, sons, husbands, ministers, generals and citizens. And why? Because they lack foundations. All their philosophy, all their principles arise only from their own self regard; the least mishap throws them down, with no resources to fall back upon.

The man Maria Theresa chose to reconcile in practice this profound and peremptory faith with the improvement of secular education for secular ends (but at this stage there was to be no teaching frowned on by the Jesuits) was a Dutchman, a noted physician, Gerhard van Swieten, to whom, as to all her advisers once she had chosen them, she gave her utter trust.

Van Swieten was born in Leyden in 1700. At Leyden and at

Lyons he became the favourite pupil of Boerhaave, the great founder of modern medicine. His studies completed, he won for himself at Leyden a European reputation for his lectures in pathology and anatomy, stirring up jealousy and intrigue on the part of his senior colleagues to such a degree that, in the end, he was forced out of the university on the pretext of his Catholicism.

Maria Theresa first heard of him in 1744 when her only and most beloved sister, Marianne, married to Prince Charles of Lorraine, now Statthalter of the Netherlands, fell ill in Brussels shortly before being confined. A few days later she gave birth to a stillborn child and was to all appearances dying. Van Swieten was sent for by the temporary acting Statthalter, Count Königsegg-Erps and by Count Kaunitz, who was political adviser to the Lorraines. He was reassuring and assiduous in his treatment, but two months later the Archduchess died.

That, one might have thought, would be the end of van Swieten as far as Vienna was concerned. Maria Theresa was desolated by her sister's death; worse, she had allowed herself to be buoyed up by van Swieten's encouraging messages. She was already deeply interested in the man and, three years on the throne, actively searching still for men she could trust. She knew about his general reputation, and Kaunitz in Brussels sent her enthusiastic reports: he was entranced, he wrote, by the Dutchman's wonderful mind and depth of knowledge. On the strength of this, Maria Theresa had declared her intention of inviting him to Vienna as her body doctor. It was one more sign of her remarkable mixture of detachment, enthusiasm and steadfastness that, with Marianne dead, far from consigning the optimistic, as yet unseen, and failed van Swieten to the outer darkness, she not only considered herself bound by her promise but also wrote to him personally in the warmest terms. She was also attracted – as so often this natural autocrat was attracted – by the Dutchman's independence of mind. She had sent out to Brussels her own body doctor, Engel, a man of great conceit and tiresomeness, whom she did not like. He was, after all, the formal emissary of the Queen. . . . But van Swieten had handled him beautifully, respectfully, without on the one hand yielding ground or, on the other taking umbrage at the pretensions of an ignoramus. Now Maria Theresa wrote to say that she was deeply impressed by his behaviour, to say nothing of his universal reputation. No monarch could have too many men like him. If only he would consent to come to Vienna she would see to it that he would meet no trouble from 'that unhappy man'. But she would not press him too hard. She shrank from tearing him 'from that sweet peace you have so far enjoyed and which is the only happiness on earth'. Nevertheless, please come. And if you come 'so strongly do I wish to see you here as soon as possible, I will make all arrangements for you to enjoy the fullest freedom'.

Van Swieten gladly responded to the call. Excluded from preferment in Holland, it is likely that he would have settled down as a useful but by no means inspired physician, building up a quiet body of written work on anatomy and clinical medicine. He was already forty-five and with his *Commentary on Boerhaave's Aphorisms* he had constructed a useful monument based on his own shorthand record of the utterances of this teacher and diagnostician of genius, who pursued his course of instruction, the most famous in the world, in his two little wards at Leyden, each with only six beds, one for men and one for women. Maria Theresa was to give van Swieten the chance not merely to celebrate Boerhaave in his *Commentary*, but also in due course to establish in Vienna an exact replica of the master's teaching wards, presided over by another Dutchman and fellow-pupil of Boerhaave's, de Haen, who was the first physician to systematise the keeping of case histories and to employ the clinical thermometer as the basic tool in exploring and recording a case history. Van Swieten, in a word, was to be the real founder of the great Vienna Medical School, which was finally institutionalised by Joseph II, with his inauguration of the celebrated complex of buildings known as the *Allgemeine Krankenhaus* (the Vienna General Hospital) and the *Josephinum* for military surgery.

He was to do more than this. It became his self-appointed task to launch the process which was to bring a Jesuit-ridden society into the age of the Enlightenment. He so thoroughly won the trust of the Empress that she allowed him to reform not merely the medical faculty of Vienna University, but the University as a whole. It was to van Swieten, too, that Jean Paul von Riegger, Karl Anton Martini and Joseph von Sonnenfels, the three great reforming minds of eighteenth-century Vienna, owed their security and their firm base.

Nothing better illustrates the extraordinary complexity of Maria Theresa's make-up than her relationship with van Swieten. He stood for tendencies which she abhorred but of which she seems to have recognised, with an unacknowledged part of her mind, the inevitability, if not the desirability. In some way reassured by his devout Catholicism, she stood by in close support while his experimental mind and his appreciation of the development of ideas outside the Empire brought him into almost violent collision not only with the University establishment but, more particularly, with the Jesuits who had been so confident of their hold on the Empress that they had come to take it quite for granted.

Nobody anywhere at any time or in any matter was able to take Maria Theresa quite for granted – or if they did so, it was their undoing. She displayed not only the complexities of her own mind and temperament, which were such that in all but one or two matters her political instinct, as it developed, was able to overcome her inborn prejudices, but also the capacity of a born ruler to establish and sustain the most delicate balances between opposing points of view, while retaining the devotion of individuals antagonistic to the point of mutual destructiveness. Thus, in general, she stood by the Jesuits to the end – to their suppression, that is, in 1774. She defended them gently against van Swieten as she was later to defend them furiously against her son, Joseph, finally against the Pope, whose claim to the property and assets of the suppressed order she quietly ignored. She chose a Jesuit as her personal confessor. But with all this she listened to van Swieten, infuriated her Jesuits by appointing him chief censor (still leaving the censorship of theological works to them), and was openminded enough to accept very hard words from van Swieten when he thought it necessary to say them. Thus, in December 1759, frustrated and disgusted more than usual by Jesuit intrigues, he addressed his Sovereign: 'I am in a position to offer the most certain proof that the true aim of the Society has always been one and the same, to enrich itself, and that religion has been only the pretext for abusing the piety of Your Majesty and her glorious ancestors.'

Van Swieten was able to say these things because he proved to Maria Theresa's satisfaction his absolute devotion to her and her realm; because, also, as censor, he had the sense to compromise and show a sense of deep responsibility. He took up the censorship appointment because he believed, correctly, that he and only he so knew how to handle the Empress, and so weaken the barriers she had set up in her orthodoxy against the infiltration of ideas from outside. If, to retain her confidence, he had to ban Voltaire, Fielding and others, it could not be helped. It was the price he had to pay for what he considered more urgent necessities – as, for example, the publication in Vienna of Montesquie's *L'Esprit des Lois* after a bitter struggle with his opponents on the censorship commission. He was able to stop the raiding of bookshops and the arbitrary burning of undesirable volumes found on the premises. He had trouble not only with the Church in general (Cardinal Migazzi above all) and the Jesuits in particular but also with Maria Theresa's personal blind spots. Thus in 1764 he allowed a Bavarian periodical to circulate in Vienna which contained sharp and ironic characterisations of notable contemporaries. Both malice and irony were anathema to Maria Theresa who, although she could always make a joke against herself, detested joking at the expense of others and, anyway, preferred buffoonery to wit. She objected. Van Swieten sought to justify: the periodical, he said, contained 'gracefully and elegantly written articles, ridiculing national vices and absurdities'. In all ages, he went on, irony had been the approved weapon 'for criticising and improving humanity'. Maria Theresa would have none of it. 'For myself I dislike irony in any form; it improves nothing, it only embitters, and I consider it uncharitable, moreover. Why waste time either writing or reading such things? There are so many better things to be done, to which we should apply ourselves.'

Van Swieten lost that round, But he won many more. He was unresting. Not content with establishing his own position close to the Empress, and, with her help, holding it against the most powerful enemies, he was ready to endanger his whole career in defence of his juniors. Thus, as late as 1766, when the young Sonnenfels came under heavy attack not only from Archbishop Migazzi and Count Chotek but also from the Empress herself, van Swieten formally offered his resignation as chief censor, and Maria Theresa, who was herself outraged by Sonnenfels's attacks on reaction, secular and spiritual, climbed down completely and gave way.

Van Swieten pursued three careers simultaneously. He worked like an ox. He was one of those commanding, easygoing men with double chins, who combine unlimited intellectual vitality, a natural authority, and great benevolence. He was busy all the time and could not take a walk or carriage exercise without brooding over a current problem or sparking off new ideas. In conversation with his intimates he was lively and amusing, but he kept himself to a very narrow circle, and it was only by secluding himself and making himself inaccessible to the men who flocked to see him from all over Europe that he was able to cope with work which would have been more than enough for a dozen lesser men. With all this he was unremittingly kind to his patients and his students, many of whom he kept alive by gifts from his own pocket.

He started off modestly enough as the Empress's personal physician and director of the Court Library; and it was in an improvised lecture-room in Fischer's superb baroque monument, not in the University itself, that he started his own two-year course of lectures in medicine which established him as a teacher and decided Maria Theresa to give him carte-blanche to reform the official medical faculty: from her point of view what she was doing was depriving the medical faculty of its ancient autonomy and chartered privileges and putting it under state control. From van Swieten's point of view he was being given the opportunity to introduce to Vienna the spirit of Leyden. In the end he developed his authority to such an extent that for all practical purposes he was an unofficial minister of education. He had to fight his own battles, and although he was sure of the empress's support in principle, these were often savage. Churchmen, Jesuits, old-established university professors, courtiers too, all regarded him with jealousy and suspicion, often with malevolent hostility. He was a new broom and swept vigorously, often tactlessly, in many dusty corners, speaking his own mind with a directness foreign to an all too servile society, riding purposefully over hallowed customs, caring little for wounded vanities and nothing for vested interests. Khevenhüller had one more man to grumble about, and fulminated in his diary against the pretensions of 'this by all means cultivated, but also extremely rude and insolent medico, who has made himself uncommonly well-hated by all and sundry'. To survive in this atmosphere, he needed all the protection Maria Theresa could supply.

Her loyalty was characteristic. The irony of the situation was that this man who had been brought to Vienna as her personal physician was not an outstandingly good doctor. He raised the level of medicine in Vienna to a new height, both directly and through his fanatical protégé de Haen. He put an end to the situation in which patients admitted to hospital were thereby more often than not sentenced to death. He reconstructed the examination system, so that instead of the native Viennese going abroad to qualify, foreigners swarmed to qualify in Vienna. He built a new anatomy school and, under the patronage of Francis, started the famous botanical gardens under Jacquin at Schönbrunn. He did many other things besides. But when it came to keeping the imperial family alive he did not shine. He was too busy, too full of his own thoughts, to be a good diagnostician. More particularly, for too long he allowed himself to be influenced by de Haen in the treatment of smallpox. De Haen, for all his innovating ways, was firmly, passionately, indeed, opposed to the new idea of inoculation against smallpox which had spread from England. Van Swieten at first took his word for it and did not change his mind until after the catastrophic year of 1767 when in a matter of weeks Maria Theresa lost her daughter and her daughter-in-law and almost died herself. After that van Swieten changed course, applied to Sir William Pringle, George III's physician, for a skilled practitioner, and allowed experimental inoculations. These proved so successful that soon the Empress had her younger children treated, and also offered free inoculations to the children of the poor, in order to give Viennese doctors further practice in the technique.

But she never reproached van Swieten for being so slow to adopt a treatment which could have saved the lives of members of her own family. With him, as with so many other trusted friends and servants, her remarkable gift for recognising the inevitable limitations of gifted and beloved men, was most perfectly displayed. She trusted him to the end, as she argued with him to the end; and her trust was not removed when it became clear to her that his reforming ideas were undermining the system she was determined to maintain.

Chapter Twelve

Prince Kaunitz

Tarouca, Haugwitz, van Swieten – to these must now be added the most brilliant, soon the most powerful, of all Maria Theresa's advisers: Wenzel Anton, Count Kaunitz-Rietburg, later Prince Kaunitz. His reputation is a legend. His name, in advance of the legend, has already cropped up. It was Kaunitz, in Vienna, who warmly recommended Haugwitz to Maria Theresa; it was Kaunitz, in Brussels, who was enraptured by van Swieten. Who recommended Kaunitz? Where did he come from?

Unlike so many of the Empire's diplomats and statesmen, he was a born Austrian. His father belonged to the nobility, undertook diplomatic missions, and settled down to be the viceroy of Moravia, where the family estates were situated. Wenzel Anton was a second son, the sixth of sixteen children. He was intended for the Church, and his father was able to establish him, at sixteen, in a sinecure in Munster, intended as the first step towards a useful bishopric. But the young Kaunitz was not cut out for the contemplative life, and although his lack of faith would have in no way deterred him from presenting himself as a prince of the Church, he hankered after a wider stage. So he released himself, embarked on a grand tour, which included England, and went through the motions of equipping himself for the law. At twenty-four, in 1735, he joined the offices of the Imperial Court Council. There he idled away his time, made a useful marriage into the Starhemberg family, and soon entered the diplomatic service.

It was in Turin in 1742, when Maria Theresa was working hard to attach Charles Emmanuel of Sardinia to her cause, that Kaunitz had his first glimpse of Machiavellian diplomacy, in the person of the Marchese d'Ormea, a shining light of equivocation and a master of that *Realpolitik* (the term was not then invented) which, disregarding all considerations of morality and human decency, thinking only in terms of self-interest, all too easily is found also to have disregarded considerations of common sense. The young Kaunitz was fascinated, and the fascination stayed with him.

He was also suddenly ambitious. He did not in the least flatter himself that Sardinia came into the war on the side of Austria as a result of his intelligence, skill or charm. It was not in his nature to underrate these qualities in himself, but he knew that in this context they had been irrelevant: Charles Emmanuel decided to back Vienna because Austrian troops had been doing well in Italy. That was how things should be done. Here was an ambition worthy of an intelligent and cultivated man: back the right horse and then fix the race to make sure. Such exercises, to carry them out in style, call for the deployment of a large range of special qualities. As much as any man who ever lived, Kaunitz had them; and no man was ever happier in his work. He was gay as a lark, industrious as a bee, clever as a fox. Like a cat, he knew instinctively how to work within his powers; but his powers exceeded those of any other contemporary statesman. Music and art he loved, women too. He found time for them all. The only apparent cloud over the sunniest of existences was an extreme hypochondria. But no doubt he took pleasure in that too: he had energy to spare for anything. His Sovereign came to cherish him as the apple of her eye. He was everything that she was not: vain, promiscuous, atheistical, showy, arrogant, greedy, self-dramatising, cynical to a degree. He became her Disraeli.

All this took time to develop. When he was in Turin, as soon as he perceived the light of his own nature, he set to work to establish himself. He wrote a memorandum which he sent to the aged Sinzendorf, outlining with extreme boldness and total disregard for conventional morality a master plan for dealing with Prussia and making Austria a stronger and more coherent power. It included operations of the kind later to be approved by Joseph Stalin, involving, for example, offering Naples to Charles Albert of Bavaria (then an emperor without a base: General Khevenhüller was sitting in Munich) in exchange for Bavaria and presenting Sicily to Charles Emmanuel of Sardinia in order to eliminate his pressure on the Milanese. Subsequent quarrels between the two minor monarchs, both exposed to British maritime importunity, could be of no possible consequence to Vienna, save in a negatively advantageous sense. It was all a dream. The subsequent progress of the war put an end to such projects. But it helped Kaunitz to make his mark as a coming man. When, in 1744, Maria Theresa sent him to Brussels to act as political adviser to Prince Charles of Lorraine it may have looked like a backward step, but it was not. Maria Theresa was devoted to her brother-in-law, and closer to Marianne than to any other woman. In sending the young Kaunitz to advise them she was bringing him directly into the family councils: it was a mark of extreme confidence, and a test.

He survived the test, and his next major assignment was to represent Vienna during the peace-making at Aix-la-Chapelle. In this thankless position he completed his political education. Turin had introduced him to the world of *Realpolitik*; Brussels had shown him that there was no useful future for Austria in the Netherlands; Aix-la-Chapelle convinced him finally that Eugene's ideal of a firm alliance with England in face of France had now been invalidated by the Prussian challenge. At Aix-la-Chapelle England and France ran the show between them, relegating Austria to a peripheral position. Kaunitz, who believed firmly with his Empress that the efforts of Austria must from now on be directed singlemindedly towards reducing Prussia and regaining Silesia, saw clearly that she would receive no serious help from England in this struggle; more, that further association with an England interested only in a continuing struggle with France would only strengthen the bonds between Paris and Berlin. In a continental land war Austria could not hope to smash this dangerous coalition, which, therefore, must be undone by peaceful means. Thus it was that in 1748 this remarkable virtuoso of thirty-seven, occupying no seat of power, set himself to reverse an age-old policy and achieve an alliance with the hereditary foe. This involved retaining the alliance with the English and the Dutch, while loosening it a little; working to turn Paris and Berlin against each other; developing friendly relations with the hostile court of Versailles; and, for good measure, cultivating Russia.

First he had to win over Maria Theresa herself to this new policy, and this he did with astonishing ease. In the early spring of 1749 Maria Theresa required each member of the State Conference to put into writing his recommendations for the future course of Austrian policy. Broadly speaking, all spoke for a continuation of the pact with the Maritime Powers, the development of civilised relations with Prussia (without prejudice to future claims on Silesia) and working to achieve defensive alliances with Saxony and Hanover in Germany and Russia outside. In a word, the general aim was the neutralisation of Prussia and a grand coalition against France. Francis himself came out very strongly for the maintenance of traditional ties with England. All took it for granted that France was the main enemy and could never be anything else. All except Kaunitz, the youngest of them all, who exposed his deeply pondered conclusions in an elaborate memorandum as long as a book.

Maria Theresa was at once impressed. Here was a younger man of obvious subtlety, boldness and brilliance confirming her in her own passionate belief that nothing in the world mattered so much to Austria as the recovery of Silesia. He gave her arguments which hitherto she had lacked, or at least not clearly seen, to support her passion and her instinct. She was sharply conscious of the material consequences of the loss of her richest province, with over 1,200,000 souls. The personal humiliation was deep, and she was alarmed at the rise in Germany of a strong new independent power capable of challenging and defeating imperial designs. But now Kaunitz showed her that if Prussia was allowed to continue in the possession of Silesia the whole imperial idea, or what was left of it, would fall to the ground, and that once this was understood the Habsburgs would have no reliable hold over the Slav populations of Bohemia and Moravia. He also demonstrated coolly and lucidly that England had no conceivable interest in the Austrian recovery of Silesia; further, that even with the best will in the world she could never provide the continental forces required to enable Austria to subdue a Franco-Prussian coalition. Silesia, thus, could only be recovered with the active assistance of France. Once this point was grasped, it followed that the active pursuit first of friendship, then of an alliance with France must be the supreme aim of Austrian policy. Such a consummation could not be achieved without sacrifice. But compared with the recovery of Silesia the surrender to France of territory in the Netherlands or in Italy would be a bagatelle.

Maria Theresa perused this elaborate essay with mounting excitement and wild surmise. All the members of the State Conference must read it at once, she insisted, and give her their views. They did so. Only Count Rudolf Colleredo was determinedly opposed. He refused flatly to believe that France, eternally jealous of the Habsburgs, could ever bring herself to work for their aggrandisement, at no matter what price. Francis still clung in principle to the English alliance, but was not prepared to make an issue of it: he was not a man for issues. The others ranged between sudden enthusiasm for a new and world-shaking idea and the feeling that there was nothing to lose by trying – but how? The how was soon answered. The Empress's solution was to maintain in the eyes of all the world the *status quo*, so as to avoid alarming England and alerting Prussia, while working by secret diplomatic means, but slowly, towards the fulfilment of the Kaunitz dream. Kaunitz had thought up this exciting possibility; Kaunitz believed it to be practicable: very well, Kaunitz should go to Paris as Austrian ambassador and launch from the front line the scheme he had conceived at headquarters.

It was a mission after his own heart. He presented himself as an accomplished courtier-diplomat, surrounded himself with the utmost splendour, entertained on a wildly extravagant scale, and sounded out the ground. The ground, as he had fully expected, was very firm. France, her eyes always on England, depended on a strong continental ally, which she found in Frederick, and, at the same time, required a divided Germany at her back. There was no question of Prussia unifying Germany, but a visibly strengthened Austria could well, at the expense of a weakened Prussia, especially in alliance with Russia, become once more an active threat. And indeed there were good reasons for assuming the undying hostility of Vienna. France's breach of her pledges in the matter of the Pragmatic Sanction were not lightly to be overlooked, nor the dire consequences that flowed from this. To make matters worse, the French undoubtedly assumed that Francis was burning with the determination to recover his beloved Lorraine which, not to put too fine a point on it, he had been persuaded to surrender under false pretences. Thus the new ambassador was treated – with perfect courtesy – less as an emissary of peace than as a high-grade spy, a harbinger of revenge.

But with all his brilliance and boldness of attack, Kaunitz was also the soul of patience. He was in no hurry at all. A lesser man would have been cast down by the bland refusal of Paris to respond to his delicate hints or to take in the least seriously the stories he quietly circulated to illustrate the perfidy of Frederick. A lesser man would also have been driven to indignation and despair by the ineptitude of Ulfeld and the clumsiness of Bartenstein, his masters in Vienna. Kaunitz took it all in his stride. There was a moment when he faltered and, bowing to the evidence of his eyes, advised his imperial mistress that she had better patch up the quarrel with Prussia. But all he needed from Vienna was a signal to persist, and he returned to the attack. During his three years in Paris he achieved nothing tangible. When he returned to Vienna in 1753 the general situation was unchanged. In fact, in a way which could not be paraded, he had done wonders: he had won the sympathy and interest of Louis XV and, far more important, the confidence of the Pompadour, then at the summit of her remarkable career. He was content for the time being to rest on that. When an occasion arose to make the French take a fresh look at the international situation he, Kaunitz, would be in a strong position to influence their thinking. With luck, very soon, he would even be in a position to manufacture an occasion.

With his mistress, the Empress, he was perfectly in accord. She, too, knew how to be patient. During these years she knew for the first time what it was to be happy in her work. Immensely fortified at home by the characters and activity of Haugwitz and van Swieten, she rejoiced now in having found in Kaunitz a man who was fit to be her prime minister. With him and through him she experienced for the first time that delusive excitement, that last infirmity of able rulers, that she was moving along a preordained course, no longer reacting more or less helplessly to forces beyond her control. She was, as far as can be judged, working on a larger time-scale even than

Kaunitz. The idea of a new war in the foreseeable future repelled her: she needed more years of peace. It was not only to foreign ambassadors that she disclaimed any intention of returning to the fight with Prussia. To the Dutch ambassador, Count William Bentinck, for example, she freely admitted her dissatisfaction with the state of Europe and Austria's part in it. Austria had to be strong, if only to stop the rot in the German states. The only way to hold them together was to convince them that Vienna had more to offer to satisfy their vanity and greed than Paris. But, no matter what might be said, she had no intention of going to war. She would seek an alliance with Russia to neutralise Prussia and Turkey; but England was the only country which could afford to subsidise Russian troops. For the rest, she was content to leave matters to the future and her successor.

That this was more than diplomatic subterfuge is suggested by her reply to Kaunitz in the spring of 1751 when he had to report that the prospect of getting anywhere in Paris was entirely dim.

Write to Count Kaunitz [she told her secretary, Koch], that he knows my intentions better than anyone, that I certainly have no preference for France, but that nothing would be more repellent to me than to bind myself to the King of Prussia in the way he suggests at the end of his despatch, and thus for ever renounce all chance of one day recovering possession of Silesia. . . . that I certainly do not flatter myself that Silesia may be won back in my lifetime, that I desire the continuance of peace more urgently than anyone; but, having said all that, I refuse to bar the way to the reconquest of Silesia on the part of my successors, as I should do by adopting this proposal.

It is probably fair to say that Maria Theresa was sincere in her expressed determination not to go to war for Silesia. She had experienced eight years of war and was deeply conscious of the misery it brought to her people. But in 1751 she was only thirty-four. She was in the first full flood of her powers. She had taken hold of her realm and could see her army and her treasury growing beneath her eyes. Even though she may not have admitted it to herself, she must have been filled with the hope that, without an act of aggression on her part, the occasion would arise in her own lifetime to strike a retaliatory blow at Frederick. Certainly Kaunitz acted on this assumption, and she knew her Kaunitz. Early in 1753 she recalled him from Paris. She felt strong enough now to get rid of the Ulfeld–Bartenstein combination and make the ablest of her subjects her first minister, or chancellor.

Kaunitz's first act was to make a clean sweep. He established a completely new office, a bureau of foreign affairs, which he staffed with his own men. Soon, as part of the centralising tendency, the chancellor took over all the business of the Italian and Netherlands possessions. Under the Empress, Kaunitz held all the affairs of the dynasty in his hands. The Prussians lamented. It had been much easier to uncover the secrets of Austrian policy under Bartenstein and Ulfeld. 'But now not only is Count Kaunitz himself incorruptible and much too circumspect to betray himself; his subordinates too are virtually inaccessible.' Austria was entering the modern age. Others were slower to grasp the change of approach. Thus, the English ambassador to Dresden, Sir Charles Hanbury Williams, who saw a great deal of the new chancellor in these days, could report in all good faith, that Kaunitz was now convinced, as he had not been when he undertook his mission to Paris, that the House of Austria could expect neither friendship nor support from Versailles; that the Empress must pursue a sensible policy designed to insure her against French ambition, that, in consequence, necessity demanded that the empress should strengthen ever more firmly the bond of friendship with her old and natural allies.

This was true as far as it went. It did not look into the future. And one of the main reasons why Williams, like many others, was deceived by Vienna's fair words was because during the thirteen years of Maria Theresa's rule diplomats and statesmen everywhere had come to believe in her absolute honesty and integrity shining in a world where these qualities were rare – always with the solitary exception of Frederick of Prussia, who never for one moment imagined that they could ever exist. Maria Theresa, in a word, without herself understanding what was happening (later she was all too bitterly to understand) was corrupted. She was corrupted by Kaunitz.

The other main reason was that Hanbury Williams, like so many others, took it for granted that it was indeed in Vienna's interest to cling to the old alliance with the Maritime Powers and would be clearly aware that even if a temporary accommodation could be reached between Vienna and Versailles no good could conceivably come of it. London, above all, with its gaze fixed increasingly on the broadest of horizons, with its profound consciousness of super-abundant wealth, with the clearest of views that France was the only dangerous enemy and that if France could ruin England she would also be master of the continent of Europe and a deadly threat to the Habsburgs — London above all took it as axiomatic that Austria must sink or swim with England, and that therefore England could play fast and loose with her inevitable ally. Nobody in London under-stood Vienna's fixation on Prussia which, in the context of a quasi-global conflict, formidable as it might be in the field, was a detail in the map of Europe. It was not a detail to Maria Theresa or to Kaunitz, and time was to prove them right in fearing the Prussian challenge above all others — if for the wrong reasons. It was a pro-found failure of imagination on the part of both France and England. It was not, however, necessarily a fatal failure. Kaunitz, working through Maria Theresa, erred fatally.

2

Just as the young Queen had attached herself to the inadequate and unprepossessing Bartenstein because he, and he alone, had been able to give her the answers and induct her into the labyrinth of European politics and diplomacy, so she now attached herself to Kaunitz be-cause he had a plan; a plan, moreover, which recognised her own overruling passion to put Frederick down and recover Silesia. His mind was so brilliant and bold that she was dazzled. The personal repugnance she had felt for Bartenstein must have been equally strong, though for quite different reasons, in her relations with Kaunitz. But, as already suggested, there was in her make-up an element of masochism. Just as she could love her husband as a man without taking him seriously as co-regent, then emperor, so she could value Bartenstein, Kaunitz and others without taking them seriously as men. Perhaps she was even inclined to believe that it was only impossible men who could make good advisers. There were others besides those mentioned, notably Beltram Cristiani, the stammering, loquacious, pock-marked son of a small lawyer, whose clothes were shapeless and covered with snuff, but whom, although she detested snuff, Maria Theresa entrusted with great powers in Italy because of the brilliance of his mind. Added to this was the situation in which the Lord's Anointed must find themselves everywhere, and which was to plague the Austrian monarchy in particular until the end of its course: the gulf between the monarch and his subjects, even the highest nobility, is so absolute that it is virtually impossible for him to discriminate among these subjects, so that the boldest and most assertive and clearcut, other things being equal, come out on top. Kaunitz was nothing if not bold, assertive and clearcut; and these were the qualities, far more than his wisdom, which made him chancellor.

Contrary to the legend, he was not the greatest of chancellors. He lacked the passion, the conviction, above all the broad vision of a Richelieu, a Chatham or a Bismarck. He lacked even the subtlety of a Metternich. He was a tortuously able, immensely vain man with a one-track mind. In a certain sense he was the natural precursor, though on a far grander scale, of Aerenthal, who was to bring the monarchy to the threshhold of disaster in the early years of the twentieth century. Aerenthal, too, was able. He, too, lacked breadth of vision. He brought Austria to the brink because he allowed himself to become fixed on Serbia and the threat to the Empire from Slav nationalism, centred on Belgrade – so that the world was treated to the spectacle of one of the great powers hypnotised into paralysis, blinkered to the great continental and global movements, cutting itself off from the mainstream of history in its agonising indecision about how best to cope with a Balkan nuisance which was allowed to grow into a nightmare. Kaunitz was fixed on Berlin, then still a manageable threat, and how to crush Berlin, how to ruin Prussia, in the shortest possible order. Which country had the largest and most imposing force on the continent of Europe? The answer, obviously, was France. The solution, obviously, was either to neutralise France, or, better still, engage her as an active ally. There was also Russia, the vast unknown, ruled now by Elizabeth who detested Frederick.

Russia, it was well known, could produce from her limitless interior formidable and apparently inexhaustible contingents of useful, infinitely enduring fighting men in return for cash, for subsidies. Austria could provide no subsidies, but France was rich.

England, on the other hand, richer even than France, the paymaster of Europe, drawing on her West Indian sugar and her slave trade, protected by her navy, was at best a reluctant ally, unwilling or unable to commit large armies to the European mainland, unashamedly using Austria as her convenience in her interminable struggle with France and with Spain, disputing, moreover, absolute Austrian sovereignty in the matter of the Netherlands because of her interest under the Barrier Treaty, which gave England the right to fortify a number of Belgian towns for the security of Holland. Reluctant or not, she needed Austria as the counterpoise to France. She might behave in a casual and high-handed way, wounding to Austrian esteem, over the Barrier Treaty; her ambassadors might irritate Maria Theresa herself and her ministers to the point of exasperation with their bland and sometimes patronising offers to mediate between Berlin and Vienna in order to effect a reconciliation – at Austria's expense. But, in the last resort, she stood at Austria's side in all her majesty and wealth.

The great Eugene had been through it all, had accepted humiliation and English evasiveness and slipperiness as a fact of life, had clung to the alliance. It has been claimed that Kaunitz had a wider view than Eugene. This claim is hard to sustain. Eugene would never have allowed himself to have become obsessed by Prussia, even if, impossibly, he had allowed Frederick to beat him had he been in command during the first Silesian War. He would have seen the necessity of recovering Silesia and putting Frederick down. He would have understood Maria Theresa's passionate detestation of the heretical and treacherous upstart. But he would have shrugged off Newcastle's high-pitched hectoring and would have seen to it that it was replied to firmly, sternly even, but without rancour. He would have explained to Maria Theresa the meaning of sea-power. He would have told her that in spite of Marshall Saxe, France, under Louis XV and the Pompadour, was in a bad way. He would have made her see that the Anglo-French conflict was a fight for trade and for overseas empire, and that England, always feeble in peace, in war would put out such strength that France would be wiped from the seas and broken. He would have recommended a serious mending of the Anglo-Austrian alliance, augmented by an understanding with Russia paid for by English gold. A firm triple alliance of this kind would, once England was fully engaged, defeat the combination of France and Prussia and lead to the recovery of Silesia, if not immediately, then a little later, when the German states would rally round the victorious emperor. And to anyone who said that things had gone too far to re-establish the Anglo-Austrian alliance, he would have replied, how much easier to achieve this than to achieve an alliance with France. England would dominate the seas and, with Austria, would hold the balance on the Continent.

Kaunitz had no such vision. He was scarcely aware of the seas. He could see, with all his vaunted 'algebra', no further than the destruction of Prussia. What then? The logical extension of his own line of reasoning must postulate a greatly strengthened France, drawing wealth and sustenance from India and the Americas, at the expense of an enfeebled England. Prussia would be confined. Russia was, always must be, unpredictable. There would be nothing in the world to prevent France intriguing more actively than ever among the German princelings, dominating Europe, allying herself with Spain for the conquest of Italy, encouraging Turkey.

What sort of algebra was this? The equation was never worked out. England and Prussia were victors in the Seven Years War, but only by the skin of their teeth. France was defeated, and with her Austria – luckily for Austria. The final loss of Silesia was a small price to pay for the removal of the threat from Versailles. It happened in spite of Kaunitz. The Franco-Austrian alliance was to endure. After the Seven Years War it served a useful purpose to both countries, but only because France had lost her overseas empire and was irretrievably weakened, thus posing no threat to Austria and finding necessary support from the friendship of her age-old enemy. It was to be cemented by the disastrous marriage of the fifteen-year-old Maria Antonia, the empress's youngest daughter, to the Dauphin, and it was to survive until the Revolution.

The architect of this great design, which indeed saved Austria as a power and ended with the guillotining of a Habsburg bride, was far more of a piece than is often imagined. His contemporaries could not understand how Kaunitz could be so wise and far-seeing as a states-man and so petty and foppish and vain as a man. But in fact as a statesman he was neither wise nor far-seeing: he was a wonderful calculator and manipulator, but he calculated and manipulated in a void; as a man he was much more than a fop, his foppishness being a disguise for an iron determination and a sign of fathomless arrogance. In his later years, when he was manoeuvring between Maria Theresa and her difficult son, then the Emperor Joseph II, he deliberately went out of his way to create a legend about his person, less a disguise than a smokescreen. His hypochondria was exploited to this end: it helped him to establish the image of a man who was a law unto him-self, free of conventional restraints, on no account to be questioned. He carried through the game with Maria Theresa herself, and she, seeing through it (though in the early days she had been seriously concerned about her Chancellor's health), entered into the game. After her menopause, and until the end of her life, the Empress suffered acutely and chronically from hot flushes. It was this that gained her the reputation of being an open-air woman who could not tolerate heated rooms; but for years she had danced and played cards all night without turning a hair. It was only in her later years that all the windows of her apartments had to stand constantly open, even when the snow floated in, sifting over the desk at which she sat working. Such was the position of Kaunitz that he was allowed to close the windows when he had audience of her at Schönbrunn. Later still he was excused from visiting Schönbrunn at all, although he had had a great deal to do with the final embellishments to palace and gardens: the famous Gloriette on its artificial hill was entirely his conception.

To the world at large he showed a face which combined easy and genial social accessibility with intellectual withdrawl. Sir Henry Swinburne was deeply struck by this. After dining at the Kaunitz Palace at Laxenburg he reported as follows:

After dinner the prince treated us with the cleaning of his gums; one of the most nauseous operations I have ever witnessed, and it

lasted a prodigious long time, accompanied with all manner of
noises. He carries a hundred implements in his pocket for this
purpose—such as glasses of all sorts for seeing before and behind
his teeth, a whetting steel for his knife, pinchers to hold the
steel with, knives and scissors without number, and cotton and
lawns for wiping his eyes. His whims are innumerable. Nothing
allusive to the mortality of human nature must ever be rung in
his ears. To mention the smallpox is enough to knock him up for
the day. . . . To derange the train of his ideas puts him sadly out
of sorts. . . . He is full of childish vanities, and wishes to be
thought of to excel in everything. . . . he is dressed very oddly;
his wig comes down upon his nose, with a couple of small
straggling curls on each side, placed in a very ridiculous manner.
He is extremely fond of adulation, will swallow anything in its
shape, and indeed lays it upon himself with a very liberal hand.
One of his peculiarities is his detestation of musk. . . . Prince
Kaunitz has neither bosom friends nor bitter enemies; he is cold
and insensible; has made no man's fortune nor ruined any one.

His wife was a Messalina, and after her death he took to
actresses, whose dupe he was, to his cost. He has no affection for
his children.

Sir William Wraxall made frequent visits to the Kaunitz town
palace: the visitor to Vienna, he explains, is not driven, as he is in
London, to public entertainments, he is received immediately into
the domestic company of the Great.

Here a sort of patriarchal simplicity subsists, in the midst of
those entertainments which wealth and luxury have introduced.
The upper orders seem to constitute only one large family, of
whom Maria Theresa is the common parent. The rallying point
of pleasure and relaxation at Vienna is found in the highest
circles, to which a foreigner is immediately carried. The assemblies of Prince Kaunitz and of Prince Colloredo, are the first into
which every stranger of condition is introduced after his
arrival. . . . As the houses of both, which may be said to form
part of the Imperial palace, are open every evening for the reception of company, they constitute a principal source of
amusement at Vienna. It is, besides, an attention expected from
persons who have lately been presented to those Ministers, that

they should frequently be seen of an evening among the crowd in their drawing-rooms. There is not the smallest degree of constraint imposed by the presence of Prince Kaunitz, who is usually engaged at billiards, in a corner of the apartment; and everyone is at perfect liberty to amuse himself, either at play, or in conversation as his inclinations may lead him.

He did a great deal for the arts. He was in tune with the Enlightenment, and the ideas and attitudes he veiled, or at least subdued, in converse with Maria Theresa he discussed freely with her son. He failed in his great object, the recovery of Silesia, the humiliation of Frederick and the reduction of Prussia. But, nothing daunted, apparently without a backward look or a hint of self-questioning, he steered the realm into the courses which he had believed attainable only were Frederick destroyed. He was, in a word, infinitely supple in his reflexes, and thus made up for the doctrinaire rigidities of his considered actions. His greatest failure was that it never dawned on him that Austria's supreme asset was the integrity of Maria Theresa, which he undermined with consequences nothing short of tragic.

Chapter Fourteen

The Loss of Innocence

What had been happening to Maria Theresa as a person and a ruler between the end of the Succession War in 1748 and the reversal of the alliances in 1756? There had been a period when she could do no wrong. The heroine queen, the beauty in distress, harassed and threatened beyond endurance, sustaining with her own will the faltering courage of all those around her, rewarding the brave and the loyal with words of incomparable warmth and charm, alternating pleading, flattery, teasings and sharp reproaches calculated to charm or to shame feebler vessels and doubters into standing up for her cause, she won the hearts if not the minds of all around her. She has been represented during this period as an innocent acting on impulse and carrying all before her. But enough has been said in preceding chapters to show that this is an altogether too simple view. Her impulses were genuine enough and usually warm-hearted. But she was an accomplished actress too. She knew her role, and she played it to perfection. She very soon discovered her own strength and became aware of the immense superiority of her untrained mind, her common sense, her will. In due course this awareness began to go a little to her head.

It is not necessary to take too seriously the first veiled criticisms of Khevenhüller, confiding to his diary that the 'young woman' was apt to be despotic in her ways. That was in 1743, two years after her accession. She was certainly acting then and knew how to keep the old men on their toes by contrived outbursts – the sort of outbursts she used to discountenance Robinson with his moralistic prosing. But it is clear that towards the end of the Succession War she was getting the bit between her teeth and allowing all her suppressed impatience to show itself in bursts of ill-temper which were to grow into a habit. They never got out of control. They were almost invariably calculated; but they were sometimes miscalculated.

Petty in small things, great in large, was a generally accepted criticism; but this in itself tells us little. It has been true of most outstandingly powerful individuals possessed by a sense of purpose whether engaged in politics, the professions or in the arts. The genius is also human, but he knows instinctively how to preserve from his human pettiness the pursuit of his great design, whether the painting of a picture, the winning of a battle or a war, the organisation of a great business, the wooing of an ally or the execution of a great reform. Some, built on a lesser scale, possessed by neither the capacity nor the desire to bend others to their will, to harness them to their purposes, or even in the privacy of studies and studios to penetrate and make articulate the secrets of the universe — some of these, though by no means all, may bring to small things, to the business of daily intercourse and living, the harmonising solvent of love and abnegation. But to look for such qualities in a man or the occasional woman committed to the concentration and deployment of all his forces on the realising of a dream, whether secular or spiritual, is absurd. Sometimes it happens, and then it is a miracle. The extraordinary thing about Maria Theresa was that even as she coarsened she never forgot her good and splendid impulses entirely; and, in due course, she found herself again — but not before she had done much harm.

When discussing the development of her nature it is necessary to distinguish between failures arising from faults of character and failures arising from ignorance and faults of taste. The latter were to be with her always. She was, as we have seen, ill-educated and she had no conception whatsoever, no comprehension, of spiritual questioning, or divine discontent, of the meaning of either philosophy or art. There was nothing to question. She was brought up, like millions, to believe in God and the Catholic Church, and, like millions, she never questioned this belief. Nothing else mattered. So far as the arts were concerned, these were entertainment and nothing more at all — as for millions of others. One was amused by a painting, a building, an opera, or one was bored. If one was amused it was good; if one was not amused, it was bad.

Her defects of character were less absolute than her defects of sensibility. Some of those defects were really virtues. For example, she has been criticised, and frequently, for her interference in practical matters over which she had no control at all. These examples range from her letters to commanders in the field to her constant demands for information about the provenance of quite small sums of money. They comprehended the whole range of ministerial and social activity in between. They needed to. Apart from Browne and General Khevenhüller in those early days her generals were unimaginative, slack and slow; her husband was not the man to stir them up; her beloved brother-in-law turned out to be as inadequate as Neipperg himself. Hurry, hurry, hurry, she entreated, she commanded — without effect. If she offended against protocol by writing to junior commanders in quasi-independent commands over the heads of their superiors, urging the supreme importance of this and that, she was not engaged in undermining the authority of the commander-in-chief, rather, she was instilling morale by showing colonels in ticklish positions that she was aware of their existence and their problems; she may even have hoped that they would do something.

As for her interventions in detailed matters of administration and finance, again, faced with inertia, muddle, corruption and obstruction all down the line, she was determined to show to all and everyone concerned that they were observed and accountable. She was dealing with men who knew a great deal more about affairs than she herself could know; but they were also the men who had allowed, sometimes positively encouraged, her father to bring her inheritance to the edge of ruin. It is safe to say that her minute overseeing of every financial transaction, of every quartermaster's duties, was not the result of an overweening conviction that she and she alone knew best but rather of a determination to instil the fear of the monarch, if not of God, in every individual who was supposed to be acting on her behalf but who all too frequently was engaged in feathering his own nest or obliging friends, relations and patrons. 'How about the excises on beer and wine?' she would write – and expect a detailed answer. 'A certain Burckhardt, lessee of the Upper Austrian mines, has again offered an advance of cash; I must be informed, and I shall decide whether his lease is to be renewed and his terms accepted.' Again: 'Starhemberg will make immediately available the 675,000 florin contribution from Styria; but he must also be given the Styrian bonds to pay 42,000 florins for horses in Italy.' And again: 'It is illegal to commute tax for deliveries of cloth or wheat – the latter being, anyway, inferior and charged to me at twice the market price.' Again: 'I want to know where those 900,000 florins can be found in Koch's statement, and whether they have been received. Dates!'

Evidently she was leaning on the financial talents of her husband in teaching herself the rudiments of imperial finance. No less evidently she threw off these notes and memoranda in very much the same spirit, and with very much the same drive, as Winston Churchill, two centuries later, was to throw off his innumerable war-time memoranda on every subject under the sun: 'Pray explain . . .' 'For action this day . . .' To the layman one of the recurring wonders is the manner in which his rulers (I speak of our democratic age) manage to insulate themselves from the practical problems of existence. Men who come to office in early middle age, who for half a lifetime have had to wrestle with the consequences of bureaucratic idleness, ineptitude, inertia and evasiveness, suddenly, on achieving power and sitting back in their chauffeur-driven motor-cars, allow themselves to forget everything they have ever known – or lack the energy to remember it. Part of the greatness of Churchill, who had led a more sheltered life than most of his political contemporaries and who was an autocrat into the bargain, was that he kept in touch with life and found the energy to nag the bureaucrats and the place-men and frighten them to death. A large part of the greatness of Maria Theresa, born in a palace, ignorant when she came to the throne of almost everything in the world, from accounting to soldiers' boots and knapsacks, was the way in which she understood how those whose job it was to attend to such things were betraying their professions and, even if she did not understand, knew how to give the impression that she understood, and made people work for their lives: 'No supply officer, supervisor, baker, or whatever name such men have, will be sent to Italy, the Netherlands, or anywhere in the Empire. . . . They are to be dismissed; I cannot afford them.' Bang went a dozen sinecures, bang went a score of rackets . . . And so it went on.

How tedious, how irksome, how frustrating she must have found the necessity to nag, to teach herself enough detail to confound the men who were paid to look after detail, is shown most vividly by what happened when at last she found men she decided, rightly or wrongly, she could trust. With Haugwitz in charge of the economy, van Swieten in charge of, broadly, education, Kaunitz in charge of imperial affairs, Daun in charge of the Army, she stopped nagging and, while always insisting on being informed, sank back with relief. She was not a busybody. She was a woman of immense vitality and profound common sense – with a woman's practical eye into the bargain – who was faced with an estate in ruins. Working for its restoration she was at first compelled to operate through the very men who had ruined it. She had no choice. But, quite reasonably, she trusted none of them out of her sight.

It must have seemed to her in those first half dozen years that she was the only individual in her great realm capable of taking a quick and firm decision – and acting on it. No wonder she grew impatient with the men she had to work through. . . . And though she might sometimes raise her voice in anger, so that her scolding could be heard through the doors into the anteroom, the remarkable thing about her was her forbearance and the restraints she placed upon herself, her tongue and her actions when she decided it was politic to do so – or, more admirably by far, when she was convinced that an individual who had served her well, only to fail later, had been doing his best when he failed. Thus, on the one hand, hotly bent on punishing those nobles and officials of Lower Austria and Bohemia who had deserted her and recognised the sovereignty of the Bavarian pretender, she listened, angrily no doubt at first, to the counsel of older men who suggested that mercifulness would make a better foundation for her reign than vengeance and pointed out that to come down heavily on the Bohemian nobility would arouse unhappy memories of the wholesale banishments and expropriations inflicted on his Protestant subjects by Ferdinand II after the Battle of the White

Mountain in the Thirty Years War. Indeed, in her desire to conciliate and to use the men who could serve her best, the queen at times succeeded in alienating those who had been loyal in the moment of crisis, but whose brains and abilities did not measure up to her demands.

Most of our insights into Maria Theresa's behaviour in the late 1740s and early 1750s comes from the Prussian ambassador to the court at Vienna, who was the son of Frederick's foreign minister, Podewils. The young Podewils was by no means a denigrator of his master's most devoted enemy. He was struck both by her beauty and her talents, and said so quite openly. At the same time, it was his duty and his pleasure to report on the weaknesses of this very remarkable woman. He scraped together all the gossip that came to his ears, and he was clearly incapable of separating gossip from intelligence or in distinguishing malice from goodwill in his informants. It is a pity (for he had a lively and observant eye) that he simply must not be believed except when his information can be checked from other sources. Even Khevenhüller will not serve us here, because, as already observed, this sterling creature was temperamentally incapable of telling when his royal mistress was play-acting or when she was deadly earnest: he was the most literal-minded witness in the world. The probability remains that she did, in confidence turn on her chancellor, Ulfeld, and tell him he was 'a jackass, and likely to remain one', a remark the effect of which would not have been softened by its manifest truth (later, as already mentioned, she bought Ulfeld out of office, in favour of Kaunitz, by the simple expedient, as has been said, of paying his appalling debts.) And that her increasing acerbity and high-handedness became disturbing to her well-wishers, besides playing into the hands of her ill-wishers, is shown by a painful and laborious attempt by Tarouca to persuade her to show more frequently her better side.

I cannot deny that certain complaints have reached me, some resentment of Your Majesty's lack of confidence in men who have served you for a certain time. It may stem from wariness on your part, or from an inability to compromise with their shortcomings. They may still do justice to the essential goodness of

Your Majesty's character. But your treatment of them affects the feelings of their families their friends, their servants. Must one call an over-cautious or over-suspicious and sensitive minister 'just a fool'?

He went on to give her a lesson in the need for reciprocity in trust and respect. 'Every human being has some imperfections, some weakness, some streak of pettiness. If he does not tolerate these in others, how can he flatter himself that others will make allowances for him? Love and trust will cool.'

We do not know how Maria Theresa took this homily. We do not even know whether Tarouca himself had felt the lash of her tongue and, with dignity, was reminding his mistress that she had engaged him to tell her the truth about herself. On the face of it he was reproaching her for her too impatient dismissal of the pretensions of advisers well known to be inadequate. There may have been undertones, audible only to her, referring to her treatment not only of Tarouca but, quite possibly, of her husband. The only thing we know in this connection is that Tarouca was able to write as he did and to retain the respect and affection of his most royal pupil.

In a different connection we also know that quite early in her married life Maria Theresa was shocked into awareness of her beloved husband's inconstancy. For quite a long time, for ten or fifteen years indeed, Francis refrained from serious affairs, if refrain is the word for a man easily susceptible, who liked to be amused, but was not made for passion. He had an eye, as they say, for the girls, and the girls were eager to catch that eye. Moderately sensual in his own tastes, he enjoyed relaxing in the company of rakes and debauchees, provided they could laugh and tell a good story and were ready to play cards for high stakes. Maria Theresa liked playing cards herself, dancing too, as we have seen. Good, healthy, cheerful excitement and exercise she would have called them, not at all the things to mix with sex. Francis was hers and she turned a fiercely jealous eye on all company which might make him forgetful of this fact, more indirectly on all influences that might conduce to a lowering of moral tone in the company that Francis kept. Such influences included the new peripatetic companies of dancers and opera singers, mainly from

Italy, which had replaced the Court singers and dancers of her father's day. Unlike all other women faced with this sort of complication, Maria Theresa was in a position to do something about it—or thought she was in such a position. She had only, she thought, to command, and illicit sex would be abolished. Command she did. In the autumn of 1747, the year in which all her energies broke out in the cause of a root and branch reform of the economy, Haugwitz's reforms, she was clearly in a mood to make herself felt, after so many years of frustration at the hands of the generals and the diplomats. She established a ludicrous organisation known familiarly as the Chastity Commission, whose duty it was to strengthen the moral tone of her realm in general and in particular to combat the sort of loose attitudes which might encourage her Francis to stray.

The Chastity Commission, as such, did not last long. It was quietly abolished, according to Khevenhüller, six months later having been received first with incredulity, then with outrage, then with ridicule by the populace at large. It also made Maria Theresa absurd in the eyes of Europe for a time. The commissioners were empowered to search houses on suspicion, to arrest any man found entertaining an opera singer, a dancer or any other woman of presumed loose morals. Similarly, offending ladies could be locked up in a convent or banished from the realm. At least two companies of players were formally expelled for alleged scandalous behaviour, and one of the most celebrated sopranos of the day, Santini, was arrested in Vienna and taken all the way to the Venetian border by agents of the commission.

Even though the Chastity Commission as such was quickly done away with, the puritan streak in Maria Theresa, evident at the very beginning of her reign when she took exception to one of the Harrachs' affairs with 'lowly women', persisted until the end of her life. Twenty years after the episode of the Commission, some of the original commissioners found themselves forming the nucleus of the celebrated corps of police informers whose special task was to keep an eye on the intramural activities of ladies of high birth who might suddenly find themselves translated from Vienna to Trieste – or Olmütz – as a consequence of a clandestine affair which turned out not to be discreet at all.

Perhaps one should say the jealous, rather than the puritan streak. Or, rather, the puritanism was latent. So long as Francis lived Maria Theresa was in no sense averse to the pleasures of the flesh, and it was only after his death in 1766 that she entered deliberately on a course of self-mortification. Even then she smiled on the pleasures of others, so long as they were conducted in accordance with the book. She was the mother of her people. As a born headmistress she was indulgent and kind, but she was headmistress all the same. And this meant, among other things, that, not to put too fine a point on it, she was the only person in the school who knew just how to behave and could be relied upon to do so. The boys and girls were hopeless and had to be kept in order for their own good; her subordinates were not to be relied on. Thus it was that in her later years her educational reforms, which gave the Empire what was incomparably the finest and most comprehensive system of elementary education in prerevolutionary Europe, were inspired less by respect for learning than by concern for public morals. And the ageing woman, who at times seemed to be obsessed by the temptations offered to provincial youth by public dances, could at the same time embark on that strange correspondence with Marie Antoinette about ways and means of coping with the impotence of the Dauphin, her husband.

The coarsening process of maturity is nowhere more clearly seen than in her early relationship with Kaunitz, who taught her how to lie. Tarouca had done his best to instruct her in the art of dissimula-tion. Is it really necessary and desirable, he asked in effect, for Your Majesty to express all her feelings quite so openly? 'Unlike simula-tion . . . dissimulation is not a vice. Rather, if guided properly by prudence and patience, it is a virtue.' She came to learn in time and, in later years, deliberately exploited her reputation for extreme and impulsive openness as distinct from being carried away by impulse. Kaunitz went further, in recommending to her the necessity for a *bissel Falschheit* – a little mendacity. Soon she was learning. She allowed Kaunitz to give Frederick the ostentatiously evasive reply about Austria's offensive intentions which drove him, as she hoped it would drive him, to attack in 1756. And she lied quite positively to the new British ambassador, Keith, in May 1756 when he sought audience with her to deplore the new alliance with France. 'It was not

I who abandoned the old system, but Great Britain who abandoned me and the system by concluding an alliance with Prussia. . . . How can you be surprised when I follow the example set by England in concluding her treaty with Prussia and myself arrive at an understanding with France?'

This air of injured innocence was something quite new in Maria Theresa. She was at her worst, arrogant, overbearing and disingenuous throughout the process which culminated in the Seven Years War. It was Kaunitz who inflamed her pride, played on her old resentments, excited her with the prospect of diplomatic masterstrokes, touched her with the dream of winning back Silesia, crushing Prussia, and at the same time teaching England a lesson. But she was a willing pupil. She would have done much better to stick to her original resolution and concentrate on developing and consolidating the prosperity of her realm, leaving it to her successors, operating from strength, to find ways to redress the wrong that had been done to her by Frederick. But for a time she had become like any other monarch, and to salve her conscience she used her chancellor as an alibi. She was to have plenty of time to repent, and repent she did. Five years before her death she wrote to her old friend, the Countess Enzenburg: 'I pass the years, the months, the weeks, the days in the same simplicity, the same grief as the first day [after her husband's death], and often I find comfort in the knowledge that those days that are gone can never return, and that each moment brings me closer to the end, but not without trembling at the terrible account I shall have to render.' She was thinking not only of the always deeply felt disgrace of the Partition of Poland, into which she had been bullied by Kaunitz and her son – and of which more later. For on another occasion she made a great accounting of her sins of ommission and commission, and first among these, which included anger, envy and inertia, she placed 'having made war out of pride'.

It was during the course of this war, the Seven Years War, that she began to rediscover her true nature.

Chapter Fifteen

The Seven Years War

The chance to animate the great design, the reversal of alliances, presented itself to Kaunitz unexpectedly and accidentally. The action which threw Louis XV into the arms of Maria Theresa, who held him in extreme distate, was, in the eyes of the Duke of Newcastle, who committed it, a harmless manoeuvre in this familiar game, the only game he knew, of insuring against France. This Pelham was far from being an inspired statesman. He could not see far beyond his nose, and he oscillated between panic fears and hectoring. But he had held office of one kind and another since joining Walpole's cabinet in 1724, and in 1756 he had been prime minister for twelve years. Like most British prime ministers and foreign secretaries he possessed a minimal knowledge of Europe, but he knew that money talked and that Britain had plenty. For a long time he had been pressing subsidies on every German principality and electorate that would accept them, making Frederick wonder whether, perhaps, London and Vienna were preparing the ground for an attack on Prussia: he may also have rather covetously contemplated all that money. At the same time, through his envoy Sir Charles Hanbury Williams, now translated from Dresden to St Petersburg, he had been bribing the Russian Bestuzhev in an effort to effect the renewal of the 1742 subsidy treaty with Russia.

The policy of bribery, of subsidies (nowadays called economic aid), of laying out cash in return for soldiers or professions of neutrality, was so well tried and, on the whole, so successful — so sensible, indeed — that it is astonishing to find a distinguished twentieth-century American historian raising his eyebrows at Newcastle's policy: 'He actually believed that if England paid a high enough price everything and everybody could be bought, including the Tsaritsa of Russia. He regarded the subsidy treaty as a legitimate commercial operation, and agreed with his colleague, Holdernesse, who said, "As we pay the piper, it is not unreasonable for us to have the tune we like."' Professor Dorn's book was first published in 1940. He would have to write differently today. Eighteenth-century England, indeed, France too, had far more excuse for behaving in this way that mid-twentieth-century America. In the eighteenth century there was no popular nationalism to complicate the cool financial calculations of the monarchs. Even then, however, eyebrows were raised and gentle protests registered at the way the subsidies were sometimes spent. Maria Theresa herself was reproached for using British money, intended for her army, to build Schönbrunn (a charge she hotly denied: it came from the Jews).

Newcastle lived in easier times. And, of course, his propositions seemed perfectly reasonable to his European contemporaries. For example, Kaunitz knew very well that Russia had to be bought. But somebody else must be paymaster: Austria had no money to spare. At first Kaunitz was happy to let England pay; but his great design depended on the ultimate willingness of France to take over the burden, and this is what France did.

The international situation in 1755 was of especial complexity and interest. Two separate revolutions, one continental, one quasiglobal, were converging. The explosion, when it came in 1756, was the Seven Years War. Just as the War of the Austrian Succession had been the last dynastic war, so the Seven Years War was the first imperial war in the modern style. The unsettling elements injected into the European system arose from the establishment of a new great power in the form of Frederick's Prussia and the break-out of Russia, transformed from a portent into a European force. At the same time, England and France were fighting for trade and empire overseas. The only man who saw the imperial struggle for what it was, William Pitt, was so obsessed by his vision that at first he made the almost fatal mistake of thinking that he could turn his back on

Europe entirely. On the Continent not one of the main actors, including Kaunitz, who saw himself as the mainspring of the whole vast operation, had a clear idea of the nature of the forces at work. Like Maria Theresa, Kaunitz saw Prussia in terms of a local challenge, a challenge to Austria and to the Empire. Russia, he thought, as several of his successors were to think after him, he could fix whenever it was convenient. In fact he fixed her this time only because of errors of tact on the part of London and Berlin.

As late as 1754 all the rulers wanted peace. Kaunitz alone was preparing for a war to recover Silesia, but this was still a distant goal. England was playing fast and loose with her raids on French Atlantic shipping, and suddenly, in 1755, the two countries were formally at war. Formal conflict had not been desired either in London or in Paris, and at first neither side had any intention of convening, as it were, a continental war. Both were fighting for colonial trade, a matter in which the central European powers had little direct interest. Each, nevertheless, had its own system of agreements with other continental powers, France above all with Prussia, Britain with Austria. France also had arrangements with Denmark, Sweden and Turkey; Britain was allied with Holland. Russia at this moment was still floating, having broken her connection with France and Prussia. In spite of the Tsaritsa's dislike and distrust of the English, Britain and Russia were drawn together by considerations of trade. In spite of her contempt for Maria Theresa, the contempt of a cynic and a rake for virtue mistaken for hypocrisy and cant, Russia was also being drawn to Austria as the natural ally against Turkey. And, anyway, Elizabeth's likes and dislikes could hardly count when it came to the sticking point. She had even less love for Frederick and Louis XV than for George II and Maria Theresa.

Britain's immediate concern, as she saw it, was to secure Hanover and the Austrian Netherlands (Belgium) against France and Prussia. Newcastle still believed that Austria, when it came to it, must join him in this task; there was, as he saw it, no other path open to her. In spite of the constant bickering over the Barrier Treaty and the status of Austria in the Netherlands, it had never occurred to him that Maria Theresa, guided by Kaunitz, had written off the Netherlands as indefensible and saw continued Austrian occupation as benefiting nobody but England. As for Hanover, Maria Theresa said she would by all means detail troops for its protection, but only if Britain would agree to join her, together with Russia, in an offensive treaty aimed at the destruction of Prussia. Other considerations apart, this was an open invitation to a continental war, the very thing which Newcastle was determined to avoid. Still with the limited objective of securing Hanover, he decided quickly on his next step. If Austria would not help him, then he must do a deal with Prussia. Frederick, who had reason to fear a coalition between Britain, Austria and Russia, leapt at the chance. Newcastle had already expressed his dilemma: 'We can do nothing without the Dutch, the Dutch can do nothing without the Austrians, nor the Austrians without the Russians.' With this in mind he had at last, in September 1755, secured the renewal of the subsidy treaty with the Russians, who were also bound to Austria by the defensive treaty of 1746. If England was desperate because of the Austrian cold-shoulder, so now was Frederick. By the Convention of Westminster of January 1756 Britain and Prussia agreed to oppose the passage through Germany of any foreign, that is to say French and Russian, troops.

France was outraged by the defection of Frederick, who, in any case, was heartily disliked by Louis XV. Russia was dumbfounded by an agreement partly directed against her and barring her entry into Germany only four months after the conclusion of the subsidy treaty designed to effect precisely this. Britain congratulated herself on ensuring the safety of Hanover. Frederick had lately been assured by France that she had no intention of invading Hanover, so he was offering his guarantee against a non-existent threat. At the same time, convinced that Russia would never fight without subsidies and knowing that Austria could never supply them, he saw the Austro-Russian menace recede into the distance. He had been very clever indeed. But he had reckoned, as Newcastle had also reckoned, without Kaunitz. He had reckoned too without the surpassing ineptitude of Louis XV.

Frederick's mistake was not to take the French king into his confidence. Louis, indeed, had no intention of attacking Hanover; it is on the cards, though nothing can be certain, that had Frederick told him how he was treating with the English, and why, he would have agreed to the neutralisation of Germany. Be that as it may, Frederick's secret volte-face in his policy towards England, coming after a long series of betrayals, made Louis very angry indeed, so that at last he was in a mood to allow the anti-Prussian faction at Versailles, very much a minority, to have its head. Similarly, if Newcastle had warned the Tsaritsa of his dealings with Frederick, and the reason for them, he might well have kept Russia in play, instead of providing Kaunitz with the chance to stir up trouble. It was one thing for Russia to be bought, another to have it demonstrated to all the world that in return for subsidies the Tsaritsa would do anything that England told her to do: Elizabeth might be a ruin of debauchery, but she was still a woman of extreme pride and spirit. She had agreed to the subsidy treaty only because Bestuzhev had been able to persuade her that Britain would call on Russian troops for employment solely against Prussia. Bestuzhev, one of the supreme rogues in Russian history, managed to keep his own position (and his British pension) because Elizabeth could find nobody to replace him. But in spite of his intrigues with the young Catherine, whose husband was a fanatical admirer of Frederick and who was persuaded by Bestuzhev that Austria was working against her succession, Elizabeth could not be restrained. Broken as she was, in her forty-eighth year, she had convinced herself that the new Prussia was a direct threat to her empire, and Kaunitz had all his work cut out to curb her in a scheme to start an offensive war against Prussia, in alliance with Sweden, Saxony and Austria, in the summer of 1756. She coveted East Prussia.

Kaunitz was not ready. The Convention of Westminster, he saw immediately, was the chance he had been waiting for to reverse the alliances and get France on his side. But this would take a moment. And, in any case, Austria herself could not be ready until the spring of 1757. The first thing to do, while holding the Tsaritsa in leash, was to exploit the indignation and resentment against Frederick at Versailles. This was where Madame de Pompadour came in.

Historians have argued ever since as to the precise role played by the Pompadour in the negotiations that followed, whether she actively persuaded Louis to treat with the Austrians first, later to submit to their terms. All that matters here is that Louis was persuaded. He had always detested Frederick and now he felt betrayed by him. He had for long had a sentimental hankering for a rapprochement with Maria Theresa, as between one Catholic dynast and another, but had been blocked by his pro-Prussian ministers. The Pompadour had conceived a liking for Kaunitz, who had gone out of his way to flatter her, encouraging the illusion that she was a woman of state. All this smoothed the path for Starhemberg's initial approach. Success was assured when Louis decided to entrust the negotiations to the ambitious and basically irresponsible Abbé Bernis, who, bypassing the proper channels, went with the Pompadour to meet Starhemberg in conspiratorial secrecy at a château outside Paris. Starhemberg, the Austrian ambassador to Versailles, had a master diplomatist behind him and the personality to play the part exactly written for him by Kaunitz. Frenchmen who blame the Pompadour for what followed, the ruin of the French Empire, fail to put first things first: the responsibility for the Marquise de Pompadour, née Mlle Poisson, lay wholly with the King.

At first the French were wary, as well they might have been, and Kaunitz himself was moderate and cautious. 'A great Power,' he wrote to Starhemberg, 'has to be convinced that the whole political system which it has hitherto pursued has been directly opposed to its true interests.' The first Treaty of Versailles, negotiated by Bernis with the Pompadour at his side, provided for nothing more than a declaration of neutrality in the Anglo-French conflict on the part of Vienna and a pledge by France to leave the Netherlands alone should Austria march into Hanover. There was a mutual guarantee of each country's European frontiers and possessions. More important, each would come to the aid of the other with 24,000 men if attacked by any continental power. From the point of view of France it was absurd. France could have had Austria's neutrality in the war with England for nothing: Kaunitz had offered it as a sign of goodwill nearly a year before. She could have bargained for the Austrian Netherlands. She could have insisted on Vienna breaking its ties with England. She did none of these things. There was no offensive alliance it is true, but who in Vienna expected one at this stage? The thing was that a great historical movement had been set in train, and at no cost to Austria, under the eyes of an astonished Europe. The two hereditary foes had made it up. Kaunitz, of course, wanted more, and he knew that he would get it if he played his cards well and restrained the Tsaritsa from precipitating offensive action. He was working for a treaty with Russia, and in January 1757 he got it, the Convention of St Petersburg, which committed Elizabeth to armed support of Austria for the reconquest of Silesia: she herself proposed to seize East Prussia, a prospect acceptable to Kaunitz but which filled Maria Theresa with profound and well justified foreboding.

By then the initial move had been taken. The man who moved was Frederick, who saw himself encircled by an unthinkable combination of France, Austria, Russia and Sweden. In those days the word encirclement had not been used in this context, but Frederick was far more entitled to use it than any of his successors, who were to make so much play with it in the next two hundred years. As far as one can be certain of any of Frederick's motives, he acted now out of fright. From his extremely competent service of spies and informers he knew what Kaunitz was up to and he decided to put a spoke in his wheel.

On August 29th, 1756, secretly, without a declaration of war, he marched into Saxony. He needed Saxony as a bastion for Silesia and as a jumping off ground for the invasion of Bohemia. But there is nothing to suggest that he was deliberately seeking to start a European war which would involve him in head-on conflict with Austria and Russia (he still did not believe that France would ever fight for Austria). Rather, he saw it as a preventive action. He moved only after he had received two evasive and highly equivocal replies from Kaunitz to his blunt question whether Austria proposed to attack him either in 1756 or 1757 – replies which drove at least one of Maria Theresa's ministers to protest. Frederick, he said, must be firmly reassured. Francis thought so too. Even before Frederick moved he assured Maria Theresa that he would withdraw his troops as soon as she gave him her word that Austria would not attack. The word was not forthcoming.

In fact, Frederick, well informed as he was, was still unaware of the extent and imminence of the danger to Prussia. He knew that Russia was only waiting to fall on him. He also knew that she could not do so without money. Austria had no money: it was England that held the purse. He failed entirely to foresee that France would provide the money. And so he moved, setting in motion the Seven Years War, which was to change the face of Europe and leave behind it the complex of forces and interests which were to form the armature of what we call the modern world and to govern all political and diplomatic activity until, in 1945, that world was repolarised into East and West.

2

For Austria the Seven Years War began and ended as the third war for Silesia. From start to finish both Maria Theresa and Kaunitz had one object and no other: the recovery of the lost province, with the consequent reduction of Prussia and humiliation of Frederick. Everything that happened in the course of that ruinous and far-ranging conflict was seen from Vienna in the simplest terms: would it help or hinder the great Object? The grim struggle for maritime supremacy, for trade and overseas empire, between France and England meant nothing to Vienna – except in so far as for some time it diverted from the European mainland British troops which might have given direct aid to Frederick, and then weakened the French will to fight on as a consequence of the resounding exploits of Clive at Plassey in 1757, Wolfe at Quebec and Hawke at Quiberon Bay in 1759, Eyre Coote at Wandiwash in 1760.

It was the same with the process which brought about the first major penetration of Russia into the West, the crushing defeat of Frederick at Kunersdorf in 1759. This process was to transform Catherine's Russia into an effective European power, no longer to be thought of simply as a useful reservoir of unlimited manpower to be paid for and exploited by her allies of the moment. Henceforth Russia was to be an active contestant in the power game, a development which, a century and a half later, was to accelerate the destruction of Austria herself.

It is interesting that Maria Theresa, eager as she was to dish Frederick, was herself apprehensive at the prospect of an accretion of power to Russia. Her deep, unschooled political instinct was operating here, not merely her sharply voiced distaste for the Tsaritsa's morals. But on the eve of the Seven Years War she was still in thrall to Kaunitz, and in his presence that streak of diffidence in her otherwise overwhelming nature was at its strongest. She was also, quite simply, pleased to shed the main burden of decision-making, which she had been called on to bear too soon.

Kaunitz for his part was exhibiting that special sort of blindness, or short-sightedness, which was to distinguish Austrian diplomacy for the Empire's remaining term, to culminate in the events of the summer of 1914. It was a blindness to the larger movements of history, aggravated by a tendency to concentrate exclusively on the immediate short-term goal, or even the irritation of the moment. Frederick and Silesia in the mid-eighteenth century; Cavour and Lombardy in the mid-nineteenth century; Serbia in the early twentieth century. The very brilliance and success with which Kaunitz set about organising Europe for the recovery of Silesia tended with its dazzle to obscure the existence of vast imponderables in the surrounding shadows. He was, in a word, too clever by half. His perception, so marvellously clear and acute, was also so narrow, that when the imponderables materialised he had no alternative plan, no room indeed for manoeuvre, no way left open to him to exploit a changed situation. France, the great new ally, virtually threw up the sponge in 1761. It still seemed that nothing could save Frederick. But a few months earlier George III had come to the English throne, with him the peace party led by Bute. Pitt fell. And in 1762 Elizabeth of Russia died, to be succeeded briefly, until he was murdered, by Catherine's mentally retarded husband, Peter III, who idolised Frederick, and, as his sole act of kingship, took Russia out of the war. Maria Theresa, stubborn as ever, was left alone to go on fighting on her own against a Prussia miraculously restored. In February 1763 she at last had to see that there was no more help from anyone and that Austria could fight no longer. The Peace of Hubertusberg marked the end of the struggle begun twenty-two years earlier. Silesia was signed away for ever. Prussia was established as a power.

3

In the earlier stages of the Seven Years War, after a disappointing start, there had been every justification for Maria Theresa's profound conviction that Austria would win. Once more it was Maximilian von Browne who first took the field against Frederick, a field marshal now, and almost at once to be awarded the supreme patent of nobility, the Order of the Golden Fleece; then to die. He was not in the least impressed by Frederick's reputation, which he considered grossly inflated. The fact that, under Neipperg, he himself had suffered defeat by the Prussians at Mollwitz in 1741 seemed to him neither here nor there. That battle had been lost because of the inferior generalship of Neipperg and the staunchness of the new Prussian infantry: Frederick had run away. Now at Lobositz in Saxony in 1756 he was to fight a much greater battle which augured well for the future. It was an indecisive battle, because Browne was fighting what was intended as a holding action to stave off the imminent invasion of Silesia. But before it was over Frederick had run away again. He was so shaken indeed, that he looked round for a mediator to negotiate peace, while at the same time shouting loudly that he had won a great victory. Since at the end of it all Browne had not advanced (it had never been his intention), and since there arose a great scandal about the disgraceful conduct of part of the Austrian cavalry, Maria Theresa never fully understood that Browne had done brilliantly well and might be trusted to follow up against a very much chastened Frederick with a more decisive blow.

It was not to be. Court politics now took a hand, and Maria Theresa's brother-in-law, Prince Charles of Lorraine, was once more appointed commander-in-chief. This was in deference to Francis; partly, no doubt, also to soothe the feelings of aristocratic generals who did not like serving under a parvenu Irishman. More particularly, Maria Theresa all her life had held a great warmth of feeling for Prince Charles. With his pock-marked face, his virile, jolly nature, his frequent drunkenness, she seems to have valued him as a reassuring and cheerful link with a coarser, less complex, more full-blooded world than the one she herself inhabited. Perhaps he reminded her of her own rather dizzy youth and stood for the fun she could have had if things had been different. It was to prove an unfortunate predilection.

Charles was not wholly unequipped for command. It might have been better if he had been. By eighteenth-century standards he was a competent soldier in the pre-Frederick, pre-Browne manner. He had not shone in the War of the Succession, though he had done a great deal better than his brother, Francis. But he was slow, hesitant, unimaginative, and no match for Frederick at all. During the long winter recess Frederick, as always, had recovered his nerve. It was this resilience which was his supreme quality. He was not, as is widely believed, a man of steadfast and unquestioning courage, imperturbable. Faced with a sudden crisis or the unforeseen disruption of a careful plan he was apt to fall into despair and run. But always he bounced back to fight again, a characteristic by no means rare in great generals, though in Frederick carried to spectacular extremes. Now, in May 1767, he had quite recovered from the panic induced by Lobositz, and tough, sun-dried, hard-bitten, stripped of all superfluous impedimenta, he was ready, as always, to step out of his tent and give battle with the minimum of fuss and headquarters apparatus. He knew everything that was going on in the Austrian camp, and his spirits must have lifted when he heard that the enterprising, highly professional, resolute and generally unpredictable Maximilian von Browne was to be subordinated to Charles of Lorraine, now posting up in the general direction of Prague in the wake of a personal baggage train of immense and luxurious proportions, which would not have been despised by Louis XV himself.

It was Browne's turn for things to go wrong. He was ill, and Charles arrived to find him in a highly nervous state. But he had a good plan to defeat the Prussians as they moved in to take Prague, and when the day came all his hesitations were forgotten. He fought brilliantly and heroically, without repining when he saw the ruination of his plans by Charles's clumsy and reluctant movements. The Prussians conquered. Browne himself lost a leg and had to be carried to safety when what was left of his army fled and shut itself up inside the city walls.

The Battle of Prague was a bitter day for Maria Theresa: it seemed to be Mollwitz all over again. But this time she had a card up her sleeve. Marshal Daun, who had been in charge of her earlier army reforms, now President of the War Council in Vienna, emerged from his headquarters at the head of a powerful relieving army, while the Queen bombarded her brother-in-law with instructions to hold on at all costs. Daun, also, was an eighteenth-century general. He had no intention of rushing Frederick while the Prussians gathered themselves for the kill at Prague. He spent some days looking round for the perfect position, his main object being so to dispose his forces that Frederick would have to give up and fall back, allowing Prince Charles's garrison, 25,000 strong, to move out of the city and join up with his own army of 54,000. And, indeed, this should have happened. Instead, with one of his strokes of reckless courage, Frederick broke all the rules and decided to attack. Still Daun was careful. It simply had not occurred to him that the attackers were inferior in numbers, and it was not until midday that it dawned on him that the waves of Prussian infantry that had broken themselves against his cannon and his grenadiers were finally spent. He had been steadily holding on and hoping for the best. The best, when it came, was a miracle. The rest was slaughter.

That was the Battle of Kolin, of June 18th, 1767. Once more Frederick galloped from the field without waiting to see the end. But this time the end was total defeat. Frederick had lost a third of his army and nearly fifty guns. Prague was relieved. Prince Charles was once more in command. 'Phaeton has finally crashed to the ground,' wrote Frederick's jealous brother, Prince Henry, with characteristic malice. 'We do not know what will become of us. The eighteenth of June will for ever be a baleful day for Brandenburg. Phaeton took care of his own person, getting away before the loss of the battle was sure.'

All that remained now was to deliver the *coup de grâce*. The French were at last on the move. Russia and Sweden had burst into East Prussia and Pomerania. Frederick himself was on the edge of suicide. But Prince Charles made no decisive move. He made no serious attempt to follow up and destroy the Prussian forces, contenting himself with securing Bohemia. Frederick was to be given time to survive a further blow: the defeat of the Duke of Cumberland, who had to give up Hanover. Worse still for him, most of the German princes now jumped on the band-wagon, belatedly remembering the obligations to the imperial crown. Over thirty of them sent contingents to be combined with a French army under Soubise, which marched to the relief of Saxony. Even though at this moment, the late autumn of 1767, the Russians pulled out of East Prussia on the strength of a false report of the death of the Tsaritsa Elisabeth, there seemed no escape for Frederick. But he still had his genius, and now his will came suddenly flooding back. With the Austrians moving into Silesia, he turned sharply west and, at Rossbach, cut Soubise to pieces by sheer brilliance of attack; then, not resting, he turned his army round to race back to Silesia and shatter the Austrians at Leuthen in an exceptionally bloody battle.

Rossbach and Leuthen made him Frederick the Great. He was the wonder of the world. But he looked like being a shortlived wonder. At the end of 1767 Prince Charles was at last removed from the command. Daun, the victor of Kolin, was now in charge, and he had with him two generals of remarkable ability, Laudon and Lacy, both, like Browne before them, soldiers of fortune. Laudon's ancestry went back to Scotland, but his family had been settled for centuries in Lithuania. He himself had started in the Russian army, tired of it and offered himself to Frederick, who had misjudged him, as Louis XIV had earlier misjudged Eugene. He had moved on to Vienna, and now in the service of Maria Theresa he was to distinguish himself extremely. His approach was more radical and imaginative than Daun's. In conference he was gruff and inarticulate; but when it came to fighting all the energies of a very remarkable character were concentrated into a rapid, cool, farseeing eye and a swift decisiveness, concealed behind the countenance of an amiable horse. Lacy, like Browne, was of Irish extraction, easygoing, cheeful and fond of good living, but very quick in his thinking, also bold, and with, perhaps a little surprisingly, a talent for organisation in general and A and Q work in particular which was rare in that age. The combination of Daun, Laudon and Lacy was formidable indeed. It first hit Frederick and overwhelmed him in a boldly improvised battle at Hochkirch in the spring of 1768. Maria Theresa was triumphant. The Prussian monster had been smitten at Kolin, had recovered and struck back at Rossbach and Leuthen, had been smitten to the ground again. And now the Russians, ponderously moving, were bringing their weight to bear. For one intoxicated moment the Empress threatened to revive in all its force the ancient authority of the imperial crown, and put under the ban of Empire, outlawing in a word, not only Prussia but also the few German princes who still supported Frederick (Hanover, Hesse, Cassel and Brunswick) unless they changed sides. Events were moving very fast. At Kunersdorf came a powerful Russian victory in which Loudon played a leading part, and it was after Kunersdorf that the Hungarian general Hadik made his spectacular raid on Berlin. But now things started going wrong. The Russians refused to follow up their victory. The Russian commander Soltsiev declared that he had done enough. He had won two battles with great loss of life. 'I now,' he said to Austria 'expect two victories from you.' He was on no account prepared to allow Austria to fight to the last Russian. Ignoring Daun's achievements and the new spirit that had inspired the Austrian forces since the recall of Prince Charles, he demanded, in effect, a second front. Had the united pressure of Austria and Russia been resolutely applied in the autumn of 1758 there would have been no hope for Frederick. Even as things were the campaigning season of 1759 opened with Maria Theresa full of confidence and Frederick in despair.

But for three more years the war went on. Daun calculated and manoeuvred with the greatest skill and coolness: his always careful, sometimes inspired generalship in face of any other foe but Frederick would have more than compensated for his lack of fire. But Frederick was an electric eel. He lost not regiments but armies. He formed new ones. He was saved again and again, now by the French defeat at Minden, now by his own great feats as at Liegnitz and Torgau. At the one Laudon lost 10,000 men, eighty officers and eighty-two guns; at the other Daun was badly wounded and carried out of the battle, which cost him 20,000 men. But Austria and Russia had more men to lose. Frederick's dwindling forces were green, hungry and exhausted; the Prussian economy was run into the ground; the Prussian coinage was debased.

Between 1759 and 1762 the soldier king was fighting for his very existence. His only hope was to keep moving, to keep the imperial forces guessing, to prevent them concentrating an overwhelming force against him. His moves were unceasing and desperately swift. They were always miraculously in time. And somehow, again and again, when he faced annihilation his genius would flare up to illuminate the tortuous path to another critical victory. He no longer rode away from the field of battle to save his own skin. He no longer cared. 'Is there no bullet for me?' cried Laudon as he rode out in front of his shattered army at Liegnitz. It was in this mood that Frederick was now fighting all the time. Again and again his horse was shot under him. But he survived.

He survived until England had swept France from the seas and won her empire. Then he had only Austria and Russia to reckon with. And he survived until the Russian miracle, the death of Elizabeth and the withdrawal of her armies from the field. Maria Theresa now had had enough. Like Napoleon III, a hundred years later, she might have exclaimed: 'I have had enough of war; there is too much luck in it!' What she was saying in her heart was that no object, not even Silesia, was worth this suffering. It was never to happen again. She also knew that she had sinned.

She did not repine. Nor did she turn on her generals and her Kaunitz. Daun, whom she had overwhelmed with honours after Kolin, remained her trusted hero to the end of his life. She had fought the war until nearly the end, convinced of the righteousness of her cause, and as she had fought the Succession War, with a surer touch, with undiminished stubbornness, repeating many of her mistakes, and exhibiting once more her familiar virtues. She was forty, stout now, but still a splendid figure when the war started, and on the face of it her character was set. The Succession War had been a formative experience of the first order. It had taught her the realities of power; it had opened her eyes to the rule of selfishness and inertia among the privileged and the worldly. It had taught her to appreciate her own strength and it had taught her how to rule. It had taught her, finally, that honesty was not the best policy. She had been a rapid pupil. Contemplating her equivocal behaviour on the eve of the war and her singleness of purpose throughout its course, one might conclude that this woman with all her splendid qualities had been so corrupted by the world that she could hold no more interest for us. But in fact the Seven Years War was a formative experience too.

She had never quite lost herself. She had coarsened; her impetuous high-handedness sometimes threatened to harden into the stereotype of the domineering woman of whom everyone went in awe; her quick impatience had sharpened, but the old warmth of spirit still persisted. She could still charm and enslave; she could still surprise the men she decided to trust with her loyalty and the generosity of her gratitude; she could still blurt out the truth as she saw it. Above all, she was still growing. And since the shabby attitudes which had distinguished her final challenge to Frederick had led to a dead end, to grow meant to retrace her footsteps and return to her true self. This she did.

We do not know what went on in her mind as she accomplished this great reversal. She never spoke of it. She did not apologise and she did not explain. She did not seek to abdicate (this was to happen later under the impact of the death of Francis). She did not disown her advisers. She remained every inch a queen. But as she contemplated the appalling ravages of the war she had so confidently entered, and as she looked back on the diplomatic manoeuvres which had preceded it, she was clearly at some time overcome with a renewed sense of the vanity of worldly ambitions and of the wickedness of lies. Certainly she discovered again, even before the fighting was over, that honesty was her destiny and that princes who made war and sacrificed their subjects to personal ambition betrayed their duty and their calling, their Christian faith. She had known this once by instinct; by the time the war was over she knew it with her mind. There were to be no more wars, unless in response to direct aggression, so long as she lived; further, as Empress, she would apply to politics the morality she applied to her private life. Of course, in some particulars she failed in this resolution. Sins of omission were her failure in part to restrain (in spite of heroic efforts) the belligerent ambitions and specious politicising of her son (who became the Emperor Joseph II and co-regent after the death of Francis in 1765). Sins of commission included the exploitation of her children, above all the unfortunate Marie Antoinette, as expendable pieces in the political game. But she succeeded well enough in the seventeen years that remained to her after the Peace of Hubertusberg for the persistent and peremptory warrior-queen of the first half of her reign to be transformed, in legend, into the queen of peace.

PART FOUR

The Queen Mother

Chapter Sixteen

The King of the Romans

At the end of a letter to her old friend Countess Enzenburg Maria Theresa added a postscript: 'I had to write this in four instalments, six children in the room with me, and the Emperor too; it reads like it.' That was in 1752. There were very often children in the room. At Schönbrunn there is an amusing gouache by Marie Christine, the second and most gifted of the young archduchesses, which shows what they looked like when they were at home. It is five minutes to nine in the morning by the grandfather clock in the corner. Francis, his head done up in a towel instead of his wig, sits in a dressing-gown and slippers before an open fire. Maria Theresa is about to pour coffee from a silver coffee-pot. The children, four of them, are starting their day as children do. By the time of the Seven Years War there were a dozen altogether: four of the sixteen had died. In 1760 the eldest, Marianne, was twenty-two; the youngest, Maximilian, only three. Between them came Joseph, the heir, already nineteen, Charles, a little younger, and Leopold the next in age; then three girls getting to be grown up, and three more girls and another boy still in the school-room. Their mother took great pains with them and went to endless personal trouble to supervise their upbringing; but that upbringing was strict.

So far as the girls were concerned, it never seems to have crossed Maria Theresa's mind that it might be a good thing to equip them better than she had been equipped herself. She, who complained in later years about her own narrow and useless education, inflicted much the same sort of upbringing on her own daughters. The eldest, Marianne, was becoming a chronic invalid. The next, Marie Christine, was highly intelligent, quick, shrewd, humorous, as well as beautiful; she was the sort of girl to make her own way against any background, and she was her mother's favourite. Others, notably Marie Antoinette, were never taught to use their minds at all. Their lessons were dull and learnt by rote. None except Marie Christine, Mimi to her mother, ever learnt to concentrate. Maria Theresa loved Mimi because she had a mind, but she did nothing to develop the minds of her weaker sisters. Remarkably, too, the first quality this least docile of women required of her daughters was, precisely, docility: 'They are born to obey and must learn to do so in good time.'

That sentence occurs in a long instruction, written at some time in 1756, for Countess Lerchenfeld who had been appointed *aya* to two of the younger children, Johanna and Josepha. After outlining the manner in which she expected the countess to look after the children's health, informing both her, Maria Theresa, and van Swieten of the least mishap, the Empress developed her views about food: van Swieten, she said, would prescribe their diet, but they must be made to eat up everything put before them.

I insist on their eating everything, with no fault-finding and no picking and choosing. Further, they must not be allowed to criticise their food. On Fridays, Saturdays, and all other fast-days they will eat fish. Although Johanna in particular dislikes it, she must not be indulged. The sooner the habit is broken the better. All my children had the same aversion, and all had to overcome it. . . . I don't like to see them eating much sugar, see that they have as little as possible.

Then cleanliness: 'Cleanliness is to be observed most strictly; they must be properly washed and combed, every day without exception.' Then the passage about obedience:

They must not be allowed to talk to door-keepers and stokers, or to give them orders; they are born to obey. . . . I fear that Johanna is pig-headed, though she is clever enough in other ways. Josepha still seems to be a good child, but not so capable. And never must they be allowed to be afraid, neither of thunderstorms, fire, ghosts, witches or any other nonsense. The servants must not talk about such things or tell horror stories. You are not to let them be frightened of illness, so you will talk in a perfectly natural way about everything of this kind, even smallpox and death; it is all to the good to familiarise them with such thoughts in good time. They must not be allowed to show aversion to anything, still less to anybody: no familiarity with the servants, politeness towards all, and particularly towards strangers.

With all this they had plenty of time for amusements. Countess Lerchenfeld was given an entirely free hand here. And, indeed, in this sense, the children were spoilt. Four years earlier Khevenhüller had gloomily asked himself in his diary whether so much play-acting, dancing, singing and dressing up might not turn their highnesses into flibberty-gibbets. They were at it all the time; an endless succession of comedies, operas, ballets, all elaborately dressed and mounted, often with libretti by Metastasio, displayed the talents of the imperial children and carefully selected contemporaries to specially invited audiences. Maria Theresa herself had given up going to the theatre as a regular thing, but she remembered her young days, she liked to show off her children and see them happy, above all she was trying her best to please Francis. Clearly she saw in Francis's delight in his children a bond to be exploited to the utmost. She was at her best on such occasions, young and gay and benign. They gave her something to hold on to in the days when Francis, effectively excluded from the business of state, was always off and away entertaining a lady friend in his curtained box at the old Burg theatre, attending private parties with his cronies, hunting at Laxenburg or Hollitsch, and using both as a cover for his moderate but persistent infatuation for the Countess Wilhelmina Auersperg, a lady of reckless and extravagant tastes, who took a great deal from him without ever concealing the fact that others shared her favours. Francis had given her a small house at Laxenburg (Kaunitz, and many other great figures, had built there too) and Maria Theresa knew it. This was one of the reasons why, on the eve of the Seven Years War, she bought Schlosshof as a present for him after the great house-party described in an earlier chapter, the one which led to the composer, Gluck, being summoned to Vienna.

It was in the same spirit that in 1762, when all her dreams of a successful outcome to the Seven Years War were being extinguished, she commanded the child Mozart and his sister Marianne to appear at Schönbrunn. '. . . Now there is only time to tell you that we were so graciously received that as I tell it it will be reckoned a fairy-tale. Let it suffice that Wolferl sprang on the lap of the Empress, put his arms round her neck and vigorously kissed her. We were with her from three to six.' Thus Leopold Mozart wrote back in haste to his wife at Salzburg in the seventh heaven of delight. He allowed himself to expect great things for his children from the Empress. But Maria Theresa was happy to be amused, genuinely enchanted by the child. Of the genius she was unaware.

2

One of the children stood outside all such affairs, regarding the goings-on of his mother, his father, his brothers and sisters, at first with sulky reserve, soon with increasingly arrogant disdain. From his childhood onwards, Joseph brought out the best and the worst in his mother: the best because she sought unceasingly, to the point of obsession, to find ways and means of bringing him out, developing his obvious gifts, humanising him and winning his confidence; the worst because, finding in him a character no less stubborn than her own, but also cold in a way she could not understand, she was lost, alternating between pleading and nagging, always unsure – a state of mind she was not well equipped to enjoy. Further, as time went on, Joseph's extreme contempt for her own instinctive values and his unyielding championship of foreign and heretical ideas caused her to close her mind to the new ideas which van Swieten and Kaunitz had so well known how to persuade her, however reluctantly, to accept. One result of this was that in her old age she was made to appear as a bigoted reactionary. Her own reforms were largely forgotten, and it was Joseph who was credited with the still greater reforms of her last fifteen years, the period of his co-regency.

She was uneasy from the beginning of her eldest son and heir, as well she might have been. What seems to have happened with all the imperial highnesses was that they were badly spoilt in very early infancy and then, when they were six or seven, handed over to their tutors to be disciplined and knocked into shape. This, over the ages, has been the common lot of most upper-class children everywhere. As a rule it worked out fairly well. Sometimes it did not work at all. It did not work with Joseph. But to blame Joseph's character defects on a faulty upbringing, as has frequently been done, is unfair. His brothers Charles and Leopold, for example, were brought up in exactly the same way. Charles had an easy and facile temperament, very much his father's son, which carried him cheerfully through all difficulties. Leopold was the most unpromising youngster imaginable – awkward, sulky, arrogant, deceitful, rough, apparently unfeeling. In 1762 his *ayo*, Count Francis Thurn, reported to Maria Theresa on his character and the way it was developing with a directness and honesty which few modern headmasters would dare to emulate. His report was broken down into twenty sections, covering every imaginable aspect of character and ability. Each section was unrelievedly adverse. Any mother reading it would believe she had given birth to a monster. Against each paragraph of bleak criticism, Count Thurn noted improvements made during a given period. These, often considerable, still left a great deal to be desired. Yet Leopold turned into a highly personable youth and, in due course, as Grand Duke of Tuscany, developed into the wisest, kindest, most imaginative ruler in the Europe of his day. With him the system worked. With Joseph no system would have worked, because he had no heart, his later passion for poor Isabella of Parma notwithstanding: he was as complete an egotist as it is possible to be. And his solitary passion was simply another aspect of this egotism. He was unaware of Isabella as a person: briefly she fed his self-love.

He could never persuade; persuasiveness implies the recognition of other points of view. He could only command. The solitary obstacle was his mother's will, and even this was almost more than he could bear. He was, of course, bursting with ideas, and many of these were good. But his reforms did not spring from love of his peoples, or even pity for – as an example – the starving peasantry of Bohemia: they sprang from self-love tempered by abstract ideals of justice and from disdain of all who differed from him. The Habsburg monarchy must be whipped into shape to be a credit to him, as autocrat. The betterment of his peoples meant, most joyously, the smashing of the Jesuits and the disciplining of a detested aristocracy.

He started quite young. Maria Theresa, as so often, gives us the essentials in her instructions to Count Charles Batthyany whom she chose, as a soldier, to knock some sense into Joseph at the age of nine, after his civilian tutor had all too manifestly failed. 'He *tutoyers* everybody,' reported Podewils to Frederick of the six-year-old crown prince. 'His countenance reflects pride and haughtiness, and so does his behaviour. He has the most exalted conception of his station. . . . The Emperor tries to rid him of such airs, but his great love for the boy weakens his authority.' He must, indeed, have been intolerable. At six he already had a name for flatly ignoring all those around him who were not of the highest rank, and he publicly made fun of the inferior station of his father's family, the father he was later to dismiss as 'an idler surrounded by flatterers'. Playing at soldiers, given, absurdly, a real regiment to command, he turned on the great Haugwitz, then engaged upon his great army reform: 'Did you ever do service in the army? . . . Then why do you meddle in matters you do not understand? I warn you not to touch my own regiment with your reforms, for I would not tolerate them.' This was not intended as a joke. Somebody had put the child up to say this, and Maria Theresa could never find out who it was. But she was determined, a little belatedly, to put a stop to that kind of nonsense. Hence Batthyany:

Because my son, a pledge so dear and important to us all, has been brought up from the cradle with the greatest tenderness and love, it must be admitted that his desires and requests have been deferred to too easily in many ways, particularly by those who serve him, who have flattered him too much and allowed him to develop a premature conception of his exalted station. He expects to be obeyed and honoured, finds criticism unpleasant, almost intolerable indeed, gives way to all his own whims, but behaves discourteously, even rudely, to others.

He had somewhat improved, she went on, under his first tutor, who had brought out 'a remarkable liveliness, which until then nobody had suspected', but he still had a long way to go. He lacked any sort of application and made life a misery for his teachers by answering them back. He was not without intelligence, but this made it all the harder to cope with him, because he was clever enough, 'particularly when he is excited, to answer back violently and engage in arguments likely to embarrass a superior who tries to avoid unseemly quarrels'. Above all she was distressed by

> the pleasure he is prone to take in seizing on the shortcomings, physical or otherwise, of others and pouring ridicule on them. . . . The *ayo* will do his best to keep from his presence men who flatter him too much, pander to his consciousness of his high birth, or try to ingratiate themselves with laughter, jokes and malicious gossip. He must be stopped from amusing himself at the expense of others – a failing especially reprehensible in the great, who can so easily hurt or embarrass those who cannot defend themselves.

But the horrid youth could not be stopped. He was impervious. The characteristics which distressed his mother when he was still in the nursery remained with him all his life. He was unkind and cruel to the point of sadism. Hectoring, rude, impatient, bitter, this man born with every advantage in the world behaved like one of those sad schoolmasters who find fulfilment in bullying little boys with heavy sarcasm and personal remarks about the colour of their hair, the size of their ears, the deficiency of their understanding, the shortcomings of their parents. But Joseph was not a third-rate schoolmaster. He was the head of the most illustrious house in Europe and master of a great empire.

Later, in the years of conflict between mother and son, it will be important to remember these early days. Maria Theresa's unhappiness was not, as is usually supposed, primarily due to her distaste for her son's reforming zeal (though she certainly objected to many of his ideas), the real cause of her distress was her all too intimate know-ledge of his character. She might, and did, object to his treatment of the Jesuits (but she herself saw the need to cut them down to size) and his bullying of the nobility (she herself had set her face against aristocratic irresponsibility when Joseph was in the cradle). What she objected to far more was the arrogant and overbearing manner of his attack. She knew all about his ambition too, above all his ambition for aggrandisement and military glory. And when she was told, as she sometimes was, that brash and harsh as he might be, her son, in his concern for the underdog, was on the side of the angels, she must have wondered often and long how he reconciled his championship of the peasantry with his unregarding determination to use them as cannon-fodder in unnecessary and rather disgraceful wars.

There was a time when she could allow herself to hope that this difficult and unloving son (he constantly protested his love in words, constantly denied it in his actions) was turning over a new leaf. In 1760, at nineteen, he married and fell in love. The girl was Isabella of Parma, and the original idea had been to reinforce the new bonds between Vienna and Versailles by marrying Joseph to a Bourbon: Isabella's mother was the favourite daughter of Louis XV. The idea was collapsing owing to the death of Louis's daughter, but Joseph had seen a picture of Isabella, dark, olive-skinned, with wonderful eyes, and he liked what he saw. Maria Theresa, with Austria on the verge of bankruptcy in the death-throes of the Seven Years War, threw herself into the affair with a return to all her old gaiety, energy and extravagance. After the proxy marriage at Parma, the young bride was escorted to Vienna for a round of celebrations on a scale to take the breath away. Joseph, who had already embarked on the course of a dynast who despised outward show and everything that went with it, and Isabella, who had spent her childhood and adolescence in conventual obscurity, to emerge as the companion of a widowed father whom she adored, and who had more brains, intelligence and taste than any other prince in Europe, had to submit.

Nobody knows just what Isabella made of Joseph — or what she would have made of him had she lived. She was a Brontë-esque girl whose brooding habit of mind went with striking looks and a most incompatible gift of winning hearts and charming everyone she met into believing that she would be the ideal wife, the ideal daughter-in-law, the ideal empress. Maria Theresa quickly came to love her as a daughter. Joseph gloried in her. She had to convince this self-centred and suspicious youth (he was no more than that), who prided himself on intellect and clear vision, that her own wisdom, though outstanding and an asset to him, was in no way superior to his. It must have been a hard task, but she succeeded to perfection. And she succeeded also in concealing from him that the great love of her life was his sister, Marie Christine.

The correspondence between Maria Theresa's favourite daughter and her adored and cherished daughter-in-law was for generations a source of almost intolerable embarrassment to biographers. Marie Christine was a splendid, healthy girl, later a devoted wife. Isabella was on the face of it a girl of extraordinary attractions, great and varied gifts, intelligent, widely and deeply read, an almost perfect wife and consort: she could join her husband in his music-making, his only real delight, and apply herself to problems of state, of economics too. And yet . . . And yet in two hundred letters over a period of three years she not only made it absolutely plain that her love for Marie Christine was the biggest thing in her life (and Marie Christine accepted it and returned it in large measure), but also that, conscious of her guilt but unable to overcome its cause, perhaps not even willing to overcome it, she made herself fall in love with death as the only way out. Biographers writing in a less permissive age had to discount the seriousness of the love. Even Alfred von Arneth, who had the honesty to publish many of the letters, could never make up his mind whether to reprobate poor Isabella flatly (it would have meant reprobating Marie Christine too) or to shrug off the whole alarming correspondence as the product of an excess of youthful romanticism. He seized triumphantly on two lines in a single letter to prove that all the time Isabella really loved her husband. Joseph had been ill, and was recovering. Isabella wrote to Marie Christine to give her the news. She finished up: 'Deeply as I love you, I discovered yesterday that the Archduke comes first.'

Set against this we have all the other letters:

'Believe me that my greatest, indeed I can say my only joy, is to see you and be with you. Never in heaven or on earth, neither because of absence or anything or anybody else, shall I change in this.'

Again and again she reiterated her eternal fidelity. Again and again she wrote begging for reassurance:

> Here I am again, my all too cruel sister, on tenterhooks until I know the effect of what you have just been reading. . . . I cannot wait to know my fate, whether you think of me as somebody worth knowing, or worth throwing yourself head-first into the water for. It is too much to bear. I can think of nothing but that I am head over heels in love like a fool; if only I knew why? Because you are so cruel that you really shouldn't be loved, yet how can one help it when one knows you?

Marie Christine did not reject Isabella. Her passions were less intense than her sister-in-law's, but she did not reproach her. She returned affection for affection. Never once, as far as is known, did she suggest that her brother was not getting a fair deal; indeed, it is clear from Isabella's own letters that Marie Christine herself could be demanding. Joseph was hardly mentioned between them, though Isabella discussed, with great penetration and shrewdness, most other members of the family. In fact the only time Isabella reproached Marie Christine – as distinct from charging her with coldness – was on one of the few occasions when she referred in detail to her husband. Joseph had hurt and infuriated his sister with one of his sarcastic comments, and Isabella sprang to his defence:

> My deep love for you prompts me to send you this note. I conjure you in the name of that love to listen to what I say. You know what happened yesterday. It can lead to endless trouble if you go on like that. I have convinced the Archduke that he was in the wrong. Actually you were too; but let that be. I beg you therefore when you meet him next time to behave as though nothing has happened. If he is stiff with you, take no notice. If he refers to the quarrel, treat it as a joke. If you do this I can make him feel more guilty then ever. . . . But do try to give way to him more and not take him too seriously.

And again, when Marie had been complaining about Joseph's coldness:

> His nature is not primarily emotional. Caresses and endearments he sees as flattery, unless you have established a sure claim to his esteem. Given esteem, friendship follows as a matter of course.

Conversely, when Marie Christine reproached Isabella it was not because of her passion but because of her constant brooding on death:

> Allow me to tell you that your great longing for death is an outright evil thing. It means either that you are selfish or else that you want to seem a heroine. It has nothing to do with your own loving nature. You ought to be ashamed of uttering sentiments so grievous to people who are absolutely bound up with your existence.

But Isabella went on talking about death. In the intervals of preparing long studies of the political situation, of the economic situation, of problems of trade; in the intervals of writing the most extraordinarily perceptive 'profiles' of the imperial family – of Maria Theresa, whom she loved deeply, but whom she saw as her own worst enemy because of her diffidence and her 'clinging and trusting nature', so sedulously concealed, which delivered her into the hands of false advisers; of Francis, who needed to be respected as his wife's equal, but who could not be trusted and talked to with absolute candour, because he had become the creature of the Countess Auersperg – she brooded on the crowning mercy which was to remove her to ultimate peace. Never once did she ask herself what would happen to Joseph if she died; but she asked constantly what would happen to her mother-in-law, whose confidant she now was – and she left a long testament urging Marie Christine to be ready to act in her place, and explaining just how to handle the Empress best to influence her.

This was the woman of whom Albert of Saxony, later to marry Marie Christine, was to write:

> This truly amazing woman, who was still not twenty years old, was endowed not only with all the qualities of heart which made her estimable, but also combined all the knowledge and the talents one might hope for in the most accomplished of young men. . . . But in spite of all the efforts she made to conceal it, her expression showed a tendency to sombre thoughts which indicated that she was not entirely happy, and on the subject of which she never clearly explained herself, even to those in whom she placed the greatest confidence.

She died at twenty-one. She had borne Joseph one daughter, the infant Theresa. She was pregnant again. There was typhus about. The fourteen-year-old Archduchess Johanna caught it. Isabella herself opened her own arms to destruction. She wanted only to change places with Johanna, who would not die. In an extraordinary series of daily letters to Marie Christine, Isabella reported with clinical detail on the long-drawn-out struggle between death and the child. 'Johanna will not die,' she wrote, as though she herself was the power of death and could give final comfort to the child. Johanna died. Isabella lived. But, very soon there was smallpox. Marie Christine went down with it, so did the infant Marie Antoinette, then Isabella herself. The others recovered, Isabella did not. On the third day of her illness she suffered the premature birth of a girl, who died at once. Five days later she was dead, in Joseph's arms. It was the end of one of the most fascinating might-have-beens of history.

Joseph wrote to his father-in-law in Parma:

I have lost everything. My adored wife, the object of all my tenderness, my only friend is gone. . . . You have known my love for her and now will be smitten by the same misery as I: Judge of my situation! Agonised and beaten down, I hardly know if I am still alive. This terrible separation: shall I survive it? I shall, but only to live in misery for ever.

And a fortnight later:

My only comfort is to be alone in my room, to gaze at the portrait of my beloved wife and read through her writings and papers. . . . Often I seem to see her before me; I talk to her and this illusion sustains me. When she withdraws herself and I see only nothingness, imagine my despair. I cherish the tiniest scrap of the writing she left behind, because I want to be able to show the whole world what a helpmeet I had in her and how truly she deserves to be mourned. Although you are also saddened, and the loss of such a daughter is terrible for you, your loss seems but a shadow compared with mine. All the world knew the excellent qualities of my wife, the tenderness of my love for her, the friendship, the respect, the perfect confidence we shared. It was the best marriage that had ever been. What blessed peace I enjoyed in my own house, in the arms of a wife I still adore! When I had to leave her, what joy to return. Honestly sharing all joys and sorrows, we lived the happiest of days. And in five days it was all destroyed for me. Who can measure the loss for our State, for our whole family, and for my wretched self. Irreparable is the only word, for never was there a princess, a woman, like her. And it was I who possessed this treasure and had to lose her when I was only twenty-two.

Years later, when people were trying to account for the aloof and cold disdain of the mature Joseph, the story went round that Marie Christine had given her brother Isabella's letters to read. She had done this, it was said, because she could not bear to see Joseph suffering so deeply for a delusion – the delusion that Isabella had loved him as he had loved her. As a result, Joseph had turned against all mankind, womankind in particular, and was never to trust anyone ever again. But nothing could be more absurd. Marie Christine was soon to be happily married to a sane and decent husband with whom she had long been in love. She never cared for Joseph, and he never cared for her. She was a sensible and level-headed girl, neither a fool nor a monster. She kept her secret well. It is plain that neither her husband nor her mother ever came to suspect it. Above all Joseph needed no encouragement to despise mankind. He had been doing little else since his nursery days. His love for Isabella, had it been allowed to grow, might have changed him, or at least developed stunted aspects of his nature. The loss, so soon, of the one person who could take him out of himself for a moment was quite enough in itself to turn him back on himself for good. It is worth noticing in this context that in his letters to his father-in-law, later, in his letters to his mother, the whole emphasis is on self-pity. Isabella's death was an outrage perpetrated upon him. Not by so much of a breath does he indicate a feeling for Isabella, so young, so eager, so wonderfully endowed, so brutally extinguished. Nor does he seek companionship with his father-in-law in a shared loss. Isabella is dead at twenty-one. I, Joseph, am the victim.

Maria Theresa has been sharply blamed, even by some of her champions, for what happened next. While Isabella lay dying the empress wrote to Kaunitz: 'The life of an angel draws tragically near; I don't think she can last out this night. All my happiness, all my peace is dying with this enchanting and incomparable daughter, whom I have owed to you.'

She meant it. But once Isabella was dead and buried, life took charge. Joseph would one day be Emperor. In preparation for this he must first be crowned in Frankfurt as king of the Romans, and already there were plans to marry him again.

The mixture of arrogance and self-pity in this twenty-two-year-old crown prince must have been hard to bear. His mother knew him all too well and she must have found it impossible to accept at their face value the bitter lamentations of a son whom she knew to be self-centred, inconsiderate and cold. It was as though, partly aware of his own failure, he was finding in his breavement a chance to make a virtue of it. If Joseph had been really determined not to marry again, or at least to postpone remarriage, no power on earth could have compelled him. And if he had gone to his mother and asked for her support in face of the activities of the marriage-brokers he would have gained it. There was plenty of time. Maria Theresa herself was only forty-six. But although Joseph lamented incessantly, he did not refuse. Half the courts of Europe were putting candidates forward, and Kaunitz was happy in his scheming. The coronation certainly could not wait, and when Maria Theresa read her son's letters written on his journey to Frankfurt with his father and sponsor, the Emperor, she may well have thought that the sooner he was brought back to earth the better. 'Unless to prove my love for you, dear mother, I shall never marry again,' he wrote from Munich. 'These recent days have brought a cruel tearing open of my wound. . . . I cannot keep back my tears as I write these words; you will know by that the greatness of my sorrow.'

And again, from Frankfurt itself, *en fête* for the coronation:

My existence now is strained to breaking point. With a heart aching with grief I have to appear delighted with a position of which I feel all the burden and none of the pleasure. I with my love of solitude, with my difficulty in being at ease with people whom I do not really know, have always to be on view, and ready to enter into conversation with every chance stranger. Think of me, with my limited command of words at the best of times, having to chatter and pay compliments the whole day long.

And again:

> My election took place on March 27th, four months to a day
> since the departure of that dear spirit. On the 29th, four months
> to the very day since they took that dear body away, I had to
> make my bow. . . . Forgive me, my very dear mother, if I
> grieve you with my words. But have pity on a son who is ten-
> derly attached to you, and who is plunged into despair.

These protestations on the part of a young man who had never had
a kind word for anyone, who was notorious, moreover, for his delight
in wounding, made very strange reading. To Maria Theresa it must
have seemed that her unaccountable son was determined to figure as a
martyr. On his return from Frankfurt he announced that if he must
marry he would choose Isabella's fourteen-year-old sister, Louise,
who would at least have something of poor Isabella in her. He knew
perfectly well that the child was already betrothed to the Spanish
Infante, and although Maria Theresa did her best to persuade the
Spanish king to release Louise from her engagement to his son,
Joseph seized the opportunity to sulk and declare that if he could not
have Louise he did not care whom he married. In the end, after a
great deal of undignified manoeuvring, the choice narrowed down to
Princess Josepha of Bavaria or Princess Kunigunda of Saxony. Both
were unprepossessing. Joseph wanted neither, but instead of putting
his foot down he contented himself with sniping at his parents and
his would-be bride. 'I am persuaded,' he wrote, 'that the political
considerations are not worth the sacrifice; but who can resist the
promptings of filial affection, especially for a mother so dear and
worthy of reverence?'

Of Josepha, whom he ultimately married, he wrote when he first
saw her: 'She is twenty-six. She has never had smallpox, and the very
thought of the disease makes me shudder. Her figure is short, thick-
set, and without a vestige of charm. Her face is covered with spots
and pimples. Her teeth are horrible.' He invited his parents to
choose for him. Kaunitz wanted Josepha because of the Bavarian connection, so Josepha it was. To Isabella's father he sent off a long, self-
pitying letter. He had nothing in common with his new wife, he
said; but her character was irreproachable and he was sorry for her.

'I will keep to the path of honour, and if I cannot be an affectionate husband, at least she will have in me a friend, who will appreciate her good points and treat her with every imaginable consideration.'

Words again. As time went on he did more than treat poor Josepha with perfect frigidity. He showed his contempt for her and went out of his way to wound and humiliate her publicly. No matter how much he detested her, there was no need for this. He had every opportunity to avoid Josepha in private while behaving politely in public. Marie Christine once wrote: 'I believe that if I were his wife and so maltreated I would run away and hang myself on a tree in Schönbrunn.' He behaved worse that Frederick of Prussia, whom he came to admire so much. Frederick at least behaved as though his wife did not exist. The only member of the family who took poor Josepha under his wing was Francis, and when Francis died, all too soon, she had not a real friend left in the world: 'He never made any difference between me and his own children,' she wrote after his death. 'And I loved him and honoured him as if he had indeed been my father. His memory is graven on my heart, and my gratitude to him will cease only with my life.' She was a lonely soul, decent and loyal, who was to die quite soon – glad, one imagines, to leave a husband who could say of her to an acquaintance: 'My wife has become insupportable to me. . . . They want me to have children. How can one have them? If I could put the tip of my finger on the tiniest part of her body which is not covered with pimples, I would try to have a child.'

Chapter Seventeen

The Great Change

Seven months after Joseph's second wedding, on August 18th, 1765, Francis Stephen died quite suddenly, and Maria Theresa's life fell apart. She was forty-eight; her husband was fifty-seven and his death was wholly unforeseen. The whole Court was at Innsbruck to celebrate yet another wedding — the marriage of Joseph's brother Leopold, Grand Duke of Tuscany, to the Infanta of Spain, a blue-eyed beauty of great liveliness and charm. It was to be a glorious occasion, but Maria Theresa was worried about Leopold, who had outgrown his strength and had now caught a chill on his journey over the Brenner Pass to meet his bride at Bozen and bring her back to Innsbruck. On the wedding day he was so ill that he could hardly get through the ceremony and had to be carried off to bed immediately afterwards. He had gone down with pleurisy, and for several days lay in a critical condition. His mother could think of nothing else. But he rallied, and then it was decided to go through with the rest of the festivities without him, while he collected his strength for the journey back over the Brenner and through the Appenines to Florence in the August heat.

On August 18th there was a gala performance at the theatre, which Maria Theresa decided not to attend, to be followed by a large supper party at the palace. Francis, who had been the life and soul of the party during those anxious days, had suffered a slight seizure during the previous night, but felt better in the morning and behaved quite normally — except that he cut the last act at the theatre to snatch a moment's rest before the supper-party. Joseph went back with his father to the palace, which was connected with the theatre by a covered passage. At the end of this passage Francis was stricken again, as he had been the night before and had to lean for a moment against the wall. Joseph urged him to sit down while he fetched a doctor, but Francis waved him away, insisted that he would be better in a moment, and told him to go on ahead and tell nobody. Joseph pretended to obey, but hid in a doorway and was in time to run back and catch his father when, taking a few steps, he swayed and began to fall. Now the alarm had to be given. Francis was already unconscious. Physicians and confessors appeared from nowhere to bleed him and to pray. The Emperor was carried into an anteroom. But he was dead.

They tried to keep Maria Theresa out of the room, but she was already there; the uproar created by courtiers tearing about in search of doctors had alarmed her, but for what she saw she was not in the least prepared. She was shattered. She did not speak and she did not weep; she simply knelt by her husband's body, soundlessly, until in the end she had to be raised up and led away by force. The whole palace was in pandemonium. 'Never shall I forget that evening,' wrote Albert of Saxony, Marie Christine's future husband, to his mother. 'Imagine it. The Emperor dead, the Empress supported to her apartments by my brother- and sister-in-law, who were almost as overcome as she herself; the Archduke ill in bed; the Archduchesses prostrate with grief; and the guests all the time arriving for supper and bursting into tears until the whole palace seemed to echo with weeping and wailing.'

Only Maria Theresa had nothing to say. She would allow nobody, nobody at all, neither family nor servant into her room with her. But in the morning she called one of her ladies to help her dress, at first as though nothing had happened. But when she prepared for the long, elaborate dressing of the still beautiful hair, the woman was shocked by the command to cut it short. During the morning the Empress sent for all the family, and they all came, even though Leopold still had to be carried in. She regarded them attentively, hoped they were as well as could be expected, and then sent them away. All that day she gave no orders. Or only one: Francis's shroud was to be sewn in her own room, and she would help with the sewing. All day she sewed and prayed. Her great realm might not have existed.

It was in this way that Joseph came to take command. Somebody had to give orders. He was pleased to do so. Thus without formality, the King of the Romans automatically became the Emperor Joseph II.

But Maria Theresa was still Empress. More to the point she was the crowned Queen of Hungary and of Bohemia, and would remain so until she died or abdicated. The new emperor had no power other than the power she chose to vest in him.

At first she was in a mood to cede to him all her power. The reason for her life, she thought, was gone. She reproached herself bitterly for not making more of Francis, for her jealousies, her impatiences, her sins, imaginary and real, against the beloved object. She went out of her way to be kind to the Countess Auersperg. This lady was at Innsbruck with the rest of the Court, and the moment the Emperor was dead, everyone expected that Maria Theresa would send her packing – and behaved accordingly: men and women who had made up to her for the Emperor's favour, now, overnight, cold-shouldered her. Until the Empress went up to her before her departure for Vienna, and said, 'How much we both of us have lost!' Later she found that Francis had promised a large sum to the Auersperg. Maria Theresa regarded it as a debt of honour and paid it. Her generosity was worthy of a better cause. Wilhelmina Auersperg was one of those creatures who gave beauty a bad name; greedy, libidinous and cold. But she had spirit. The Empress could have ruined her yet did nothing of the kind. All she asked was that the Auersperg and all the other ladies of the Court should refrain from rouging themselves for a period. 'Is it possible,' the Auersperg exclaimed, 'that one cannot be mistress of one's own face? I got it from God, not the State!'

The regulation against the use of rouge was characteristic of the new mood at Court. Soon it was rescinded, except for the unmarried Archduchesses who still lived at home. But Maria Theresa herself was to abandon make-up and jewellery, to dress herself in mourning, for the rest of her life. There is no doubt at all that for some time she was also abandoned to grief. To her old friend Tarouca she wrote on New Year's Day, 1766: 'I hardly know myself now, for I have become like an animal with no true life or reasoning power. I forget everything. I get up at five. I go to bed late, and the livelong day I seem to do nothing. I do not even think. It is a terrible state to be in, but I revive a little when I see one of my old friends.' It was just thirty years since she had first written to Francis, her affianced, that she 'felt uneasy, like a little dog' when he was away from her.

Now she thought seriously of leaving the throne to live out the rest of her life at Innsbruck, where she had founded a new convent for women of high birth: she had turned the room where Francis had died into an oratory. But although she was deeply tempted to retire, and although many thought she would do just this, she knew in her heart that it would never be. She rationalised her decision to carry on by reminding herself of her duty to her children. Quite soon she was writing to Kaunitz:

In the dreary future I shall follow your advice with the same confidence as in the past. In conformity with which I am letting myself be dragged back to Vienna, wholly and solely to assume the guardianship of nine orphans. They are greatly to be pitied. Their good father idolised them and could never refuse them anything. It will be changed times now. I am exceedingly anxious about their future, which will be decided in the course of the next winter. I count upon you, and will do nothing without knowing your mind. I can trust you with the interests of my family as confidently as with the business of the State.

The one person who had no objection to the seclusion of the Empress and who looked with favour upon her rejection of worldly show, was Joseph. Almost at once she had formally appointed him co-regent, to take his father's place, and this time the co-regent was determined to make himself felt.

Joseph is usually called a doctrinaire because of the theoretical nature of his actions. Certainly he had no sense of measure, was wholly lacking in tact and pushed his ideas to their logical extremes with a contemptuous disregard for human feelings, prejudices, susceptibilities. He knew nothing of the politician's art of the possible; and in this sense he could indeed be called a doctrinaire – except that he was not a politician; he was a highly self-conscious autocrat; and to an autocrat everything is possible provided only he has the will.

Joseph had plenty of will. He was, in fact, rather a fantasist than a doctrinaire. He saw himself as the state embodied, and the state was stripped down to a slim figure plainly dressed in black or grey, or in field marshal's uniform, for ever on the move, brisk, purposeful, the willing and tireless servant less of his peoples than of the principle of autocracy. Many of his ideas were good, some fruitful, most what is nowadays called 'progressive'. But he did not sacrifice himself to those ideas: they served his image of himself. That image was clear enough on the surface, incoherent in depth. A study of his words and actions does not clarify this incoherence. It is impossible ever to be certain as to which of his reforms, for example, were occasioned primarily by the genuine concern for the wellbeing of his subjects, which often were occasioned primarily by fears for the future of the dynasty unless popular discontent were appeased, which of them were occasioned primarily by a delight in injuring individuals, or groups of people, who incurred his displeasure.

To make things more difficult, this reforming emperor was a convinced militarist in a manner quite alien to the Habsburg tradition, an attitude which cut clean across his professed concern for the underdog. He admired Kaunitz to excess, simply because he was brilliantly clever and perfectly unfeeling. Later he was to idolise Frederick of Prussia and Catherine of Russia. As a human being he seems hardly to have existed. If we have to doubt his word that he loved Isabella with undying passion, he had only himself to blame. Thus we do know that he despised his father and felt no more than superficial affection for him. Everybody knew it, most of all his old tutor, Batthyany. And yet to Batthyany he could write after his father's death in the following terms:

> No human being is capable of adequately expressing the acute feelings with which the heart of a son is overwhelmed, who loses for ever a father, by whom he is convinced he was loved. . . . My father had the most tender affection for me. He was my teacher, my friend. . . . I am now twenty-four years old. Providence has given me the cup of sorrow in my early days.

To his mother he was writing perpetually in terms of perfect filial affection and devotion, yet he crossed her on every possible occasion.

When he threw himself headlong into his reforming programme he seemed genuinely to have believed that nobody, least of all his mother, had ever reformed before him. He was building on her unaware of the foundations she had laid, and sometimes, rather ludicrously, he was simply repeating her actions.

Thus, one of the first things he did was to get rid of his father's great cohort of professional huntsmen and gamekeepers. Above all there was a sanguinary action aimed at the extermination of the wild boars which ravaged the vineyards, forests and farmlands round Vienna. This was carried out with great fury and panache. So was the ruthless cutting down of unproductive Court expenditure. Just twenty-four years earlier Maria Theresa herself had embarked on the same course, with a good deal less fuss, and with no sense of starting a revolution. And twenty-four years ago she had been reproached for keeping up insufficient state.

Of course she had been extravagant – though no more than was the custom of the time, and a great deal less so than some of her contemporaries. Her own father had been wildly extravagant, and she had grumbled at the consequences. But expenses had crept up. Francis, though very careful with his own money, which he had managed to multiply, also had extravagant tastes, his informal ways notwithstanding, and Francis had to be pleased. She had not the least objection to her son's retrenchment: it was necessary. What she objected to was the manner of it, the self-conscious rectitude. He did not like hunting; he did not like outward show; he detested frivolous amusements. Very well, a good thing too: it saved money! But to make a virtue of following one's natural tastes – that was something else; and to economise in the way most calculated to hurt old friends and servants – that was something else again.

She was glad now that Francis had salted away a large private fortune. At least that meant that the other children would be well looked after. But alas, for some reason which nobody could guess, Francis had left every penny he possessed to Joseph, apart from a little set aside for masses to be said for his soul, to his servants and to the poor. It was a very odd performance. Francis knew that his widow had a large private fortune (he had looked after it and made it grow), enough to enable her to do something for the younger children. But some 2 million of the 22 million he left to Joseph belonged to Tuscany, ruled over now by Leopold, and desperately poor. Joseph claimed it, and in the end got it.

He did not want the money for himself. On the contrary. Every penny he inherited from his father, including the 2 million from Tuscany, he paid into the state treasury, where it was effective in reducing the interest on the national debt, making a very considerable saving. Leopold had his own very poor and backward grand duchy of Tuscany to manage, and he was managing it very well. The peremptory withdrawl of 2 million gulden shattered all his plans, and he protested vigorously. It was this quarrel between her two sons which brought Maria Theresa back into the saddle; and, once back, she stayed. 'I stupefy myself with work, till I have no time to think or feel.'

That was to her old intimate the Countess Enzenburg, on the anniversary of her wedding day, in February 1766. Francis had been dead less than six months, and already Maria Theresa had suffered two more grievous losses, first Haugwitz died, then Daun. She still had Tarouca, but he was an old man now; she still had van Swieten; and she still had Kaunitz. But Kaunitz had always been a working colleague, a brilliant but impersonal adviser, rather than a friend and mentor. She was very much alone. But, imperceptibly she reassumed control.

With Daun gone, she put Joseph in absolute control of the army. It was a terrible wrench.

> I have assigned to my son all responsibility for the future of the army [she wrote to Tarouca]. His association with it must of necessity be closer than mine, and doubtless of longer duration. Its weal or woe depends on the measure he may take. If he likes, he can nominate his own Minister of War. Should he consult me, I see no one more competent than Lacy. The military department was the one nearest my heart. Having resigned my connection with it, it will not cost me much to relinquish anything else.

This was a mood which did not last long.

Joseph also approved of Lacy. The appointment to this supreme position of an Irish soldier of fortune was received with bitter and vocal resentment by ambitious men of noble birth. Daun, though a professional soldier, had been a member of a rich and very ancient family: the great Kinsky Palace on the Freyung in Vienna had been built by Hildebrandt for Daun's father. Things were made worse by the fact that Laudon was inspector-general of infantry. Thus the imperial army was commanded by a radical Emperor and run by two great soldiers of fortune of Irish and Scottish extraction. Gone were the days of aristocratic privilege. But the moving spirit in this revolution was Maria Theresa herself. It was she who had appointed Laudon under Daun; it was she who entrusted the army to her son; and Lacy was also her choice as successor to Daun.

2

Her return to the full conduct of affairs had not been easy. In the winter of 1766–67 Vienna had come to life again, and although the Empress herself took no part in public amusements, she made not the slightest objection to members of her family enjoying themselves as much as they could. *Fasching*, carnival time, in 1767 was as brilliant as ever, and for the rest of Maria Theresa's reign, although the Empress herself dressed always in black, and although her strong ideas about sexual licence frequently bore hardly on indiscreet trespassers, life in and around the Court was in no way overshadowed or diminished in glitter and festivity. Even those visitors who had most to say about Maria Theresa's excessive sobriety and piety, found themselves in the next breath expressing wonder at the magnificence of the circumadjacent show. Thus William Wraxall could report:

> The women dress well, with great taste, and greater magnificence. I never saw in any Court such a profusion of diamonds, unless, perhaps, at Lisbon; and they dispose their jewels with no little elegance. . . . Rouge is universally worn by married and unmarried women of fashion; but they use it in general with moderation, as well as taste: girls of fifteen wear it as much as persons of thirty. The Archduchesses alone are never rouged, the Empress not permitting them to be so on any occasion whatsoever.

In May 1767 Maria Theresa celebrated her fiftieth birthday, and preparations were going ahead for the marriage of her daughter Josepha to the king of the Two Sicilies, a most unendearing youth: yet another of those sacrifices which a mother, who had herself made a love match, reluctantly but in the last resort unhesitatingly required her own children to make in the interests of Habsburg influence and glory.

Then, at the very moment when life appeared to be getting back to normal, there came a series of misfortunes.

First Marie Christine in Pressburg became desperately ill in childbirth. Her infant daughter died within days, and for a time it was feared that Marie Christine herself was past hope. Simultaneously that other Josepha, the unfortunate second wife of Joseph, went down with smallpox. Maria Theresa was with her when the disease was diagnosed, stayed to comfort her and kiss her, and herself went down within a week. It was no mild attack. There were days of extreme crisis, and at the height of Maria Theresa's crisis, poor Josepha died. As far as is known Joseph never visited the bedside of his wife, and he did not attend her funeral. Instead, this strange man spent his days and nights in and out of his mother's sick-room, leaving her only to sleep for an hour or two in an adjoining room. It looked like the end. The anterooms were filled with members of the family and the imperial household who had lived through smallpox and were immune. Crowds gathered round the Hofburg and in every church in the city packed congregations joined in services of prayer. To the surprise and unease of everyone, Albert of Saxony came up from Pressburg, where Marie Christine had just taken a turn for the better, to pay his last respects to the mother-in-law he loved. And just as the Empress herself was seen to be out of danger, he too went down, but with a milder form of the disease.

There was now a respite. Maria Theresa emerged in public to take part in a grand thanksgiving service in St Stephen's Cathedral, and the spontaneous expressions of delight and goodwill on this occasion, not only the cheering of the crowds in Vienna, but the messages that came pouring in from all over the Empire, marked an entirely new epoch in the Habsburg history. Throughout that summer preparations went on for her daughter's wedding. The formal betrothal in

September was an occasion for balls and assemblies which brought Maria Theresa out into society for the first time since the death of Francis. But then, in October, Josepha herself went down with smallpox. Maria Theresa nursed her daughter herself, but in eleven days she was dead. Maria Theresa reproached herself bitterly for this tragedy. She had taken Josepha to the Capuchin vault to pray. She did not know that the sarcophagus containing the coffin of that other Josepha, her daughter-in-law, had not been finally sealed and that the place was still infected.

Indeed, the whole of Vienna was ridden with the disease. The Archduchess Elisabeth, so lighthearted and careless of her beauty, caught it from her sister; and, although she recovered, her beauty was destroyed: 'as soon as she knew what the disease was, calling for a looking-glass and taking leave of those features she had so often heard praised, and which she believed would be greatly changed before she should see them again'. This was the girl of whom her mother had once remarked with some acerbity: 'It did not matter if admiring glances came from a prince or a Swiss guard; so long as someone was doing homage to her beauty, Elisabeth was content.'

One of the most extraordinary aspects of the contemporary attitude to this killer disease was the way in which family and relatives exposed themselves to infection out of sheer decency or tenderness of heart. Nobody knew, of course, how the infection worked, but all were acutely aware of its existence. Nor was this remarkable and reckless solidarity in face of the disease only an imperial eccentricity. It was this same epidemic of the autumn of 1767, which hit the Mozart family, on a visit to Vienna from Salzburg, in the hope that the wedding celebrations for Josepha and Ferdinand would provide shining opportunities for the display of the children's talent. It was while they were waiting to be invited to Court that poor Josepha was laid low. All Leopold Mozart's hopes were dashed, and the epidemic was so violent and widespread that he put the whole family in a coach for Olmutz. There the young Wolfgang was found to be ill, and soon, wrapped in furs, he was delirious. The family were installed in a 'bad, damp room' in the Schwarzen Adler Inn (the very hotel where, two generations later, Felix Schwarzenberg was to humiliate the representatives of the Prussian king), but soon, for no other reason than sheer kindness of heart, they were taken into the household of the local grandee, Count Leopold Anton von Podstatsky, who put two rooms at their disposal and called a doctor. Otherwise the world might have lost Mozart in his fourteenth year. The family stayed for some time in the Podstatsky mansion. Wolfgang himself was quite blind for many days, and then his sister Marianne went down with smallpox too. It was not until January that they were able to return to Vienna, and there at last they were received at Court and by Maria Theresa in person. Her own disasters did not close her heart to the misfortunes of others. 'You cannot imagine,' Leopold Mozart wrote, 'with what kindness the Empress spoke with my wife about the children's illness and our great tour, pressing her hand and stroking her cheeks compassionately, while the Emperor spoke with me and Wolfgang about musical and other matters and made Nanerl blush very often.' He went on to add: 'You must not conclude from this affability that we shall get an exceptional present.'

Leopold was right. From the Empress they received a splendid medallion, nothing more: from Joseph nothing. What was really heartbreaking, as Leopold himself related, was that they had to keep away from Prince Kaunitz, an admirer of whom they had expected great things. They knew about the great man's pathological fear of smallpox, even the mention of it, and Wolfgang's recent connection with it could not be disguised. He had 'still many red spots, small it is true, but clearly visible in cold weather'.

Chapter Eighteen

The Betrayal of an Idea

Maria Theresa had meant what she said when, dragging herself back to life after the death of Francis, she had written to Kaunitz: 'In the dreary future I shall follow your advice with the same confidence as in the past.' She meant this, even though she must have known by now that her brilliant and eccentric chancellor had a moral outlook quite at odds with hers – if, indeed, he had such a thing at all – and actively sympathised with new ideas which were anathema to her. She still needed him as a check to her own impulsiveness and as a guide through the jungle of diplomatic chicanery, even though he himself was at heart a jungle beast. She still believed in total honesty in the conduct of affairs and had come to regret her own departure from it during the diplomatic prelude to the Seven Years War. But with that profound diffidence which her tragic daughter-in-law, Isabella, seems to have been the only member of her family and her entourage to penetrate (although it came out time and again in her dealings with all her chosen advisers: Bartenstein, Tarouca, Haugwitz, van Swieten, to say nothing of the ultramontane element, as represented by Cardinal Migazzi, archbishop of Vienna, and Count Rudolf Chotek, her court chancellor) she could not trust her instincts, or she realised they were not enough.

In some matters, though very far from all, it was almost as though she knew that her deepest prejudices were at fault: she could not, or would not, overcome them; but she took good care to ensure that she should be successfully opposed. This, in her closing years, applied above all to home affairs. There was to be an excellent example when, in 1775, she suddenly abandoned her resistance to the abolition of torture. After putting up a strong rearguard action she wrote: 'I ask the Emperor, who has studied law, and, what is more, whose sense of justice, reason and love of humanity I trust, to decide this matter without my advice. I do not understand it at all and could only act by majority decision.' There was more behind this than a tired old woman throwing up her hands in resignation. There would have been no agitation against torture at all but for the stubborn persistence of the converted Jew, Joseph von Sonnenfels, who had worked on Joseph and Kaunitz. But Sonnenfels himself would have been in no position to agitate about torture or anything else had he not been loyally protected by Maria Theresa from the venomous and unscrupulous attacks of her Chotek and Migazzi, who regarded him as evil incarnate, subversive of Church and State.

Looking back in the light of this and similar actions we may be reminded of that first occasion when, in 1741, the young ruler, determined not to compromise an inch with Frederick, gave in to the demands of Sinzendorf, Bartenstein and Robinson with her 'Very well, if it has to be, then let it be. The whole matter has been settled against my will.' It is possible, too, as we shall see, that there was something of this spirit behind her very reluctant assent to Austria's involvement in the first Partition of Poland in 1772, when again she gave in to Joseph and Kaunitz. But it was by no means always like this. There were some things about which she was absolutely sure, and then she fought, whether successfully or not, with all her strength until the end. And she could be sure and wrong, as she could also be sure and right. She *knew* that religious toleration spelt absolute wickedness, and here she would not give an inch to her son (Kaunitz had the sense to stand away from this quarrel). Equally, she turned her face against war over Bavaria in 1777, and in this matter too Kaunitz, though agreeing with Joseph, who was set on it, was content to play an equivocal role.

Certainly she did not receive in her last fifteen years the solidly good advice she looked for from her beloved chancellor. He trimmed. He was by all means in a very difficult position. To Maria Theresa he owed everything, and he admired and respected her. He was spoilt by her utterly. Only for him would the windows of her apartments be closed, even in the depths of winter. As time went on he was excused from visiting the Schönbrunn Palace altogether. Maria Theresa with her love of fresh air, her robustness, her perpetual jokes against herself, her complete incomprehension of hypochondria, fussed endlessly over this foppish little man, terrified of sickness and death, who could not walk across the courtyard in the Hofburg in high summer without covering his face with a lawn handkerchief – and yet lived until he was eighty-three, surviving her by fourteen years. He was allowed to make his own hours, and he exasperated Joseph by habitually turning up for the morning conference an hour or so late, his mother meekly accepting it and allowing the midday meal to spoil while the chancellor held forth. But he was far closer in ideas to Joseph than to Maria Theresa. Both were children of the Enlightenment and Maria Theresa knew very well that Kaunitz was an admirer of Voltaire, though, unlike Joseph, he took good care to keep quiet about it in her presence. She knew, too, that Kaunitz, again like her son, thought, with all his enlightenment, in terms of aggrandisement by force or guile. Nevertheless, his knowledge was profound, and, within the existing framework of the European system as she understood it, he deployed unrivalled skill. This she knew, too. He was, without question, Europe's most brilliant diplomatist. What he lacked, and this Maria Theresa only darkly saw, was statesmanship. She knew when his positive actions were misjudged; but she was not herself sufficiently conscious of the European picture to understand either the basic causes of his false judgment or the faults of omission which sprang from these.

Nothing exposes more sharply the contrast between the brilliance of Kaunitz the diplomat and the shortsightedness of Kaunitz the statesman than his general line of policy after the conclusion of the Seven Years War. His failure to perceive the dangers in the grand and trimphant reversal of alliances which heralded that war was understandable, perhaps to be expected. The behaviour of England made it very difficult, perhaps impossibly difficult, for a man of spirit possessed with a sense of urgency, to pursue the traditional course. The desire to crush Prussia, as distinct from containing her, a desire fully shared by his Empress, was overmastering. And, when all is said, with his superbly engineered new system of alliances he came breathlessly close to succeeding: it took an act of God, the death of the Tsaritsa Elizabeth, to bring his plans to nothing. But brought to nothing they were. Frederick and Frederick's Prussia survived. There could be no question after 1763, for as long ahead as anyone could see, of recovering Silesia. So long as Frederick was alive (this would not be for ever) a strong Prussia was a fact that had to be lived with. Kaunitz recognised this: had he been a great statesman he would have started to think again, as radically as he had shown himself capable of thinking in the 1750s. And had he thought again, seriously and freely, he would have seen that he still had a strong card to play: the reactivation of the Empire. He would have concentrated all his still matchless diplomatic skill on wooing the German states, attaching them with the strongest possible bonds to the imperial crown, inviting Prussia's cooperation by all means, but, at the same time, prepared to leave her to be strangled on the one hand by a loosely unified Germanic confederation looking to Vienna and on the other by a Russia which could be trusted to work for the detachment of East Prussia. He would have looked to the day when Frederick would be dead. There was no reason to suppose that the monster would be succeeded by another conqueror of genius. Indeed, he was not. It was to take a hundred years and the advent of Bismarck to bring the Prussian challenge to its logical conclusion. But Bismarck owed much of his advantage to the shortsighted policies of Kaunitz after the conclusion of the Peace of Hubertusberg.

In the middle 1760s the times were propitious for Austria. France had shot her bolt. England was preoccupied with overseas empire. The imperial designs of Catherine's Russia were not yet manifest. Prussia was exhausted. Austria was exhausted too, Bohemia laid waste; but her strength and cohesion were greater than ever before. Now, of all times, was the moment to offer such accommodations to a ruined Saxony and a prospering Bavaria as would cause their rulers to bind themselves to Vienna in free association beneath the imperial crown, drawing into their orbit the many lesser states who would be forced into the coalition from self-interest if not dynastic conviction. Religion was no bar. Protestant Saxony had been and again would be ready enough to attach itself to Catholic Austria; Protestant Hanover was at a much later date to take sides with Catholic Austria against Protestant Prussia.

Kaunitz was, of course, well aware of the importance of close alliance with Saxony and Bavaria. It was he who proposed that Joseph should marry either a Saxon or a Bavarian princess, and inclined to the latter because there was no male heir to the young elector, Josepha's brother. Austria, he believed, could later claim as her own at least a large part of Bavaria. But here he was thinking in parochial terms, looking not to strengthen Austria's influence throughout Germany, but only to securing a part of Germany for Austria. By thinking and acting in these terms he threw away what was to prove to be the last chance to rehabilitate the imperial idea and restore real meaning to the crown of Charlemagne, transformed from a mystery into the symbol of a tight coalition. Instead of working for the containment of Prussia he preferred to show his perfect detachment by doing a deal with her – and, fatally, strengthening Frederick in the process.

The first dire consequences of this were soon to show. Nobody at the time saw what was happening, but if ever there was a moment in history when principled behaviour would have paid best that moment was in 1772 when Joseph, aided by Kaunitz, fell over himself to reach a disreputable agreement with Frederick and Catherine of Russia at the expense of Poland. Maria Theresa, in her desperate opposition, was right, and for the right reasons – though she had no idea that she was also right, Joseph and Kaunitz wrong, in the sphere of power politics.

2

It was nearly a century later, after the reckless and heroic Polish rising of 1863, that Disraeli observed in the House of Commons that if the Partition of Poland had been a great crime, it was a crime shared by the Polish people, since their national existence could not have been destroyed without some faults on their side. This was an easy remark to make, question-begging, in itself meaningless, and dangerous in its implications. It was a remark to excuse the behaviour of the English in Ireland, to go no farther afield. It excused in advance the activities of Stalin and Hitler, indeed, any crime of violence anywhere in which the strong or purposeful destroy the weak or feckless. Certainly the Poles asked for trouble as persistently as any people in the world – not, as Disraeli said, the Polish people, but the Polish nobility, who for centuries, in strength or weakness, showed themselves incapable of organising a stable state. Too selfish, arrogant and jealous of each other to develop a governing hierarchy with a steady centre, even when the threat from the rising power of Prussia in the West and Russia in the East made this a first and imperative necessity, the freedom they vaunted was hopelessly compromised by their conduct towards the mass of the people, who were their serfs, and, more often than not, abominably treated serfs. Oppressed masses may be welded into national coherence under a strong central authority which also curbs the aristocracy. In Poland there was no central authority, only a diet, or *sjem*, of territorial magnates, each of whom possessed the idiotic *liberum veto*, the right to veto any decision arrived at by the others. And this meant, in effect, that there was no Polish nation, only rival nobles in absolute and irresponsible control of vast tracts of land and of the serfs attached to the land. There was thus virtual anarchy and constant civil war, of profit to nobody but Poland's powerful neighbours, Russia first, then Prussia.

Catherine of Russia, who dreamt of the total absorption of Poland, was at first content to instal the first of her fifty or so official lovers, Stanislaus Poniatovski, as a puppet ruler after the death of Augustus II of Saxony in 1763. But soon there were renewed troubles. Civil war led to the sharp intervention of a Russian army, in the course of which an eccentric regimental commander, Suvorov, brilliantly distinguished himself and laid the foundations of a career which was to be crowned nearly forty years later with the ruin of Napoleon Bonaparte and his grand army. Stimulated now by French intrigues, Turkey joined in on the side of the insurrectionary Poles, who, as always, redeemed themselves by reckless heroism in adversity and proved themselves capable of infinite self-sacrifice when it was too late. Catherine was so triumphant against the Turks that Europe took alarm, and nobody more than Frederick, who feared both an access of Russian strength and a general conflagration which could end badly for Prussia.

It was Frederick who persuaded first Catherine, then, a far harder task, Austria, to seek salvation in a division of Poland which was premature from Russia's point of view, dubious from Austria's, most profitable for Prussia. It was in August 1769 that Joseph first met Frederick at Neisse in Moravia. 'That man is a genius and a marvellous talker,' he exclaimed, with the air of a discoverer. Soon he was back again, this time with Kaunitz, who, also meeting the legendary enemy for the first time, improved the hour by lecturing him at tedious length on the conduct of foreign policy. Frederick listened solemnly, and made faces when his visitors had gone. Kaunitz was naturally wary. But Joseph, making his debut on the international stage, was filled with enthusiasm for all kinds of alluring possibilities redounding to his glory. Nobody wanted war, except Catherine, who was already conducting a very profitable campaign against the Turks. Joseph and Kaunitz were inclined to think that their best hope lay in acquiring a part of European Turkey in exchange for mediation with Catherine. But Frederick was playing a deeper, faster game. He succeeded in convincing Catherine that Austria would probably intervene against her if she continued her triumphal progress towards Constantinople. The best way to buy her off and avoid spreading the war would be for the three powers to divide Poland between them. Joseph helped him by mobilising demonstratively and concluding a Convention with Turkey. In fact, Frederick knew very well that Joseph was only bluffing; but the harm was done.

Whereas Maria Theresa in her first great war had fought to defend herself in what quickly developed into a struggle for survival, and in her second great war had fought only, as she saw it, to recover the territory taken from her by Frederick – and in due course came to see that her action had been wrong – Joseph was bent on aggrandisement, glorifying wars of conquest. Worse by far, he took Frederick as his model. Maria Theresa more than disapproved of this; it made her sick with shame. And she was alone, alone as she had not been since the first bleak years of her reign. Then she had been alone in courage. Now she was alone in humanity. Her supreme, her infinitely trusted Kaunitz, was on Joseph's side against her.

She was shocked and appalled to see her son and her most trusted adviser reverting to the cynical and unscrupulous power game from which she in the past had suffered so much. She fought all the way against the negotiations with Prussia. She resisted powerfully the idea of annexing part of Turkey. Now, on January 22nd, 1772, she made her final appeal in a letter to Kaunitz. Ageing, and sadly conscious of her failing energies, ugly and fat, she made one last attempt to win Kaunitz to her side against her son:

After all the false steps we have taken, steps which I thought at the time to be false, we can never get right back to the old way. . . . The despatch to Hungary of troops from Italy and the Netherlands, the Convention with Turkey, the far too menacing tone we have adopted towards the Russians, the secretive attitude we have held towards allies and foes alike – all this stems from our determination to extort advantages from the conflict between Russia and the Porte, and to extend our frontiers and secure gains we never dreamed of before this war. We have been behaving like Prussians while seeking at the same time to preserve the appearance of honesty. . . . It may be that I am wrong and that things are not as bad as they look. But . . . from the outset of my unfortunate reign we have always at least tried to follow truth and justice, to honour our pledged word, to show moderation and to be faithful in the fulfilment of our obligations. This gained for us the confidence, I think I may say the admiration, of all Europe, the respect and esteem even of our enemies. All this we have lost in a single year. I declare to you that I do not know how to bear it, that nothing in the world has hurt me more than the loss of our good name. Unfortunately I have to admit that we deserve it. It is for this that I seek a remedy. We must reject as evil and corrupting the idea of fishing for advantage in this whirlpool. We must consider how to extricate ourselves from this wretched situation by the swiftest and least harmful means, with no thought of gain for ourselves, concerned only with our good repute and the re-establishment of our good faith and, as far as we are able, the political balance of power.

It was too late. Frederick and Catherine had already decided between them that Prussia should take the provinces lying between

Brandenburg and East Prussia and that Russia should annex all Poland east of the Dvina and the Dnieper. Unless Austria took her share she would be faced with a situation which would soon lead, all too clearly, to further Russian, if not Prussian, moves in her direction.

Maria Theresa still fought back, but she knew that she had lost:

> What right have we to rob an innocent nation that it has hitherto been our boast to protect and support? . . . I do not understand the policy whereby for the sake of present convenience and possible future advantage, it is made incumbent on a third ruler to imitate the wickedness of two others who are destroying an unoffending Power. This seems to me an untenable proposition. A prince has no more justification than any private person for such behaviour. The greatness and strength of a State will not be taken into consideration when we are all called to render our final account. Only prove to me the contrary, and I shall gladly submit.

And she went on, this remarkable pioneer of unilateral decency, to say:

> I only wish I were wrong. For long, and all too well, I have understood the critical situation in which we find ourselves, and I have pondered it deeply. But one must know how to sacrifice oneself, and the moment for this is now.

After further close argument about the actual state of affairs, after a detailed prediction of the woe that would ensue as a result of unprincipled aggrandisement, she concluded:

> What will France, Spain, England say if we bind ourselves so closely with those we so desperately need to contain and whose policies we have condemned as evil? I declare that this would amount to a formal denial of everything my government has been for thirty years. Let us rather seek to check the crimes of others. . . . Let us be considered weak rather than dishonest.

She pleaded in vain. Events, it was argued, had taken control. The decision to share in the division of Poland was taken. Even Frederick was astonished by the greedy enthusiasm with which Joseph and Kaunitz bargained for the biggest possible share of that dark and backward land.

3

Maria Theresa did not abdicate. And five years later she was to go through the same sort of agony for a second time. At the time of the Polish Partition Joseph was only feeling his way. He did not want war then. But war, sooner or later, he was determined to have. How otherwise could he prove himself as a monarch? It was an age in which the title Great was conceded not to rulers who governed well but to those who, at whatever cost to their own peoples and to others, enlarged their empires. Catherine was Great; Frederick was Great; Maria Theresa, who towered above both, was not. Joseph was determined to be Great. In the Polish affair he thought he had been clever. He soon thought he saw the chance to prove himself great.

When his brother-in-law Maximilian, elector of Bavaria, died in 1776 without a male heir, he decided to move quickly and put in a claim, based on his marriage to poor Josepha, to certain Bavarian lands. It seemed too easy. The Wittelsbach family had divided, and the natural claimant to the Bavarian succession was Maximilian's cousin, the Elector Palatine, Charles Theodore. Charles, an unambitious man, was far more interested in securing his Rhenish provinces against Prussia or France than in extending his rule to Bavaria. Certainly he had no intention of fighting Austria, and he was prepared to recognise Vienna's dubious genealogical claims to part of Bavaria (the ruling families of central Europe were so mixed up that any one of them at any time could quite plausibly put forward some sort of a claim to the property of any other: it was lawyer's work, essentially) in return for appropriate guarantees. A formal Convention was drawn up to this effect, and so confident was Joseph that, as commander-in-chief, he marched in his troops to occupy the promised land before the agreement had been ratified.

Frederick in Potsdam had been watching with the liveliest interest. Austria was playing the very game he himself had played in Silesia thirty-seven years before. Now Prussia could appear upon the stage with a shining sword as the guardian of the Right. It seemed too good to be true. Frederick, a poacher turned gamekeeper, could exclaim that Austria's right to Bavaria was the right of a highwayman demanding 'your money or your life' at pistol-point. He worked swiftly to play on French fears for Alsace and successfully exploited the anti-Austria foreign minister, Vergennes, who wished to return to the ancient policy of supporting any German state, above all Prussia, in the balance against Austrian power. The celebrated Franco-Austrian alliance, Vergennes pointed out, the alliance to which Maria Antoinette was sacrificed, obliged France to come to Austria's support only in defence of the *status quo*. Frederick himself mobilised. Joseph put an army 80,000 strong on the move towards Bohemia and Moravia.

Frederick had no intention of fighting unless he had to. He was sixty-six years old, a crooked, dried-up, bitter little man, still all whipcord; but although he had stretched himself and his country to the limit in pusuit of power and glory, there was still plenty of life left in him. Joseph was just thirty years younger, untried, frustrated, greedy to prove himself and, in his strange mixed-up way, unable to see that he must choose between the good government to which he genuinely aspired and military fame. His admiration for Frederick was intense, but it paled beside his admiration for himself. To prove himself, he had to show that he was a better general than the greatest soldier of the age.

Maria Theresa watched in an agony of apprehension. It was worse than Poland. She did not know what to fear most: the shame of committing an act of aggression, or the likely consequences of that act. She appealed to reason. On March 14th she wrote to Joseph in the shadow of the Prussian ultimatum and begged him to think again.

We have to face nothing less than the overthrow of our House and of the Monarchy, even with a complete revolution in Europe. No sacrifice is too great to ward off this disaster. I am prepared for anything that will achieve this end, even the humiliation of my name. Let them call me a coward, a weakling, a dotard, if they like; nothing shall prevent me from extricating Europe from this perilous situation; there is no better way for me to spend the remainder of my unhappy days. I confess by all means that this sacrifice will cost me much, but it is called for and I shall face it steadfastly.

She then went on, for page after page, to expose in detail, province by province, country by country, the unprepared condition of the Empire and the army, as she saw it. And from that, she passed to a consideration of the superb qualities of the Prussian army and the generalship of Frederick. This, she said, in effect, is where we came in. I have been through it all, and I know what to expect. Her beloved Marshal Laudon, in whom she had great faith, was in command of the army in Bohemia, but she saw no good coming of it. Austria stood alone.

Even if our army should be lucky, an initial success would lead to nothing. The winning of two or three battles would not win us any part of Silesia; many campaigns and many years would be needed for that. 1757 was enough to prove to us that our enemy is not to be destroyed so easily. His very mode of warfare is contrived to give him time for recovery. We have to reckon that even if we were lucky we should have to go on fighting for three years, or four. And this would give time for all Europe to join in the struggle to ensure that we do not grow too strong. We are distrusted enough as things are. I cannot think of a single friend or ally on whom we could count. . . .

And she ended her argument and appeal: 'After saying all that I must declare that I cannot be brought always to act against my conscience and my conviction. I am not writing out of pique or personal cowardice. I feel as strong as I was thirty years ago, but I will never connive at the ruin of my House and my States.'

This remarkable document, written out by her secretary, she read aloud herself to Joseph and to Kaunitz whom she had summoned. In vain. Out came the old excuse, still the favourite excuse of politicians everywhere: there is no other way, events have taken charge – the events, of course, being the inevitable consequences of their own past actions. She listened to them. Afterwards, in her own hand, she added the words: 'I tortured myself in vain. . . . If it comes to war, then count on me no more. I shall retire to the Tyrol to end my days in total isolation, lamenting the unhappy destiny of my House and my Peoples and seeking a Christian end to my miserable life.'

She did nothing of the kind. She went on resisting. Joseph was convinced that Frederick was bluffing. Maria Theresa insisted that she knew him better, as she did. She was deeply concerned with the moral aspect of affairs: '. . . unfortunately it is we who are at fault, for we will not speak out clearly. And we cannot speak out because we covet that to which we have no right.'

She had learnt that lesson in a very hard school. Even though, as she had long known, she herself had brought about the Seven Years War by not speaking out clearly, at least Silesia had been hers by right, torn from her by force. But Joseph was now reducing himself to the level of Frederick, nullifying the very principles she had clung to for so long. To complicate matters he appeared to be slightly mad. It was bad enough to have Frederick in his inimitable manner proclaiming himself as the champion of law and order and the defender of the integrity of the Empire, *her* Empire. ('As for me,' he had written to Joseph, 'as a member of the Empire . . . I find myself directly engaged in maintaining the immunities, the liberties, and the rights of the Germanic body. . . . I have no personal interest in the matter.') But Joseph trying to speak with the voice of Frederick was absurd. He had already forgotten his initial boasting to his brother: 'Everybody has their hands full. . . . I flatter myself that this coup will succeed without war, and our acquisitions even though incomplete, will be got for nothing.' Now he wanted nothing less than war. He seemed incapable of thinking of anyone but himself. His mother reminded him in vain that 'the wellbeing of thousands upon thousands of men' was at stake. In his manic mood he could even contemplate defeat with equanimity: what shame could there be from suffering defeat at the hands of 'the hero of the century'? To Frederick himself he wrote in terms that require no comment:

It appears to me that you remember too much that you have been a successful general, that you have an experienced army of 200,000 men, and a colonel who has written a commentary on

the *de bello Gallico* of Caesar. Providence has given this advantage
to several other powers besides Prussia; if it gives your Majesty
pleasure to lead 200,000 men to the field of battle, I shall be
there with the same number; if you wish to discover whether
you are still a successful general, I am ready to satisfy your lust
for fighting. . . .

I hope to find you on the banks of the Elbe, and when we shall
have fought, and given Europe a spectacle of obstinacy, we shall
return our swords to our scabbards.

The thirty-seven-year-old Emperor was not as preposterous as that
all the way through, but we are not here concerned with unravelling
the complexities of a very strange man. We are concerned primarily
with his impact on Maria Theresa, to understand that she had good
reason to fear and to fear for him. She still loved him as her cherished
son. A stranger to Maria Theresa knowing nothing about her but her
weary quarrelling with that son, might well conclude that her professions of profound affection were hypocritical. How could she love
this man, her co-regent, who disagreed so violently with her on
almost every point of substance, who seemed to go out of his way to
torture her? She could love him, and did. To the end of her life she
retained that extraordinary quality, first noticed in her attitude towards her father's mistakes, then, for thirty years, in her relations
with her husband, of being able to love with eyes wide open to the
defects of the beloved object, even when, as with Joseph, the defects
must have seemed to her little short of monstrous. He for his part
knew how to charm when it suited his purpose; to amuse as well.
But his mother found no comfort in him.

It was the same now with Kaunitz, who had already brought her
grief in the squalid affair of Poland. It was Joseph who had the bit
between his teeth in the matter of Bavaria, but it is Kaunitz who
must be blamed for allowing him to bolt. Had Kaunitz made
common cause with Maria Theresa, Joseph would have had to submit
to being overruled. But at first, when it had looked as though a little
skilled blackmail would be sufficient to acquire half Bavaria for
Austria, Kaunitz had encouraged Joseph and actively assisted in the
tortuous intrigue. When he saw that he would have to reckon with
Frederick he began to have second thoughts and envelop himself in

gloom and enigmatic silence. By then things had gone so far that he lacked the courage either to back Joseph to the hilt or to turn round and explain to his impatient Emperor that what had seemed a good idea when Bavaria could be had for nothing made no sense at all if he had to fight Prussia to get it. Instead this man of bold and radical decisions virtually abdicated for the time being, contenting himself with offering elaborate analyses of the situation, for all the world as though he were a backroom civil servant, and exasperating Maria Theresa by 'never saying what he thinks'. He never was to say.

What followed was sheer farce. Joseph and his young brother Maximilian, amiable and unambitious, 'a neither here nor there kind of youth', in the words of a contemporary English visitor to the Court at Vienna, set off on an April dawn in a state of high emotion to join the troops in Bohemia. Frederick and his brother, Prince Henry, were waiting for them, commanding some 160,000 men and over 850 guns. When the young Emperor arrived to take over the supreme command from Laudon he had all told, deployed behind the Elbe, nearly 200,000 men and nearly 700 guns. For those days these were extremely powerful and unwieldy forces. They were destined never to clash. Frederick had no intention of fighting unless fighting was forced upon him. He had had his share of military glory; he wanted no more immediate territorial gains. It had cost him quite enough to mobilise and bring his armies into Bohemia; he was prepared to let them sit there, live off the country, die of disease; but he was not prepared to risk them, still less his guns and ammunition, in a pitched battle which would cost him a great deal in replacements even if he won. Loudon, for his part, was equally anxious to avoid fighting. He thought the war absurd, referred to it as 'this political dog of a war', and suddenly showed himself, this man who knew so well how to strike decisively, a devotee of that mid-eighteenth-century warfare of manoeuvre, marching and countermarching, which first Frederick, then he himself, had long ago consigned to limbo. This left Joseph fretting for a glorious and decisive battle. But he had no idea of how to organise a major attack, and, in any case, inhibited from pressing too strongly for a wholehearted committal of the Austrian forces by the opposition of his mother and the lukewarmness of Kaunitz in Vienna.

All that happened was that large tracts of Bohemia, barely recovered from the ruin of the Seven Years War, were once more ravaged – by the Prussians, raiding and eating up everything in sight like a plague of locusts, by the Austrians seeking to deny the enemy further sustenance.

Maria Theresa was indeed active. Without consulting Joseph she took advantage of the deadlock to send a secret messenger to Frederick urging that in the name of common sense there was still time to call the whole thing off. This was not treachery. She had had two letters from Joseph expressing his complete frustration and despair. In one of them he had written: 'If there were some means of making peace under honourable conditions it would be a great relief.' Maria Theresa thought she saw the means. She was driven now not only by her original fears – fear for the good repute of her dynasty, of the misery which war must bring to her people, of the possibility of military disaster – but also by extreme concern for the personal safety of Joseph and Maximilian. If the Emperor in the field felt unable to initiate a move towards peace, she in Vienna suffered no such inhibitions. But she had misread Joseph's mind. He had written from the depths of frustration and self-doubt; now he had pulled himself together and was his old self again, determined to strike and strike hard. His mother's intervention for a moment blinded him with rage, and it took all Laudon's steadiness and patience to prevent him throwing in his hand and rushing off, not back to Vienna, but to demonstrative retirement in Italy.

Instead he stayed on and stuck it out through a terrible winter of hopeless inactivity. His great armies were reduced to living on potatoes which they dug from the sodden fields, their morale in steep decline. While the central finances in Vienna quietly melted away, the supply system collapsed entirely. It was not enough for Joseph to live among his men and share their hardships: at first they had admired him and respected him for this, for his personal courage too. But what was it all for, and where would it end? Frederick's troops were also dying fast of exposure and disease, but Frederick was prepared to stick it out. Joseph was caught between two immovable forces: his mother's determination to bring this sad war to an end and Frederick's determination not to fight. Frederick had more than time on his side. He was receiving good news from Russia. Catherine, with Turkey for the time being out of the way, and with time to turn outwards again after the suppression of the most terrible of all Russian peasant rebellions, saw profit in presenting herself as a European arbiter, giving point to her new ambition by moving troops up to the Galician frontier. And in face of this new imponderable Joseph gave up. The peace of Teschen of May 13th, 1779, Maria Theresa's sixty-third birthday, added to his natural bitterness: the humiliation of that absurd but very costly war was to fester in his heart and, after his mother's death, drive him to further disastrous military adventures in an attempt to realise his broken dream of military glory. His own personal defeat counted with him far more than the historical meaning of that defeat. Prussia had maintained her new position in Germany without fighting; more, she had presented herself effectively as the grand protector of the lesser German states. Russia, lately strengthened by her first slice of Poland and her immense acquisitions at the expense of Turkey, which had brought her to the Black Sea and the lower Danube, now, by appearing as the guarantor of the Peace of Teschen, was finally established as a European power with a voice in the affairs of Germany. Maria Theresa, with less than two years to live, experienced such deep relief at the liquidation of the war, which, in the end, brought to her only the narrow strip of the Innviertel between Upper Austria and the Tyrol, that she could think of nothing else.

> I am overjoyed. Everybody knows that I have no partiality for Frederick, but I have to do him justice now and recognise that he has acted nobly. He has promised to make peace on reasonable conditions, and he has kept his word. For me it is an inexpressible happiness to have prevented a great effusion of blood.

The real thoughts of Kaunitz about this whole ill-conceived operation which would never have been mounted but for his own failure of vision, or carried through, once he saw the danger, but for his dereliction of duty, have never been revealed.

Chapter Nineteen

Reaction and Enlightenment

It was against this background that the reforms of Maria Theresa's last decade took shape, as also the conflicts between mother and son, Empress and Emperor, arising from them. It is impossible to penetrate Maria Theresa's mood unless it is remembered, as it rarely is remembered, that in 1772–73, and again in 1777–78, she was wrestling with Joseph, and with Kaunitz too, using all her strength, to frustrate two of the more disreputable actions of eighteenth-century history: the Partition of Poland and the War of the Bavarian Succession. When she came into head-on collision with her son on other matters she was not colliding with him in a void. She was not opposing simply the new ideas of a representative of a younger generation (this came into it too). She was bringing all her tremendous weight and authority to bear against the policies of a man whom she loved with all the Habsburg possessiveness and more besides, who had yet shocked her to the depths of her being by betraying all her ideas of decency and honour. After 1772 how could she trust him in any way at all?

Conflict, of course, had begun much earlier. At first it was his attitude that she found hard to bear. With a modicum of tact, of common sense even, Joseph could have carried her a long way in the direction he wanted to go. The tragedy was that more often than not it was the necessary direction. In theory Joseph was the model of the enlightened despot; in practice his reforming actions appeared arbitrary and harsh. Charity he possessed, but it was a selective charity, undermined and often rendered null by uncomprehending contempt. Humility he lacked entirely. He wore his hair shirt like a blazon. Throughout the fifteen years of his co-regency there is no recorded instance of his seeking to persuade. From the very first he set the tone and started laying down the law which he had no authority to impose. He was still only twenty-four when he informed his mother as to the correct manner of conducting affairs:

> Instead of twelve ministers and councillors, one man should be at the head of the internal administration. Instead of limiting and checking zeal and activity, rewards and punishments should be awarded. . . . The task of the councillors should be to see that the imperial decrees are carried out, to listen to complaints, to decide upon the enactments of the ministers, and to settle conflicts among them.

It was not unnatural for his mother, who had been managing people fairly well from the days when she carried Joseph in her womb, to raise her eyebrows as this peremptory young man went at things headlong, regardless of national, provincial or individual susceptibilities. Where Joseph's own interests were concerned it was wanton foolishness. He had great potential power: through the Empress he could have exercised virtually total power if he had shown that he was capable of using it wisely. Had he been interested more in the fulfilment of his aims and less in getting his own way, and being seen to have got it, he could have achieved greatness. But he hectored. It was only to be expected that he should regard his mother as an outdated obstacle to progress. But his failure to comprehend, or even desire to comprehend, her nature, her particular greatness, her weaknesses, her prejudices and convictions, to say nothing of the magnitude of her past achievements, made him, for all his exalted station, one with those drearily destructive figures, the rebel, ignorant of the past he has set his face against. Worse, he could never refrain from jeering, and in so doing he was a traitor to his own purposes. He could not conduct an argument about education without sneering at those

> good souls [he meant his mother and her friends] who believe that they have done everything possible to form the character of

a great statesman when their son attends Mass, tells his beads, confesses once a fortnight, and never looks into a book which the narrow understanding of his spiritual director has branded as objectionable. Would anyone venture to dissent from the general verdict, 'That is a charming young man. How well he has been brought up'? True enough, I would agree, if our State was a cloister and the neighbouring peoples monks!

Again, writing of the new Pope, Lorenzo Ganganelli, Clement XIV, who was to suppress the Jesuits, so close to Maria Theresa's heart, and whose election he had helped to engineer, he chose to introduce him to his mother in a deliberately offensive way: 'This new Pope, who is of the lowest origin, whose brother is still a cabinet-maker and whose nephew plays the violin in taverns, will thoroughly displease the whole Roman nobility, especially the Jesuits, whose sworn enemy he has always been.'

Time and time again Maria Theresa found herself stiffening in opposition not because of Joseph's positive ideas but because he lacked both common sense and common politeness. She had always been too tender towards the more useless members of the nobility who moved about her court and sponged on her, and she knew it. But she had also done a good deal to promote, encourage and protect gifted individuals of low birth. Joseph could have made her do a great deal more if he had gone about it quietly. Instead he had to rail against hereditary privilege in general and the idle rich in particular:

If he has means, every family tries to capture him and uses its influence at court to create a position for him, regardless of his abilities, in order that he should marry somebody's daughter or niece. The title of Privy Councillor cannot be denied him, no matter how much of a fool, simply because once upon a time there was a sensible and honest individual in his family. . . . If the court and ministers would not only withhold honours from all these vapid and useless members, but would also regard them with contempt, there would soon be a change.

How true! Maria Theresa no doubt sighed to herself. But also how like dear Joseph not to perceive that what is sauce for the goose is sauce for the gander! Where would Habsburg be if merit was all, ancestry nothing?

His own hereditary privilege he accepted without question. He was loftily conscious of it. 'If I conversed only with my equals,' he once retorted to a comment on his democratic ways, 'I should have to spend my days in the imperial vault.' He treated not merely the idlers but also worthy and able noblemen with perfect disdain, though he might hobnob with a drayman. Maria Theresa watched at first with incredulity, then with dismay, then anger as he set about snubbing men of great distinction who had served her for decades. After one particular episode she finally let herself go:

> Do you honestly imagine that you can keep faithful servants by behaving in this manner? I fear very much that you will become the tool of rascals who, to achieve their own ends, will put up with treatment from you of a kind that no truly devoted soul could tolerate . . . but what hurts me most of all was that you spoke as you did not in sudden anger, but twenty-four hours after you had heard the news; that is to say, you decided after full reflection to plant a dagger in the hearts of men whom you yourself regard most highly and whom you have exerted yourself to keep at our side, with your sarcasm and your exaggerated reproaches. . . . And it is not the Emperor, not the co-regent who utters such biting, sarcastic, ugly words: they come from the heart of Joseph. It is this that fills me with alarm, it is this which will spell the wreck of your own life and the downfall of the monarchy and all of us. I have flattered myself that I should live on in your heart when I am dead, that your great family like your States will lose nothing by my absence, would rather gain. Can I go on hoping this when you go on in a way that excludes all kindness, all friendship?

She goes on to suggest an analogy between Joseph's behaviour and Frederick of Prussia, whom Joseph so deeply admired:

> Has he a single friend? Is he not compelled to distrust the whole world? What a life when there is no humanity! No matter how great your talents, you cannot know everything. Beware of falling into spiteful ways! Your heart is not yet evil, but it will

become so! It is high time you ceased taking pleasure in witticisms and clever remarks which do nothing but wound others or hold them up to ridicule, so that all decent men hold aloof.

At this point she allowed her disgust and indignation to boil over, to remind her son that she too had a tongue and could wound:

You are an intellectual cocotte. You chase after what seem to you clever ideas without the least shadow of discrimination. You catch on to any idle word-play, any telling phrase you read in a book or overhear in conversation and come out with it yourself at the first opportunity, without asking whether it is relevant or not.

She was so upset that she finished suddenly and, unconsciously, ambiguously: 'I ask nothing, nothing, but that you should be treasured and loved by all the world as you deserve.'

The amazing thing was that mother and son managed to work together, somehow, for fifteen years. Now Maria Theresa would be threatening to retire, now Joseph – and now Kaunitz, caught between the two. But all three of them went on. Compromise on any issue was rare. Maria Theresa had learnt to compromise since those terrible days at the outset of her reign when, facing Frederick, she had refused to yield an inch. But Joseph did not know what compromise was. Sometimes he got his way by exerting intolerable pressure, as in the matter of the first Partition of Poland; sometimes Maria Theresa got hers, as in the matter of religious toleration, by refusing to give ground. The tragedy was, from her point of view – from the point of view of the monarchy too – that Joseph's crass and overbearing demands, all along the line, gave her no time to think. Her own natural conservatism was stiffened by the constant challenge of his radicalism. Naturally as she aged she became more set in her ways. Added to this, as her old advisers died or became enfeebled, she felt ever more vulnerable and alone. In the end, she ceased to grow. She was aware of this, and sometimes it made her desperate. Thus once in 1773, when Joseph formally wrote asking to be allowed to resign from the co-regency, she spoke her heart:

I must confess that my capabilities, my looks, my hearing, my skill are swiftly declining, and that the weakness which I have

dreaded all my life is indecisiveness, made worse by discouragement and lack of faithful servants. The loss of you, of Kaunitz,
the death of all my faithful advisers, the irreligion, the de-
terioration of morals, the jargon which everybody uses and which
I do not understand, all these are enough to overwhelm me. I
offer you my whole confidence and beg you to point out any
mistakes I may make. . . . Help a mother who for thirty-three
years has had only you, a mother who lives in loneliness, and
who will die when she sees all her efforts and her sorrows gone
to waste. Tell me what you wish, and I will do it.

Joseph did not resign. Maria Theresa did not accommodate herself
to all his wishes. The business of the realm went on.

There were reforms in education, in justice, in the condition of the
peasants, in administration, in trade and finance, in the censorship.
By 1780, when Maria Theresa died, the state had been transformed.
The one thing she was adamant about was heresy: there was to be no
toleration of Protestantism. And it was Joseph's inability, or refusal,
to see that he must in this matter proceed with an extremity of care
which brought out the stubborness in her more than any other single
thing. Her religion, hitherto taken cheerfully, unthinkingly, for
granted, worn loosely like a garment, now became her armour. She
herself in the past had been at considerable pains to separate, as she
saw it, the true faith from its associated superstitions. In face of papal
disapproval she had heavily reduced the number of feast days and
fast days in the interests of secular needs. She had curtailed the
activities of the Jesuits, whom she loved. In 1773 she had most
reluctantly, and grieving, assented to the publishing of Clement's
Bull dissolving the Austrian Province of the Society of Jesus – though
making sure that this was sufficiently delayed to enable the Jesuits to
realise their assets and gather together their property before they
migrated elsewhere – mostly to Protestant Prussia, where the atheist
Frederick knew how to find a use for them. She knew very well that a
reform of the monasteries was overdue, and if properly handled,
would have agreed to the suppression of some of them (immediately
after her death Joseph was to reduce them in number from 2,163 to
1,065 and to collect over the next nine years some 60 million gulden
to be used as a special fund for the welfare of the state). But faced

with the demand to treat the Catholic Church like any other church, she refused absolutely to move.

> Among the many fundamental principles [she wrote in 1775], the three most important are: Free exercise of religion, which no Catholic prince can permit without heavy responsibility; the destruction of the nobility . . . for which I see neither the necessity nor the justice; and the so frequently repeated liberty in everything. . . . I am too old to accommodate myself to such ideas, and only pray to God that my successor will never try them.

And again, in 1777:

> There can be nothing more ruinous than your persistence in religious toleration. . . . But I still hope, and will not cease to pray and let more worthy persons pray, that God will preserve you from such misfortune, the greatest disaster that ever afflicted the Monarchy. In your striving to save useful workers you will destroy the state and cause the damnation of innumerable souls.

That was in reply to a letter from Joseph, written from Paris, stimulated by his mother's reaction to a mass conversion of some ten thousand Moravians to Protestantism:

> Things cannot be done by halves [he wrote]. Either complete freedom of religion, or you must drive out of your lands everyone who does not believe as you do. . . . To drive away the living, good farmers and excellent subjects, in order to save the souls of the dead — What arrogance of power! . . . To save people's souls in spite of themselves, to coerce their conscience! So long as men serve the state, obey the laws of nature and society, and do not dishonour your Supreme Being — what right has a temporal ruler to interfere in other matters . . .? This is my conviction, and Your Majesty knows it; and I hope I shall never be forced to change my mind.

Maria Theresa thought she had not only the right but also the positive duty to save as many souls as she could, regardless of whether they wanted to be saved or not. She also, like Joseph (himself never an atheist, but a good Catholic), had an eye to utility. If Joseph feared the wholesale emigration of useful workers as a result of his mother's bigotry, Maria Theresa saw the ruin of the state as a result of religious freedom:

> What, without a dominant religion? Toleration, indifferentism, are precisely the means to undermine everything. . . . What other restraint exists? None. Neither the gallows nor the wheel . . . I speak politically now, not as a Christian. Nothing is so necessary and beneficial as religion. Would you allow everyone to act according to his fantasy? If there were no fixed cult, no subjection to the Church, where should we be? The law of might would take command.

Alas, the law of might now took over in Moravia. First Maria Theresa sent out men to set up new churches. Then she despatched troops to drive people into them. Those who resisted were not hung or broken on the wheel, but the more stubborn were exiled to the remote Carpathian mountains, others were conscripted into the army, forced to do hard labour, or, in the case of women, sent to the workhouse.

Joseph, back from Paris, and gone to Moravia to see things for himself, was beside himself with rage. Again he offered to resign. Maria Theresa for once found herself on the defensive and tried to blame the State Council for the decree. But she pulled herself together: 'I do not believe it when you say that my actions and ordinances cause you shame. You go a little too far in your ideas. In a private person such activity is admirable, but he who commands must reflect and act according to the laws of the land . . .'

Once more the resignation threat. In the end, as so often, the whole affair was resolved by Kaunitz. After a deputation of Moravian Protestants come to plead with Joseph in Vienna had been arrested on Maria Theresa's orders, Kaunitz, seeing that a disastrous explosion was inevitable if mother and son were left to themselves, at last intervened on Joseph's side. He knew how to appeal to the deep humanitarian as well as the deeper religious side of Maria Theresa, where Joseph could argue only in utilitarian terms. So the delegation was sent home and the Protestants were in future left alone.

2

I have dwelt on this quarrel in some detail because, together with the Polish and Bavarian crises, it goes to the heart of the relationship between mother and son, Empress and Emperor. It also shows, better than anything else, what lay behind the public image of Maria Theresa in her last decade, the image of the complaining widow, perpetually in mourning, withdrawn from the world, and opposing with all the bigotry of a Catholic fanatic her son's attempts at secular reform.

It is a pity that the most voluble foreign travellers did not begin to flock to Vienna and Prague until this time (Lady Mary Wortley Montagu, on her way to join her husband in Turkey half a century earlier, was an exception). And it is ironic that Vienna now attracted them precisely because Maria Theresa had made it worth visiting. They heard all the gossip about her bigotry, about the unremitting rigour with which she pursued immorality of every kind. They found a stout old woman, her face marked not only with smallpox from that dreadful year of 1767 but also scarred by a more recent carriage accident. They heard of her morbid posthumous devotion to her dead husband. Thus, according to William Wraxall:

> Maria Theresa never fails to repair on the eighteenth of every month, very early in the morning, to the vault of the convent of the Capucins in Vienna, where his remains are deposited. Even in winter she is there long before dawn, notwithstanding the rigour of the season and her many infirmities. The vault is lighted up, while on her knees she pours out supplications for the repose of his soul. The whole month of August she considers as a penitential time, dedicated to his memory; and she generally passes it at the palace of Schönbrunn, in a sort of gloomy and devout retirement amidst masses, Requiems and services for the dead.

But, as with Victoria of England, a hundred years later, a great deal was going on behind the image of retreat. As we have seen in the matter of religious toleration, she was still very much the Empress, and she worked hard, looking into everything. Her working day began earlier now. Instead of getting up at eight as she had done under the old Tarouca programme, she would be up at five or six, hear Mass, drink a cup of *café au lait*, and set to work solidly until midday, when she would hear Mass again before eating her midday meal, often quite alone. Back to work until six, and then for the first time she would be accessible to her family (apart from Joseph, who counted as work). Then the two unmarried daughters, Marianne and Elisabeth, who still lived with her and dragged out null and weary lives, were required to present themselves and report on how they had spent the day. Then a light supper and early to her room at 8.30 p.m. But she did not go to bed. This was her time for writing.

These were the days when, in summer, she could be seen on the covered terrace overlooking the gardens at Schönbrunn, which she could reach from her own apartments without climbing any stairs. 'A sentinel, stationed at the entrance, prevents all interruption; and the Empress has a little box, which is buckled round her waist, full of papers, letters and memorials. She peruses them all, remains four or five hours at a time in this employment, marks such as appear to deserve attention, and enters in the minutest detail upon every point.'

It all sounds very sober, very passive, rather pathetically in-effectual. It was not like that at all. Nobody would guess from this description that Maria Theresa still liked receiving visitors, strangers, whom she would question eagerly, and charm. Nobody would guess that she liked nothing better than to trot off in her coach to Pressburg to spend cheerful hours in the company of her daughter Marie Christine and her son-in-law Albert of Saxony (now the Hungarian Palatine). She would ask Joseph to go with her, and Joseph would usually refuse: he had better things to do than immerse himself in family gossip, and he was perpetually irritated by his mother's lavish spending on that particular part of the family – 'My *dear* brother-in-law' he always called Albert. Nobody would guess that this old woman who appeared to be always reading was in fact giving orders, arguing incessantly, not only in bitter conflict with Joseph but also, amicably, with Kaunitz, with Migazzi, the Cardinal Archbishop of Vienna, with Sonnenfels, the brilliant converted Jew, jurist, connoisseur and man of state, who was her new link with the spirit of the times, not only about domestic affairs but about Joseph's expansionist policies in Poland and Bavaria. Nobody would guess that she revelled in her grandchildren and devoted long hours to a remarkable correspondence with her married children. Nobody would guess that from 1770 to the day of her death she was engaged in a sideline, a career in itself, which consisted of trying in vain to teach Marie Antoinette in Versailles to be a wife and queen.

3

Her positive achievements during this long period of strife and sadness, sometimes depondency, were remarkable indeed. Her religion, as we have seen, had always been the fixed point of her life. But after the death of Francis, and under the impact of her son's demands, what had started as an unquestioning faith, warm and benign, became obsessional, rigid, and harsh; it was the contrast, on the one hand, between the rigidity of her orthodoxy and, on the other, the experimental empiricism of her social policies, which complicated the steady forward movement from her father's unspeculative obscurantism to the emergence of her son as the supreme example of the 'enlightened despot' of the age of reason. In all things secular Maria Theresa herself belonged, without knowing it, to the age of reason, and she was far less of a despot than her son. It was Maria Theresa, not Joseph, who presided over the rapid transition from feudalism to bureaucratic centralism, compressing into forty years a development which elsewhere had taken, or was to take, very much longer.

For one who travelled little about her realm she had a remarkable appreciation of its diversity. She appeared to know by instinct how at least the most important of her peoples felt. It was not only that she alone among the Habsburgs knew how to handle the Magyars. She was also aware of the widely differing characteristics of, for example, the German mountain peasants of the Tirol, who had never known serfdom (though their lives were desperately hard) and the Slovenes of Carinthia and Styria, exploited by the great landowners. We saw her, early in her reign, determined to arm the Czechs of Moravia against the Prussians. Again, in Bohemia, she showed prescience in encouraging the use of the Czech language and the employment of Czech officials. She fought intermittently all her life against the pretensions of her nobles, above all in Bohemia and Moravia, although she needed their support and enjoyed their company. In a very late letter to Marie Christine, discussing chiefly family affairs, she could slip in a sharp aside to the effect that the Bohemian nobility were, as usual, behaving abominably.

The abolition of serfdom was left to Joseph after her death; but in her last decade she worked hard to lessen its rigours in face of heavy obstruction both from the landowners and from a suspicious peasantry: almost every Land and province had its own variation of serfdom, from the mild to the extremely harsh, based in immemorial local custom or in special privileges granted the landowners at various times by previous Habsburgs. It was a hopeless tangle of rights and duties which she sought to straighten out by issuing a series of Patents, most of them revisions of much earlier enactments, laying down the maximum dues or services payable by the peasants to their lords. The first of these, for part of Hungary, was issued as early as 1756, by personal Rescript, without the approval of the Hungarian Diet. But the great movement did not begin to get under way until 1771. In 1769 the peasants of Silesia struck against the *robot* and Maria Theresa set up a Commission of Enquiry, first for Silesia, then for Bohemia and Moravia. It was then found that the mass of the peasants were living in fearful poverty and a state of near-starvation, which sometimes became actual starvation. Maria Theresa had, of course, known that these lands had suffered terribly through the ravages of the Seven Years War, but the population had been rapidly increasing, and thus she had been deceived by the resultant gross increase in productivity into assuming that things were much better than in fact they were. She was surprised and horrified by what she found.

The first thing she decided was that no matter what the legal position was, no matter how much the landowners, the communes, the Church could legitimately expect in the way of dues and taxes, the individual peasant must be put into the position of being able 'to support himself and his family, and also to pay his share of the national expenditure in times of peace or war'. In other words the peasantry from now on were to function primarily as self-supporting family units with a duty to the state, only secondarily as contributors to the wealth of landlords. In fact these Patents, for one reason or another, turned out to be far less radical in practice than they were in intention, and it was left to Joseph after his mother's death to carry the idea to its logical conclusion. But Maria Theresa's intention was clear, and her peasant reforms offer a good illustration of the workings of her mind, in which a genuine and warm humanitarian impulse worked together with a clearheaded utilitarianism. The peasants must be raised up because it was wrong that the weak should suffer; it was also expedient to treat them well because they were needed in the interests of the economy, an economy that had improved out of recognition as a result of careful management and the Haugwitz reforms, so that in 1775 the miracle happened, and the budget was balanced for the first time in memory. But she was still extravagant, and still able to undo the effect of great and wise saving by making immense presents to loyal servants who had run themselves into trouble by their own extravagance.

Her later educational reforms were the fruit of the same spirit. Just as after the War of the Succession she had done much to improve higher education, so, in her last decade, she tackled primary education on a very broad front. During her reign the population of the monarchy more than doubled itself and was yet still below strength from an economic point of view. She saw the need for greatly improved elementary education if all her peoples were to be employed to the advantage of her realm. There was no incipient egalitarianism here. She herself did not speak of the mob, or the rabble, but her senior officials could do so, unrebuked, in their letters and despatches to her. She herself was moved above all by her detestation of superstition in all its forms: she did not wish to educate the children of the masses above their station, but she was determined to educate them out of superstition and into a decent, sensible and clearheaded outlook.

Her earlier reforms had been obstructed by the Jesuits, whom she loved so much, but who clung to their old formalities, neglecting the teaching of good German in favour of Latin. But in 1770 she saw the need for a far more radical approach, and so urgently did she feel about it that she brought herself to ask Frederick of Prussia for permission to consult the experience of the famous educationist, the Augustinian bishop, Felbiger, whose methods, particularly as demonstrated in his own school at Sagan in Prussian Silesia, were far ahead of his time. Frederick was amused to be of service to his old enemy, and four priests from the Tirol were sent to Sagan to learn what they could. Felbiger's influence was strong in the new school system established in 1775. The Jesuits could obstruct no longer, since their Order had been banned, but still in the new schools village priests had to act as schoolmasters.

There were to be three sorts of school: the *Normalschule*, which was the model, set up in each Land; the *Hauptschule*, of which there was at least one in every district; the *Trivialschule*, one in every small town and in every rural parish. All children of both sexes had to attend from between the ages of six and twelve. In the country children up to eight years old attended the summer school, from Easter to the end of September, while all from eight to twelve attended the winter school, from December 1st to March 31st, so that they could help with the farm work in the summer. There were special refresher schools – two hours each Sunday after Mass for youngsters between thirteen and twenty.

Naturally, as in most reforms, the situation looked better on paper than it did in practice. The shortage of teachers with the right qualification was chronic, and parents frequently objected strongly to the waste of time. In a village near Innsbruck the whole population had to be threatened with prison for boycotting the new school. But, with all its deficiencies, the system was as good as the Prussian one – i.e. the best in Europe – and more comprehensive. With all her other preoccupations Maria Theresa pursued her school-reforms with the determination she had once brought to war. And when she died, five years after the establishment of the new system, she showed her continuing concern by leaving 100,000 gulden out of her private fortune to be distributed by Felbiger among the Normal schools throughout the Empire.

Abhorrence of popular superstition, quite in keeping with the spirit of the Enlightenment which she distrusted so much, was very deeply ingrained in this Christian monarch, who saw nothing of superstition in the dogma and practices of her Church. We have already seen this coming out in her detailed instructions for the education of her own children; and in 1766 she opened a major offensive against belief in ghosts, magic and witchcraft (this had nothing to do with witch-hunting). Van Swieten had to see to it that his censors banned all 'dream and miracle books'; only 'true and accredited miracles' could be related to the *publicum*. She was no less concerned with public health. It was she who took the initiative, as we have seen, in the matter of inoculation against smallpox. Further, in her last decade she issued numerous decrees far ahead of her time. In 1770 she strictly regulated the sale of poisons. Apothecaries were enjoined to use the greatest care in handling and dispensing them. They were required by law to keep a poisons register recording the exact circumstances and quantity of every sale. If the purchaser was unknown to the chemist he had to produce two character witnesses before he could be supplied. Again, three years later, there came a decree forbidding the use of lead in any eating or drinking vessels: only pure tin was permitted.

In this sort of thing Joseph was very much his mother's son. An ordinance about beggars promulgated in 1756, when Joseph was still a child, might have formed a part of the Josephine canon. All beggars, who then proliferated, were required to return to their birthplace and stay there, to be a charge on the local communes. This milestone towards a poor law expressed very clearly Maria Theresa's practical, empirical, one-step-at-a-time cast of mind. There was nothing theoretical about it. Joseph was all theory, some of it good, some absurd, some downright injurious, rarely commonsensical. It was not so much the enactment of social reform that was meant by Josephinism as a coldly rational attitude, a highly personal expression of the Age of Reason, compounded very strangely indeed with a profound belief in the validity of absolute despotism, Joseph's own despotism, which was not rational at all, but, rather, the rationalisation of a temperamental bias.

Nothing shows more sharply the vital difference between mother and son than their several attempts to tidy up the disposal of the dead. Maria Theresa, in 1772, deploring the unhygienic and wasteful burial customs, forbade the establishment of any new burial place without the approval of the Land government and, at the same time, ordered the destruction by quicklime of all existing corpses in churchyards, vaults, walls, etc. This was quite enough for a Catholic country to be going on with; but Joseph had to go much further, making himself ridiculous in the process, and being forced by popular opinion to retreat in dudgeon. His mother had sought to regulate burial for purely practical reasons. Joseph had to import a load of theory into his decrees of 1784. It was wrong to glorify a dead man's corpse, the empty husk of the spirit; it was wrong that people should spend more than they could afford on costly and grandiose funerals; it was wrong to use valuable timber and metals in the manufacture of coffins, designed to rot; on top of this was the threat to the living from the vapours arising from corpses crammed together within the city walls. Thus Joseph's first decree laid it down that coffins must be constructed of deal, with flat lids; his second, a few months later, did away with coffins of any kind. Corpses were now to be wrapped in a sheet or enclosed in a linen bag, interred in cemeteries well outside the city and sprinkled with quicklime. Further, all those who died on the same day were to share the same funeral service and be buried in a common grave.

It seems never to have crossed the Emperor's mind that he would offend the deepest instincts of his Viennese. The whole city was up in arms: for the first time an imperial decree provoked a spate of inflammatory and abusive pamphleteering. Within six months Joseph had to retreat before the popular will – and with characteristic lack of grace:

> Since a great many subjects do not wish to understand the reasons for the regulations concerning burial sacks, which were instigated out of regard for the health of the people with a view to accelerating putrefaction; since, moreover, they evince so deep an interest in their bodies, even after death, without appearing to understand that they are then nothing but stinking corpses, His Majesty no longer cares how they bury themselves.

Maria Theresa would never have made a fool of herself in this way (when she did make a fool of herself, as with her intermittent and absurd morality drives, there was nothing grandly theoretical about it: she was being all too human). But in fairness to Joseph (who was himself six years later to be buried in state, dressed in his field marshal's uniform in the imperial vault beneath the Capuchin church), it should be stated that the Josephine spirit was so strong in the hearts and minds of the rapidly multiplying bourgeoisie, typified now by the children of some of Maria Theresa's most enlightened servants and their friends, that the rejection of the cult of the dead found many supporters among them. And it was one of these, van Swieten's son, who in 1791 made himself responsible for the interment of Mozart, arranging the notorious 'third class' funeral in a common grave out of consideration for the widow's purse and in the light of the spirit of the age.

The times, of course, were rough. Travellers in Austria during Maria Theresa's last decade were struck by the multiplicity of gibbets by the roadside, with corpses hanging from them. The wheel was still in use, but it was quickly going out of fashion. A more familiar punishment was a long sentence to the galleys. Life was also brutal. There is nothing to be gained by comparing the Theresian Empire with Catherine's Russia, where conditions were barbaric. But it is worth bearing in mind that this Catherine, who brutalised the Russian peasants to a degree for centuries unsurpassed, ostentatiously entertained the ideas of the Enlightenment, corresponded with Voltaire and Diderot, posed as the benevolent mother of her people, and ridiculed Maria Theresa, who presided over a society no less relatively humane than is twentieth-century English society to the society of Soviet Russia. Catherine was not the first Russian tyrant to disguise her peculiar nastiness as advanced morality; she was not to be the last. It was a transparent disguise; it consisted of the simple declaration, reiterated endlessly, that bad was good. Maria Theresa made no such claims. She groped, with remarkable humility for a woman of autocratic temper, towards the light – and made no bones about her groping.

More to the point, it is well to remember the grossness and brutality of eighteenth-century England. Hogarth died in 1766.

The scenes he painted continued after his death. The savagery of the English penal laws and, later, the sustained brutalities of the industrial revolution, have to be set against the remarkably high level of enlightenment which had permeated, though by no means with uniform thoroughness, both the bourgeois and aristocratic levels of society since the days of Locke and Newton — for nearly a century, that is. The measure of religious toleration in England, so far as dissent was concerned, was a reflection of that enlightenment. Nevertheless, the Gordon Riots flared up in the last year of Maria Theresa's life; and Maria Theresa was justified, according to her lights, in holding up to Joseph the English Protestants as examples of people who knew better than to tolerate their own heretics, in this case Catholics.

But if the degree of statism established by Maria Theresa, and developed furiously by Joseph, was such that Austria would never experience the inhumanities to be inflicted on the people of Britain by laissez-faire capitalism in its sickening heyday, and if the employment of the nobility as Crown officials or representatives in all the lands of the Empire ensured that the monarch would never, as in France, be hopelessly cut off from the people, surrounded by a rabble of aristocratic placemen whose one dread was to be thrown out of Versailles and sent back to their estates, there were curious anomalies. Thus, Dr Burney, who delighted in the company of Gluck and Metastasio, Hasse and Wagenseil, and who was so impressed by the high level of the popular musical culture, above all in Bohemia, was appalled by the brutality of other popular amusements. He quotes from a handbill, 'such as is distributed through the streets [of Vienna] every Sunday and festival', which offers a very crowded afternoon's entertainment, involving the baiting of three wild bulls, one of them stuck with fire-crackers; four bears; a tiger, a wolf and a wild boar. The final and eleventh item read as follows: 'A furious and hungry bear, which has had no food for eight days, will attack a young wild bull and eat him alive on the spot; and if he is unable to complete the business, a wolf will be ready to help him.'

Burney was convinced that there was no longer any bear- or bull-baiting in England. Among the circles in which he moved there was not. He was right in supposing that spectacles of this kind did not take place in London before audiences of 'two or three thousand people, among whom are a great number of ladies'. But he was wrong in believing that the British legislature had formally abolished such entertainments. It was not until 1835 that bull- and bear-baiting was finally abolished in England.

4

Emerging slowly but with rocklike solidity from the shapeless turmoil of popular passion, the teaching of the great secular reformers began to make itself felt: above all in the legal reformers, Karl Anton Martini, Paul Joseph Riegger, professors at Vienna University (who owed their opportunities to Gerhard van Swieten) and their more celebrated pupil, Joseph von Sonnenfels. If it was to Martini, himself inspired by the great judicial reformer the Marchese Cesare Beccaria-Bonesana, that the legal reforms reaching deep into the nineteenth century were due, the man who stood up to Maria Theresa herself, and later to Joseph, was Sonnenfels, the converted Jew.

Maria Theresa detested Jews, but there seems to have been little or no racial prejudice in her attitude. The Jews were heretics. Far worse, they had been responsible for putting Christ to death. They existed, very well: there was no question of killing them. But they were to be kept as far away as possible. In 1745, at the height of the Succession War, the young Queen had gone so far as to expel them from Bohemia. Those who remained in Austria were heavily restricted. It was not until the acquisition of Galicia, with the Polish Partition of 1772, that the Empire suddenly found itself entertaining an entirely new and alien concentration of Jews. As late as 1777, Maria Theresa could write: 'In future no Jew shall be allowed to remain in Vienna without my special permission. I know of no greater plague than this race, which on account of its deceit, usury and avarice is driving my subjects to beggary. Therefore, as far as possible, the Jews are to be kept away and avoided.' If she had not needed their financial talents they would almost certainly have been banished altogether. And here we have an unpleasant gloss on the empiricism and practicality which so often produced admirable results; for she herself borrowed freely from the Jews, though, ludicrously, she could not bring herself to discuss even the most important operations (such as the financing of the building of Schönbrunn by the Jew, Diego d'Aguilar, face to face: she conversed from behind a screen.

Sonnenfels was the one great exception, and this exception was made possible only because he was a Christianised Jew. He came from a family of Brandenburg rabbis, and his father, Lipman Perlin, migrated from Berlin to the Esterházy and Dietrichstein country, first to Eisenstadt, then to Nikolsburg, close to the present-day frontier between Austria and Hungary. Converted to Christianity, and taking the name Wiener, he wrote a treatise on the Holy Communion, and was soon, astonishingly, given a chair at Vienna University. In 1746 he was ennobled and changed his name again, to Sonnenfels. His son went on from there, but with a most curious digression: instead of seeking at once to exploit his father's advantage, he enrolled as a long-service private in the *Deutschmeister* regiment of foot, which enabled him to see the world, or at least far-flung parts of the monarchy, and pick up half a dozen languages in addition to the ones he had learnt at school. It was not until 1754 that he obtained an honourable discharge and started studying law, particularly under Riegger, and at the same time developed a passion for German literature and the ideas of the Enlightenment. It was his self-appointed task from 1761 onwards to bring Austria into the main current of the new European ideas and, among other things, to lay the foundations for a good German theatre and introduce the proper and lucid use of German in affairs of state.

Nobody could have appeared a less promising candidate. He lacked charm; he lacked humour. He was loquacious, pedantic, overbearing. He was fathomlessly vain. But he emerged as the most distinguished luminary of the Austrian Enlightenment in all its forms, becoming so much of a legend that Beethoven, who can have met him barely, if at all, dedicated to him in 1802 his D major piano sonata, opus 22. He also won for himself the active protection of the empress, even though he tried her mercilessly.

She was, for example, extremely proud of her new code of laws, put in train under Haugwitz in the first reforming period and finally published as the *Constitutio Criminalis Theresiana*, after nearly two decades, in 1768–69. Sonnenfels started attacking aspects of this monumental code even before it had been printed; he wrote about it and he lectured. The main points of his attack were directed against the continued employment of torture, against various forms of corporal punishment, more reconditely against the failure to distinguish between convicted prisoners and prisoners awaiting trial, or on remand, above all against capital punishment in the form of breaking on the wheel, impalement, quartering, etc., which still survived. When the Code was formally promulgated on the last day of 1768 he returned to the attack and was immediately assailed by his opponents, above all Cardinal Migazzi, and Count Chotek, who saw in his denunciation of parts of the Empress's cherished *Constitutio* a chance to turn Maria Theresa against this ungodly, subversive and intolerable Jew, whose ideas and influence they feared *in toto*. But although they succeeded in putting a damper on Sonnenfels, even though he had the support of Joseph at this time, and in this matter the unstated approval of Kaunitz, their struggle was long and arduous. It was not until 1772 that Maria Theresa brought herself to forbid him categorically to say anything more in public about either torture or capital punishment.

This was at a time, it is worth remembering, when the Empress had been brought close to despair by the Polish question, and, as we shall see, was exasperated and deeply alarmed by the behaviour of Marie Antoinette at Versailles. If at any time she could have been forgiven for turning on this disturber of the peace, this challenger of her own ideas of propriety, and rending him, it was now. She did nothing of the kind. Sonnenfels, with an extremity of courage which was a measure of the integrity which lay beneath his tiresome and, indeed, frequently offensive manner, refused to be bound. Putting his whole career at risk, he returned to the attack. Until now he had based his arguments on reason, and expediency, with the general idea of challenging Maria Theresa on her own ground. He still did so. But now he injected an element of passion: he made a direct appeal to the Empress's humanity and kindness of heart. And Maria

Theresa was touched and deeply troubled. All the diffidence which, years before, had been remarked by her beloved daughter-in-law, Isabella of Parma, came flooding back. Instead of laying down the law, she consulted one of her most enlightened ministers, Count Blumegen, who said that, although he believed Sonnenfels to be in the right, it was too soon to make a radical revision of the new code: nevertheless, Sonnenfels must be left in freedom to discuss anything he liked, but for this one matter. The Empress, to the fury of the conservatives, who had thought that Sonnenfels had at last fatally overreached himself, acquiesced in this advice. More, very quietly, she allowed the whole matter to be reopened on an official level. Soon it became apparent that most of the provincial governments were agreed that it was time to bring an end to torture. And it was after this that Maria Theresa turned the matter over to Joseph, as previously related: 'I ask the Emperor, who has studied law and, what is more, whose sense of justice, reason and love of humanity I trust, to decide this matter without my advice.'

The upshot was that in January 1776 torture was abolished throughout the Empire, except in Hungary. Maria Theresa was then sixty and had four more years to live.

A French traveller, writing of the opposition between Maria Theresa and Joseph, spoke of the division of opinion in Vienna into two parties, sharply and absolutely opposed.

The first and strongest party is that of the Empress. It consists of Cardinal Migazzi, some monks . . . and a few pious old dames. This party is always full of schemes for chastity-commissions, prohibitions of books, exile of dangerous teachers and preachers, maintenance of papal absolutism, and the persecution of the so-called new philosophy. A large part of the nobility, whose rights are tied up with those of the priests, supports this group.

The second party is that of the Emperor, constantly at war with the other. It stands for reform of justice, the promotion of agriculture, commerce and industry, the undermining of the power of bigotry and its satellites, the diffusion of the new philosophy, the reduction of the unfounded rights of the nobility, and the protection of the weak against the strong.

This *simpliste* view was evidently put about by Joseph's more ignorant or less reputable supporters. But it is a little disconcerting to find it quoted as a true reflection of reality by a reputable twentieth-century American historian. The very concept of Maria Theresa at any time of her life, let alone in her closing years, being associated, however remotely, with a party in any conceivable sense of the word, is nothing but fantasy. She was the monarch. Among her servants and advisers she had her favourites, and at one time and another she met with opposition from all of them, even, as we have seen, Prince Kaunitz. But she was supreme. And no matter how sharply she might find herself in conflict with Joseph, he was the Emperor, also set above the rest of men. The idea of entering into a league against him would never have crossed her mind. Joseph, for his part, would have regarded anyone who thought of him as heading a party of his own as stark mad. Quite a large part of his patronage of the lowly, his ostentatious rejection of extravagance, his great gestures, like throwing open the imperial parks, the Prater and the Augarten, to the Vienna public, was directed less at raising up the humble than at casting down the arrogant and proud. He was the Emperor, *sui generis*, who could agitate against his mother for the abolition of serfdom, the suppression of the monasteries, the streamlining of the state, and who was ready to give the deepest offence to all and everybody, from the highest to the lowest, needing no support from anyone at all.

Indeed Maria Theresa had a weakness for Migazzi, the Cardinal Archbishop, who was the focus of reaction; but Migazzi knew he could not count on her support. She frequently opposed him, as she did the Pope himself. Thus, on the one hand, she attacked him, as it were, from the right, when she defended the Jesuits whom Migazzi was urging the Pope to ban; on the other, from the left, when she defended Sonnenfels against him. Two successive Popes would have been surprised to hear that she was a believer in papal absolutism. We have seen her operating in the fields of education and justice as well as curtailing the 'unfounded rights' of her nobility. We have also glimpsed the manner in, which even before the Haugwitz era, she applied herself to industry, trade and agriculture – at a time when Joseph was still in the cradle. As for the protection of the weak against the strong, this was throughout her life her especial care: any failure here was failure of imagination, never of intention. Indeed, of all the Frenchman's charges, the only ones of real validity were the accusations of bigotry and, to a lesser degree, of obstructing the diffusion of 'the new philosophy'. And we have seen how her bigotry was strengthened by a well-founded distrust of Joseph's motives and her rejection, confirmed in due course by most of her subjects and the general judgment of history, of his attitude and manner. She was an old woman being rushed by a young man in a hurry, and all her prophecies came true.

Joseph, before he died, had his peoples up in arms against him. Lacking both humility and common sense, in the end his spirit was broken by the ingratitude of his subjects, who preferred to live irrationally rather than be torn up by the roots and neatly transplanted in orderly rows by the monarch who knew what was good for them so much better than they. Everything poor Joseph touched turned to dross, and he never saw why. Thus, for example, neither he nor his mother, Germans though they were, had the least national consciousness: they were supranational: the peoples existed to serve the dynasty, and the dynasty must serve them in return. But Maria Theresa, with her fine, her astonishing instinct, knew there was such a thing as local patriotism, and that the best way to harness the different peoples to her cause was to encourage its development. Hence her first great act, the dramatic appeal to the Hungarians in 1741; hence, much later, her efforts to encourage the strengthening of Czech consciousness in Bohemia and Moravia. Joseph altogether lacked this instinct. He undid all his mother's work in Bohemia by developing at a great pace a bureaucracy manned above all by Germans. He did this not because he felt himself German, or because he despised the Czechs, but because there were more able and highly educated Germans among his subjects. The Czechs should be pleased that so many admirable and efficient Germans were dedicating their lives to the administration of Bohemia and Moravia under the eye of the benevolent despot in Vienna. The Czechs were not pleased, as his mother could have told him.

For what she had been doing all her life, hesitantly and at most half consciously, was working towards the liberation of the individual. The masses were seen by her, if only cloudily, as people, with potentialities to be developed, so that they might take their place in a more broadly based society. The masses were going to develop themselves in any case, but it was this extraordinary woman's great achievement to assist them instead of, like some of her contemporaries, suppressing them until they broke out not as individuals but as a mob.

Chapter Twenty

❧

The Burden of the Years

As a letter-writer Maria Theresa was in the same class as the great Victorians. The high peak of her activity was reached after the death of Francis and when her children began to go out into the world. She was sleeping badly now and she must often have spent half the night, endlessly scribbling away in her awkward-looking squarish hand, almost invariably in her own special variety of French, sometimes in her still odder German. Most of her correspondence was with her children, but she had two or three close friends to whom she wrote as well, and she could always be trusted to come up with a warm-hearted message for her old servants or their widows in case of need. It is impossible to judge just how many letters she wrote under the flickering candles in the chilly, draughty elegance of her room in Schönbrunn or the Hofburg. But by the time Maximilian went out into the world to be Grand Master of the Teutonic Order in 1774, only the sickly Marianne and poor Elisabeth, once so lovely, now ruined by the smallpox, stayed at home. Joseph had to be written to a great deal on his frequent travels. The others had letters at least once a fortnight. Some much more often than that.

Most of these have been lost. Maria Theresa insisted that her children and their wives or husbands should burn all her letters, once read, and as a rule, they did so, including her daughter Amelia in Parma, who was running wild and causing her much grief. But Ferdinand and her beloved daughter-in-law, Beatrix d'Este, in Milan, to whom she would sometimes write three or four times a week, kept every one of theirs. Joseph kept many, and so did Marie Antoinette. The Empress herself destroyed all her children's letters, again except those from Joseph and Marie Antoinette: these she kept because they were also documents of state.

In her correspondence with Joseph we have seen her fighting a losing battle to impose her own will without exercising her absolute authority, a sanction which, had she been able to bring herself to employ it, would have been irresistible. Against this sad reading it is necessary to set her letters to her Italian daughter-in-law with whom she could relax. They show that in her heart she was still very much her old self and that her life was by no means all bitterness and tears. 'Here we are,' she wrote on her fifty-ninth birthday, May 13th, 1776, 'at Laxenburg, in the most beautiful weather. Your dear letters and good wishes came just when we were at breakfast under the trees in the garden – the Emperor, that is to say, and the two girls and myself.'

A year later she was very much feeling her age, but she had plenty of spirit:

> Your good wishes, your anxiety about my health, might re-animate a corpse. For your satisfaction be it known to you that I am quite well again – a little feeble, and by no means gay as I think of my sixty years and what they stand for. . . . There is nothing to be gained by growing old: one slackens off, and makes excuses; one loses ground instead of gaining it. Nevertheless, for the moment I am in a mood to devote myself exclusively to the pleasure of keeping alive for you, a tender mother and friend, who has no thought save for your welfare, and to give you love in return for all you give to her.

And a little later:

> I love you so dearly that I assure you I shall take care of myself. I will even coddle myself to make you happy. Only a very powerful motive could make me promise *that*.

She still knew what she liked. Writing to tell Beatrix and Ferdinand that they would find the Duke and Duchess of Gloucester on Lake Garda, where they were going for a holiday, she observed:

'They have two children, who usually go about bare-headed and stockingless, the girls with their hair cut short on their foreheads, like a boy. It is a style I dislike exceedingly. The Princess de Ligne is here with a girl of four got up in the same way. It is really too much. Soon we shall see children running about like negroes with nothing on at all.'

She lived very much for her grandchildren and was always greedy for pictures of them, as well as of their parents: 'Lacy has just been with me,' she wrote to Marie Christine in 1776. 'He found me surrounded by three Mimis and two Alberts. I have the portraits from Schönbrunn here, as well as your new one, which Lacy thought admirable, and so does everybody else.'

And again to Marie Beatrix:

The dear picture of my little granddaughter so long desired has this moment arrived. . . . But it is a frightful painting, and now I sympathise with those who told you not to send me your own picture, if it is at all like that. . . . What a frightful bonnet they have made the child wear. . . . Forgive the comparison but this bonnet reminds me of her worthy grandfather's periwig. . . . In fine, 'tis a horrible painting, but the subject is charming and dear and interesting, and a cause of great joy to me.

Week after week, year after year, for ten years this correspondence continued. During all the trials and frustrations arising from her conflict with Joseph she was able to throw herself into the lives of the family in Milan. Not a detail escaped her, every illness, every little triumph, was faithfully recorded – the prophetess of woe becomes in these letters the gay, tender, self-deprecating mother she could have been had she not also been required to run an Empire.

2

A cause of no joy at all was Marie Antoinette. And in her long series of letters to this errant child in Versailles we see, rising above her impotence in face of Joseph, laying aside the comfortable gossip with her older children, the figure of the Empress, born to command, wise in the ways of the world, level-headed and infinitely practical. But she was an Empress with a guilty conscience. She knew very well that she had failed badly in the upbringing of her youngest daughter. She knew, too, that she had sacrificed this enchanting, silly, feckless, ignorant child in the bleakest of political operations and must take on herself the blame for much that followed.

The political operation was to set the keynote on the grand Bourbon–Habsburg alliance by marrying this barely fifteen-year-old child to the Dauphin of France, himself only sixteen. It was launched in 1766, when Marie Antoinette was eleven years old, and achieved in 1770. During all these years Maria Theresa had time to prepare her daughter for the ordeal ahead. But for two years she did nothing (she was, of course, engaged in pulling herself together after her husband's death and taking the measure of the new Emperor, but it was a bad failure of imagination, all the same). Suddenly, when the child was thirteen, her mother woke up to the fact that she was virtually illiterate and that her French was atrocious. These matters must be remedied at once. What could be easier? The child was highly intelligent, quick to learn when she wanted. She had wonderful grace, she was gay, high-spirited, warm-hearted. Life would take care of her, but two things she must learn: to speak French correctly and to dance in proper style instead of romping. The great Noverre should be her dancing master; two actors from the French company in Vienna should teach her French.

Maria Theresa was surprised when Versailles, hearing of this, objected: the future Queen of France must not mix with strolling players. She revealed herself here. She would have felt the same about any future queen of Hungary. So Versailles now supplied a suitable tutor, the respected Abbé Vermond, Archbishop of Toulouse, who found, as so many were to find, that quick and clever as she was, Marie Antoinette was incapable of concentration or serious application of any kind. The Habsburgs were rarely brilliant, rarely deep thinkers, sometimes dull or feeble; but they had rarely been irresponsible or flighty, as Joseph was in his way and his youngest sister in hers, as Amelia in Parma was too. The last thing Maria Theresa would have allowed herself to think was that her husband had brought into the family a new and alien strain, incompatible with the pretensions of the first and most solemn house in Europe; but there seems no doubt that this was the case. Her own mistake, apart from her failure to give adequate supervision and discipline in the nursery, was to assume that childish high spirits and idleness could be banished the moment duty called. Who, after all, was she to stop her children enjoying their youth? None of them romped more, played or danced harder than she herself had done so long ago. It is clear from the long missives which she wrote for some, perhaps for all, her children when they went out into the world that, perturbed though she might be by this or that failure, shortcoming or delinquency, she took it quite for granted that all had in them at least a measure of the character which had transformed the gay and ignorant young woman she had herself been so long ago into a monarch of formidable parts.

Poor Marie Antoinette had character, but of a different sort; and the life she entered in her sixteenth year at the court of Louis XV was the very one most precisely calculated to stifle it before it could begin to develop. After years of extravagance and nonsense during which she indulged her empty-headedness in search of pleasure on a scale that became legendary, the woman that might have been at last emerged, but not until she was alone, without a throne, her husband executed, and she herself, as Widow Capet, waiting, stripped bare, for trial and the guillotine.

From the very beginning, from the moment of the child's departure from Vienna, Maria Theresa was touched by a foreboding which at times was no more than a well-founded apprehension about her daughter's adequacy for the role she must sustain, but which sometimes assumed an almost prophetic depth. In the last weeks she had had the child sleep with her in her own room, seeking to make up in a sort of crash course her deficiencies of understanding. The letter she gave her to take with her was longer and far more explicit than anything she had committed to paper for her other children, and she made the unfortunate child swear solemnly to read it religiously every month (her young brother Maximilian was let off with an exhortation to read his own special instructions at least once a year). She also made elaborate and efficient arrangements to ensure that she was perfectly informed about all her daughter's words and actions once she was established in her new home. One of her most trusted and subtle servants, Count Mercy d'Argenteau, the imperial ambassador to the Court at Versailles, was appointed, unofficially and confidentially, as the Empress's spy.

Or this is what his enemies would have called him; no doubt Marie Antoinette would have agreed had she the faintest idea of the detail and intimacy of his reports to her mother. Maria Theresa did not see it like that at all. As she put it in her first long letter to Mercy: 'I am apprehensive about my daughter's youth, her susceptibility to flattery, her idleness, her disinclination for any serious activity.' Mercy was to keep her out of danger, as best he could directly, otherwise by warning the empress in good time so that she herself might intervene. Once again Maria Theresa chose well. Born in the Low Countries, a man of personal distinction, infinite tact, compassionate and kind, but skilled in the ways of the world and very shrewd, an intriguer into the bargain, Mercy needed only ambition to make him a great figure. He had no desire to be a great figure. He was a rich and comfortable bachelor; he enjoyed being in the Court without being of it; he did not even wish to be a power behind the throne; he was happy to serve his Empress; and he was utterly discreet. He was more discreet, indeed, than Maria Theresa herself, who assured him that she would burn his letters with her own hand and not show them to anyone, not even to Joseph or Kaunitz. Quite often she did show them, and even had parts of them copied. It was one of Kaunitz's hidden strengths that he was never in the least jealous of Maria Theresa's 'secret' consultations with other advisers. She liked to keep in personal and private communication with quite a number of her ambassadors: it gave her the feeling that she had her finger on the pulse of things. But Kaunitz knew everything: there were no secrets from him. He thought it gave his mistress harmless pleasure of a therapeutic kind, and he was so unashamedly confident of his own information and views and ability that the idea that he might be undermined by secret intrigue never entered his head. Indeed, even before the wedding of Marie Antoinette, he had written to Mercy at Versailles suggesting, precisely, that it would give the Empress great pleasure and do no harm if he, Mercy, cared to write to her from time to time for her eye alone.

Thus arose the remarkable parallel correspondence between the Empress and Mercy and the empress and her daughter. Very quickly the ambassador established his sources, covering every moment of the livelong day:

I have made sure of three persons in the service of the Archduchess, one of her women and two of her menservants, who give me full reports of what goes on. Then, from day to day, I am told of the conversations she has with Abbé Vermond, from whom she hides nothing. Besides this, the Marquise de Durfort passes on to me everything she says to her aunts. I have also sources of information as to what goes on whenever the Dauphine sees the King. Superadded are my personal observations, so that there is really not an hour of the day as to which I am not instructed concerning what the Archduchess may have said or done or heard.

It was not of course, primarily, the Dauphine's immortal soul her mother was worrying about: it was the future of relations between Austria and France which might be, and in fact very nearly came to be, ruined by the ill-considered words or actions of the child who had been sacrificed to crown them.

The child was almost unimaginably alone. The proxy marriage in Vienna was an affair of the utmost extravagance, calculated to turn the head of a much wiser girl. Maria Theresa was showing off to France, and Louis XV was showing off to Austria: a full-dress military review, theatre galas, giant receptions at the Belvedere and the Liechtenstein Palace – all this while frantic preparations were in progress at Versailles, including the building of a brand new opera house. The duc de Dufort arrived to attend the wedding and to conduct the bride to her new home with a train of coaches and wagons calling for 340 horses and dominated by two travelling coaches of fabulous splendour, especially designed and constructed for the occasion by order of the French King.

Then, after days of mounting delirium, came, with cruelly dramatised definition, the surrender of identity. For months on end the court officials in Versailles and Vienna had been arguing about protocol. How was a Habsburg princess to be metamorphosed into the Dauphine of France without loss of dignity to either Habsburg or Bourbon? They came up with an ingenious solution. On a small island, no more than a sandbank, in the Rhine opposite Strasburg an elaborate pavilion was erected. Here, in no-man's-land, the formal induction of the new Dauphine would take place. Two anterooms looked towards the east bank of the Rhine, two faced the west. Between them a central hall was hung with costly tapestries and fitted with a throne and a baldachin. The eastward facing rooms were Austria; the westward facing rooms were France. Before she could enter France the child was required to strip to the skin in the presence of her Austrian ladies and then be dressed again from top to toe, stockings, chemise, petticoats, in fabrics of French manufacture. Not one single ring or ornament or handkerchief was she permitted to retain, even as a keepsake. She was to be, as it were, reborn. Worse, she must say goodbye for ever to all her Austrian followers and ladies. She was delivered over body and soul to the French delegation waiting for her in the great hall. Like the child she was, when the moment came, she threw herself into the arms of the Comtesse de Noailles, her new first lady-in-waiting, and burst into tears.

All this Maria Theresa, far away now, had on her conscience. She also knew that the young Dauphin was, to say the least, unattractive. So much so that when Mercy sent his first report of the splendid impression her daughter had made at Versailles (she had soon recovered from her tears) he allowed himself to express the fear that she might recoil from her husband in disgust. She did nothing of the kind, and her mother's first worries were occasioned not at all by her daughter's shortcomings but by the Dauphin's. The sixteen-year-old youth was impotent.

It was not until the early thirties of the present century that the Austrian writer, Stefan Zweig, in the course of writing his biography of Marie Antoinette unearthed certain passages from the correspondence between mother and daughter which Arneth in his exhaustive biography had seen fit to suppress. There had been no secret about the young man's unfortunate condition. Before long it was common gossip at Versailles. The Spanish ambassador to France even paid palace servants to report to him on the condition of the royal bed-linen. What the suppressed passages showed was Maria Theresa's intense and intimate acquaintance with the state of affairs from the very beginning, from month to month, until at last it was finally established as a result of Louis XV's personal intervention that there was no deep-seated psychological cause but only a slight deformity, a phimosis, which could be put right by a small, but obviously very painful operation – circumcision: then, from year to year, until the dauphin at last summoned up his courage to submit to the operation, and all was well. That was not until Joseph himself had briskly descended on Paris in 1777 to urge the dauphin to be a man.

At first Marie Antoinette did not understand what was happening. Then, in ignorance, she put it down to awkwardness and inexperience. Her mother, too, was not at first alarmed. The whole point of the marriage was to produce an heir to France who would be related by blood to Austria. But there was plenty of time. Marie Antoinette must be patient and understanding. Writing in May 1771 her mother could say that, eagerly as she awaited news of her daughter's pregnancy, she could not often enought repeat:

> On no account any peevishness, but only tenderness and caresses; for too much eagerness could ruin everything; gentleness and patience are the only things that can help. Nothing so far is lost. You are both so young. On the contrary, it is better this way for the health of both of you. You will both grow stronger. All the same, it is only natural that we old parents long for the consummation.

As time went by she forgot about patience. The couriers flew to and fro. Every fortnight *Madame ma chère mère* received the latest budget of news from her daughter and the latest report from Mercy; every fortnight *Madame ma chère fille* received the latest news and instructions. Once a month Marie Antoinette reported the due arrival of her period. Sometimes she must have wondered how her mother came to be so well informed about so many aspects of her life: her mother's comments on this or that action or remark would be there on the breakfast table in no time at all, frequently on matters which she herself had not reported. But she never seems to have suspected Mercy as the prime informant: life at Versailles was so public in almost every detail that she seems to have taken it for granted that the current gossip could reach Vienna by any one of many channels.

There was a good deal of comment, some of it sharp. While the slow drama of the retarded nuptials pursued its dreary course, the young Dauphine was innocently engaged in causing a major scandal, which was to cause her mother much alarm and heartsearching. Until her arrival the first lady of the land had been, unassailably, Madame Dubarry, who queened it over the Court in the King's name. Mischief-makers with a variety of axes to grind saw, with the installation of a new Dauphine, a chance to stir up trouble. Above all, the King's daughters, the Dauphin's aunts, had long been engaged in a futile war of attrition against this upstart, who had put their noses out of joint. They fell on Marie Antoinette and flattered her: she, the Dauphine, was the first lady and must behave as such, using her superior position to put the Dubarry in her place and make an end to a crying scandal. The silly child was enchanted in her boredom with this induction into the world of Court intrigue and a little intoxicated with the sense of her own power. She proceeded to snub Madame Dubarry on every possible occasion. Her eminence notwithstanding, the Dubarry was firmly bound by protocol: she could not address the Dauphine until the Dauphine spoke to her. And the Dauphine refused to speak. She was fortified in her silliness by her innocence. At first she was genuinely shocked by the openness of the King's connection with this woman of loose morals: she had not been brought up at Maria Theresa's Court for nothing. The shock could not have long endured; but she could still, when it suited her, work up a lively mood of moral indignation, and when the news of the scandal she was creating got back, through Mercy, to Vienna she thought at first that she would have her mother on her side. Would the Empress have for a moment tolerated such goings on at Schönbrunn? Indeed, no! Well, then . . .? Well, then . . . Maria Theresa naturally abhorred Madame Dubarry and all she stood for, but a grand alliance was at stake. The Court at Versailles was beside itself with delight at the spectacle of this child setting herself up against the King's mistress, therefore, against Louis himself. There were bets on what would happen next. Mercy was deeply concerned. Madame Dubarry was beside herself with fury and the King himself had instructed Madame de Noailles to convey a delicate warning to the dauphine. Marie Antoinette, half apprehensively, half gleefully, retailed the story to the aunts and the Abbé Vermond, who told Mercy, who decided to act quickly. A special messenger was sent express to Vienna.

Maria Theresa was indeed in a difficult position. She herself had refused to communicate direct with Madame Dubarry's predecessor, Madame Pompadour, entrusting the negotiations for the great reversal of alliances to Kaunitz, operating through Starhemberg in Paris, and considering her part well done when she caused her to be sent a costly present when the issue had been happily concluded. Now she was being required in the interests of state to instruct her daughter, flighty enough already, to make herself agreeable to a woman she regarded as a whore. At first she decided to keep out of it; Kaunitz should write to the Dauphine in his capacity as elder statesman:

> To refrain from showing civility towards persons whom the King has adopted as members of his own circle is derogatory to that circle; and all persons must be regarded as members thereof whom the ruling monarch himself looks upon as his confidants, no one being entitled to ask whether he be right or wrong in doing so. The choice of a reigning monarch must be unreservedly respected.

Marie Antoinette was not taking that from Kaunitz, or from anybody else. Who was this old fool to meddle in the private affairs of the future Queen of France? Upheld by the King's daughters she proceeded as before, until Louis himself, driven frantic by the Dubarry's constant nagging, sent for Mercy, and, after first letting Madame Dubarry loose on him (she pleaded almost in tears), hinted unmistakably, with extreme politeness and circumlocution, that something had better be done, and that quickly, if a palace intrigue was not to get out of hand and lead to serious trouble between Paris and Vienna.

This time Mercy tackled Marie Antoinette directly, spelling out the dire consequences which could ensue unless the Dauphine very quickly found a word to say to the Dubarry; so that, for once, the girl was frightened and sobered; through tears of humiliation and rage she gave her word that she would indeed speak. The day for the great encounter, and the very occasion, was fixed. Everybody knew about it and everybody looked on with eager speculation. But nothing happened. At the very last minute one of the aunts interrupted with perfect skill and timing, shattering the Dauphine's resolution. Now Louis quite lost patience, and Mercy reported to Vienna in a panic. The news of a possible rupture of Franco-Austrian relations, for so trivial a cause, arrived in Vienna at the worst possible moment. Maria Theresa was in the throes of her anguish over the projected Partition of Poland. The French, if they felt so minded, could intervene disastrously in this gross deal between Russian, Prussia and Austria, which was not the sort of thing to appeal to Louis at the best of times. Anger with Marie Antoinette reinforced by anger over Poland might even lead to war. Maria Theresa could keep out of the affair no longer. There was no help for it. She was the only person in Europe with influence over her daughter, and she would have to use that influence in order to make the girl publicly condone immoral conduct of a kind she would never have tolerated in Vienna.

So she wrote, quite back in her old form, and disingenuous as she had not allowed herself to be for many a long year:

The dread and embarrassment you show about speaking to the King, the best of fathers, about speaking to persons you are advised to speak to! What a pother about saying 'Good day' to someone, a kindly word concerning a dress or some trumpery. Mere whimsy, or something worse. You have allowed yourself to become enslaved to such an extent that reason and duty can no longer persuade you. I cannot keep silent about this matter any longer. After your conversation with Mercy and after all he told you about the King's wishes and your duty, you actually dared to fail him. What reason can you give for such conduct? None at all. It does not become you to regard the Dubarry in any other light than that of a lady who has the right of entry to the court and is admitted to the society of the King. You are His Majesty's first subject, and you owe him obedience and sub-

mission. It behoves you to set a good example, to show the
courtiers and the ladies at Versailles that you are ready to do
your master's will. If any baseness, any intimacy, were asked of
you, neither I nor any other would advise you to consent; but all
that is expected is that you should say an indifferent word,
should look at her beseemingly — not for the lady's own sake, but
for the sake of your grandfather, your master, your benefactor!

It was all over now. Marie Antoinette capitulated at last. On New
Years Day 1772 the second attempt was carried through. The
alliance was saved. Except for the mischief-makers the Court was all
smiles. At the usual after dinner reception, Marie Antoinette
turned from another lady to speak to Madame Dubarry. She said:
'Il y'a bien du monde aujourd'hui à Versailles.' It was enough.

Poor Maria Theresa, bullied by Joseph and Kaunitz, forced to
connive at the rape of Poland, harassed beyond measure by the
dangerous idiocies of the daughter she had brought up so inade-
quately, no wonder she felt her years. And, with all her other
troubles, she was to suffer from that daughter until she died. The one
object they agreed about, getting a child, was in due course achieved,
the long-awaited pregnancy announced in triumph, after many dis-
appointments, in the summer of 1778. But long before that Maria
Theresa had to suffer helplessly the distant spectacle not only of a
daughter going to the bad, but also of a Queen of France, her own
flesh, outvying the French court in the insatiability and recklessness
of her appetite for pleasure; even more deplorably, Marie Antoinette
had taken to displaying more or less public contempt for her
husband. The Dubarry had been 'cette créature sotte', her husband
she called 'une quantité negligéable'. 'She does not love him in the
least,' reported Joseph after his Paris visit. He had been struck by her
charm and elegance, but was maddened by her irresponsibility.

Louis XV died in 1774 and Marie Antoinette, Queen of France at
nineteen, soon started to amuse herself by playing politics again, in
spite of all her mother's warnings. In the following year she described one of her political intrigues in a letter to the elderly Count
Rosenberg who had taken her fancy, a letter of excessive silliness and
indiscretion in which she boasted of manipulating her husband,

whom she referred to as 'le pauvre homme'. Rosenberg was an old familiar at the Court at Vienna. When Joseph saw the letter he was outraged and wrote off at once to his young sister, who went in awe of him, in furious terms. Maria Theresa herself was appalled. She had tried so hard to instil some sense into the child; there were times when she thought she was succeeding, but it was clear now that she had failed. She herself wrote in such terms that for a century and a half her own letter, and subsequent references to it, were suppressed and hidden away in the Vienna archives, never to see the light until the monarchy itself had fallen:

> Where is the good and generous heart of the Archduchess Antoinette? I see only intrigue, vulgar spite, delight in mockery and persecution. An intrigue which would do very well for a Pompadour or a Dubarry, but never for a Queen, a great princess, still less a princess kindly and good of the house of Lorraine and Austria. All the winter long I have trembled at the thought of your too easy success and the flatterers surrounding you, while you have thrown yourself into a life of pleasure and preposterous display. This chasing from pleasure to pleasure without the King, and knowing that he takes no joy in it and only goes with you or lets you do what you want out of sheer good nature, has made me write before to express my fears. I see now from this letter that these were all too well justified. . . .
>
> Your luck can all too easily change, and by your own fault you may well find yourself plunged into deepest misery. . . . One day you will recognise the truth of this, but then it will be too late. I hope I shall not live until misfortune overtakes you, and I pray to God to end my days quickly, since I am no longer of any use to you, and I could not bear to loose my dear child or see her unhappy, whom I shall love tenderly until I die.

Marie Antoinette was shaken by this letter; she loved the Empress a good deal and feared her a little still. But it had no lasting effect, and she lived to see the answering of her mother's prayer and the fulfilment of her prophecy.

3

Ever since the death of Francis in 1765 Maria Theresa had gone about telling all and sundry that she was wholly resigned to the worst that might happen, only again and again to belie her words by energetic action. In her sixty-third year she did at last begin to let go. The high drama over the Bavarian War of 1777 turned out to be the last major crisis of her life. After that she was as busy as ever with affairs of state, above all with educational reforms, but her interventions now were in a minor key. She could still quarrel with Joseph, and to the end she was irritated and a little hurt by his passion for foreign travel. Particularly, she set herself against his visit to Catherine in Russia, fearing that the spectacle of the Emperor paying court to the Tsaritsa might unsettle the French alliance. And she was shocked when her son got on so well with this notoriously loose-living despot that, after their meeting in south Russia (this, for Catherine, was the celebrated triumphal progress through a landscape dotted with bogus villages constructed for her gratification by Potemkin) he accompanied her back to Petersburg. That was in the late summer of 1780. Almost as soon as he was back in Vienna he started making plans to visit the Netherlands and England. His mother's outburst showed to anyone who could see that she was coming to the end of the road. It was a parody of herself: 'The English are almost all deists and free-thinkers. I tremble lest confrontation with such a nation should shake your faith in everything held sacred by good Catholics.'

To Marie Antoinette, whose relations with her were happier now (there was her first little French grandchild to make much of), she showed another aspect of premature age: she wrote that it was hard of Joseph to leave her so long when she needed him so much. And indeed she needed him, his tiresomeness notwithstanding. Life was a burden for her now. Already in May of that year she had confided to her beloved Marie Beatrix in Milan that she was finding great difficulty in writing. She had so much to write, 'but my hands will no longer serve me. I am afraid of losing the use of them. This would be most awkward on account of my weight: nobody would be able to move me.'

The trouble with her hands, soon her arms, was rheumatic, and the rheumatism was induced, at least in part, by the rain and the wind coming in through her ever open windows. But if the windows were closed she could not breathe. She was enormous now. Marie Christine recorded that it was as hard for her to walk on a level floor as it had been to climb the stairs a year or two before. But her mind, though increasingly circumscribed, forgetful too, was still perfectly lucid. In her last letter to Marie Antoinette she returned again, but very gently, to a matter that had worried her for many years. It had always offended her sense of the conjugal proprieties that her daughter and her son-in-law slept separately. But it had all been argued about and finished with – until, in that last autumn of 1780, the matter was somehow brought up and Maria Theresa wrote to ask if it could be true. Marie Antoinette replied that it was certainly true. 'We have slept apart for a long time now. I thought my darling mother knew. It is the usual custom here, between man and wife, and I should not consider myself justified in pressing the King in a matter which goes very much against his way of life and personal tastes.' Marie Theresa, who had forgotten what had once been a great issue between mother and daughter, contented herself now with a gentle reproach. It was perhaps her last reproach to anyone: 'I confess that I did not know for certain that you did not sleep together; I only guessed. I must accept that what you tell me is right. But I should have liked it better if you could have lived in the German way and enjoyed that certain intimacy which comes of being together.'

Within a month she was dead. The end was very swift for a woman of such vigour and vitality. But in fact she was worn out. It has been said that but for catching a fatal chill while attending a pheasant shoot at Schönbrunn and getting wet through in pouring rain she might have lived another twenty years. Clearly she had no intention of doing any such thing. Her body had become an affliction, her mind was losing its edge, and she knew it. She also knew the proper thing to do: she was living dangerously, but with the most perfect tact. It was not necessary for her to turn out for Joseph's shooting party; it was not necessary for her to make the customary pilgrimage to the vault in the Capucin church on All Souls' day. It was not necessary for her to work at her papers day in day out. She was driving herself to the limit, but she did so with such an air of relaxed unconcern that almost everyone around her was taken in. A week after catching cold at Schönbrunn she was writing to Marie Christine in Pressburg that she was down but far from out. She had trouble with her breathing, but there was 'no fever or anything of consequence'. Within a couple of days she was back at her old routine and got off all her arrears of post. She had made her doctor bleed her against his better judgment. She could not lie down without suffocating, and for the last week of her life she slept in her chair, or propped up on a sofa.

Only Joseph now refused to see the true state of affairs. He was briskly confident that his mother was indestructible and waved aside in his no-nonsense manner the forebodings of Albert and Marie Christine, who were shocked by her condition when they came up from Pressburg on November 24th. He was also characteristically offensive to his mother's body-doctor, the successor of van Swieten, whose pupil he had been. He, Dr Störck, was making altogether too much of a fuss; he had better realise that the Emperor had seen through him: he was deliberately inflating a minor illness so that he could claim the greater credit when the Empress recovered. Two days later, nevertheless, on November 26th, he was shocked into reality when his mother calmly informed him that she proposed to receive the last sacrament before nightfall. Even then Joseph persisted, and persuaded her to wait. He was losing his head a little: in one breath sending for the scattered family to come, in the next telling them that all would be well. All was far from well. Maria Theresa was fighting hard for every breath. There were terrible spasms, from which, it seemed she could never recover. But again and again she came through. And in between the spasms, she sat quietly in her chair, writing to distant members of her family, talking to those gathered round her, even working a little. She made her doctor promise to tell her without fail when she was dying, and on November 28th he said the time had come. Very well, tell all the family that they may be with me when I receive Extreme Unction, but that there is no obligation: I shall understand if they find the whole affair too painful. Already she had told Dr Störck that she hoped the end would come quickly, before the sight of her suffering killed her poor children.

They all gathered round, and she was pleased. But even then there were two more days to live through. Once, after a particularly shattering spasm, she asked her doctor: 'Is this the end?' 'Not quite the end,' he answered, and she said: 'That must mean there is still worse to come.' It was her only complaint. For most of the time she was the comforter. She had all the time in the world to thank her children for all that they had been to her and to comfort them for when she was gone. She herself needed no comfort, only strength to meet her maker. During those two last days she sent everyone away as much as possible to spare them, but to Joseph she talked a great deal. Sitting up in her chair she signed many documents, wrote letters too, and made the alteration in her will which left that large sum to her schools. She refused all sedatives, which might prolong her life and with it the misery of those around her. 'You want me to sleep?' she said on what was to be her last evening, 'While at any moment I shall be called before my Judge, I am afraid to sleep. I must not be taken unawares. I wish to see death coming.' It came at nine in the evening of November 29th. She could scarcely breathe. She thought the windows must have been closed; but they were wide open and it was very cold. In her last efforts to breathe she heaved herself out of her chair and staggered to the sofa. As she sank down Joseph, supporting her, said: 'Your Majesty cannot be comfortable like that.' 'No,' she replied, 'but comfortable enough to die.' In a moment she was dead.

She died, as who does not, a prisoner of the past, her own past. But she had loosened the prison bars of feudal Austria and made it possible for all her peoples to move into the nineteenth century without revolutionary violence. In her remarkable person, empirical, practical, and kind, she had achieved the most that can be expected anywhere of any sort of government at any time – and more than is achieved by most. She had held her society together, encouraged its individual talents, and left it better than it was before.

Sources and Select Bibliography

Since this book makes no claim to original scholarship I have not burdened the text with notes.

Nearly all the basic material for Maria Theresa's life and reign is to be found in the ten-volume biography by Alfred Ritter von Arneth, *Geschichte Maria Theresia's* (Vienna, 1863–79). This comprehensive and immensely conscientious work was supplemented by Arneth with his editions of Maria Theresa's correspondence: *Briefe der Kaiserin M. Th. an ihre Kinder u. Freunde* (4 vols; Vienna, 1871); *Maria Th. u. Joseph II. Ihre Correspondenz* (3 vols; Vienna, 1867); *M. Th. u. Marie Antoinette. Ihr Briefwechsel* (Vienna, 1865); and, with A. A. Geffroy, *Correspondence secrète entre Marie Therese et le Cte de Mercy-Argenteau, avec les lettres de Marie Therese et de Marie Antoinette* (3 vols; Paris, 1874). It should be noted that most of Maria Theresa's letters were written in French and are so given by Arneth.

Certain passages in the correspondence between M. Th. and Marie Antoinette were either suppressed by Arneth or kept from him. These were stumbled upon in the Vienna State Archives by Stefan Zweig when he was working on his biography, *Marie Antoinette* (English translation; London, 1933). But the complete correspondence was not published until nearly twenty years later in *Maria Th. u. Marie Antoinette, Ihr Geheimer Briefwechsel*, edited and translated into German by Paul Christoph (Vienna, 1952).

The indispensable supplement to the Arneth volumes is the diary of M. Th.'s lord chamberlain, covering the years 1742–76 in great detail: *Aus der Zeit Maria Theresia's: Tagebuch des Fürsten Johann Joseph Khevenhüller-Metsch*, edited by Rudolf Graf Khevenhüller-Metsch and Hans Schlitter (7 vols; Vienna, 1907–25). A useful selection from this journal is offered in *Aus dem Hofleben Maria Theresia's* compiled by Adam Wolf (2nd enlarged edn; Vienna, 1859). M. Th.'s celebrated Memorials, first published by Arneth, are separately available as

Bibliography

Kaiserin M. Th.'s Politisches Testament, edited and with an introduction by Josef Kallbrunner (Vienna, 1952).

All more recent biographies lean heavily upon the above. The best of them is Eugen Guglia's *M. Th. Ihr Leben u. Regierung* (2 vols; Berlin, 1917). *Maria Theresia* by Karl Tschuppik (Amsterdam, 1934); *Maria Theresia* by Peter Reinhold (Wiesbaden, 1957); *Maria Theresia* by Heinrich Kretschmayer (Leipzig, 1938), and Karl Pfister's *M. Th., Mensch, Staat u. Kultur de Spätbaroken Welt* (Munich, 1949) are all useful. Until very recently the most solid biography in English was *Maria Theresa* by Mary Maxwell Moffat (London, 1911), which could be supplemented by J. F. Bright's essentially political study, *Maria Theresa* (London, 1897). But we now have a remarkable work by Robert Pick, *Empress Maria Th.* (New York, 1966; London, 1968). This covers only the first forty years of the subject's life (1717–57). It is indispensable as far as it goes and shows a superb mastery of sources; but its very brilliance makes it, paradoxically, indigestible.

Austrian and German histories of the Habsburg Monarchy as a whole and in part abound. The best comprehensive modern history is Hugo Hantsch's *Geschichte Oesterreichs* (2 vols; Graz, 1947). A brilliant and profound short book by an Austrian historian who is also an artist is Heinrich Benedikt's *Monarchie der Gegensätze* (Vienna, 1947). Oswald Redlich's *Das Werden einer Grossmacht* (Brunn, 1942) is also valuable for the relevant period; so, of course is Leopold von Ranke's *Zur Geschichte von Oesterreich u. Preussen Zwischen den Friedenschlüssen zu Aachen und Hubertusberg* (Vol. 30 of *Sämtliche Werke*; Leipzig, 1875). The best general history in English remains the greatly underrated *History of the House of Austria* by Archdeacon William Cox (3rd edn, 3 vols; London, 1847); readers may also care to refer to my own book, *The Fall of the House of Habsburg* (London, 1963).

The following are useful for the supporting cast:

Friedrich Walter's *Männer um M. Th.* (Vienna, 1951) for the men — ministers, soldiers, family — most close to Maria Theresa; Fred Hennings's *Und sitzet er zur linken Hand: Franz Stephan von Lothringen* (Vienna, 1961) for the Emperor Francis; Egbert Silva-Tarouca's *Der Mentor der Kaiserin* (Vienna, 1960) for Silva-Tarouca; F. Walter, *op. cit.*, has a valuable chapter on Gerhard van Swieten, aspects of whose career are also usefully treated in August Fournier's *Gerhard van Swieten als Censor*, published in *Sitzungsberichte der Philosophisch-Historischen Classe der Kaiserlichen Akademie der Wissenschaften* (Part III of

Vol. LXXXIV; Vienna, 1877), and in *Great Doctors* by Henry E. Sigrist, translated by Eden and Cedar Paul (London, 1933). Haugwitz has been neglected by biographers, but there is a useful chapter on him in Walter, *op. cit.*: he features strongly in all biographies of M. Th. and in writings about the economy, etc., of the monarchy during the Theresian period. For Kaunitz Alexander Novotny's *Staatskanzler Kaunitz als geistige Personalität* (Vienna, 1947) and Georg Kuntzel's *Fürst Kaunitz-Rietberg als Staatsmann* (Vienna, 1923). The atmosphere, strategy and tactics of eighteenth-century continental warfare is most readably conveyed in Christopher Duffy's life of Marshal von Browne, *The Wild Goose and the Eagle* (London, 1964), which also contains detailed accounts of Browne's campaigns in the War of the Austrian Succession and the Seven Years War; Edith Kotasek's *Feldmarschall Graf Lacy, Ein Leben fur Oesterreichs Heer* (Horn, 1956) is also useful; so, more technically, is Oskar Regele's *Generalstabschefs aus 4 Jarhunderten.*

The literature on Frederick the Great is, of course, without end. I have quoted from Voltaire, Carlyle and Macaulay. The king's own *Histoire de mon Temps* tells the story at length from his point of view. C. P. Gooch's *Frederick the Great* is useful and penetrating (London, 1947), so is Edith Simon's *The Making of Frederick the Great* (London, 1963). For an anti-Frederick book by a brilliant German writer, Rudolf Augstein's *Preussens Friedrich und die Deutschen* (Frankfurt, 1968); *Friedrich der Grosse u. M. Th. in Augenzeugen Berichten* compiled and edited by Hans Jessen (Düsseldorf, 1965) speaks for itself, and has a valuable bibliography. The reports of Frederick's Ambassador to the court of Maria Theresia are contained in *Otto Christoph Graf von Podewils: Diplomatische Berichten*, the most recent edition being edited by Carl Hinrichs (1937).

For the economy, the best and most readable general study is G. Otruba's *Die Wirtschaftlichspolitik M. Th.'s* (Vienna, 1963). An older and longer classic is Adolf Beer's *Studien zur Geschichte der oesterreichische Volkswirtschaft* under M. Th. (Vienna, 1894). For the condition of the peasants *The Emancipation of the Austrian Peasant 1740–1798* by Edith Murr Link (New York, 1949). For political economy, *Die Oesterreichischen Kameralisten* by Luise Sommer (2 vols; Vienna, 1920–5). There is an invaluable introduction to understanding the state of the monarchy in Maria Theresa's last years in the long opening chapter (over 100 large pages) to C. A. Macartney's monumental *The Habsburg Empire 1790–1918* (London, 1969). This volume, by a veteran scholar, is the most complete study *in any language* of the monarchy as a whole from the eighteenth century onwards. It contains a valuable bibliography, including useful works on the various nationalities.

The special situation of Habsburg Italy on the one hand and Habsburg Belgium on the other are conveniently studied in Heinrich Benedikt's *Kaiseradler über die Appeninin* (Vienna, 1964) and *Als Belgien Oesterreich War* (Vienna, 1965). Harold Acton's *The Bourbons of Naples* (London, 1859) may be read with profit and enjoyment for the strange relations between Austria and the Two Sicilies.

For the development of modern thought in the monarchy, and especially for the character and activities of Joseph von Sonnenfels and his relations with Maria Theresa and Joseph II, Robert A. Kann's *A Study in Austrian Intellectual History* (New York, 1960). For educational reforms Alexander Helfert's *Die Gründung der Oesterreichischen Volksschule durch M. Th.* (Prague, 1860).

For the arts, *Fischer von Erlach der Altere* by Hans Sedlmayer (Vienna, 1925) is a useful study of the chief architect of the city inherited by Maria Theresa. See also Hans Tietze's *Kultur, Kunst, Geschichte* (Vienna, 1931) and *Die bildende Kunst in Oesterreich, Renaissance u. Barock*, ed. Karl Hingart (Vienna, 1939). The latest edition of Burney's indispensable contemporary accounts of music and musicians in Austria, Bohemia and elsewhere is *Dr Burney's Musical Tours in Europe* (2 vols; London, 1959). The classic life of Mozart is still Otto Jahn's, the latest edition being *W. A. Mozart, neu bearbeitete u. erweiterte Ausgabe von Otto Jahn's 'Mozart'* by Hermann Abert (Leipzig, 1955). But the most stimulating and readable life is W. J. Turner's *Mozart, the Man and his Works*, first published in 1938 and belatedly reissued (London, 1965). *Letters of Mozart and his Family*, translated and edited by Emily Anderson (3 vols; London, 1938) is one of the most fascinating collection of letters in existence. I have drawn freely on Ernest Newman's *Gluck* (London, 1895) and Martin Cooper's more recent biography (London, 1935). I have also drawn on *Joseph Haydn* by Karl Geiringer in collaboration with Irene Geiringer (new and enlarged edn; London, 1964) which is worthy of its subject and extremely readable. It contains a most elaborate bibliography. For a general survey of music in Vienna see *Musikstadt Wien* by Alfred Orel (Vienna, 1953). The title of Francesco Algaotti's book on the Opera referred to in Chapter Eleven is *Saggio sopra l'opera in musica* (1755). For the special mood, above all human and cultural, of Vienna as a city, there is nothing to compare with *Vienna*, by Ilse Barea (London, 1966).

Revealing contemporary memoirs on which I have drawn, apart from Khevenhüller-Metsch, Podewils and Burney, cited above, include *The Letters and Works of Lady Wortley Montagu*, ed. by Lord Wharncliffe, new and revised edn (London, 1887); *The Courts of Europe at the Close of the Last Century* by Henry Swinburne (2 vols; London, 1841); *Memoirs of the Courts of Berlin, Dresden, Warsaw and Vienna* by N. William Wraxall (Vol. II, 3rd edn; London, 1806); *Denkwürdigkeiten aus meinem Leben* by Caroline Pichler (2 vols; Munich, 1914) — Caroline Pichler the daughter of Charlotte Hieronymus referred to in Chapter Nine and her memories, though vivid, are unreliable.

There remains the problem of Joseph II. The literature is immense and only peripheral to this volume. Practically all Joseph's correspondence has been published in various forms. Incomparably the best life is *Joseph II* by P. von Mitranov (Vienna, 1910). *The Revolutionary Emperor* by S. K. Padover (London, 1934) is the most useful in English, but displays a startling incomprehension of Maria Theresa's nature.

For the eighteenth century in general the following may be recommended: *Europe in the Eighteenth Century 1713–83* by M. S. Anderson (London, 1961); *Europe of the Ancien Régime* by David Ogg, a paperback in the Fontana History of Europe (London, 1965); *Europe in the Eighteenth Century* by R. J. White (London, 1965); *Competition for Empire, 1740–1763*, by Walter L. Dorn (New York, 1940). The best idea of the thinking which conditioned the English attitude to Austria in the 18th century is given by J. H. Plumb's superb *Sir Robert Walpole* (Vol. 2. London, 1960).

For vivid and useful insights into the immediate past of Maria Theresa's Austria, see *The Siege of Vienna* by John Stoye (London, 1964) and *Prince Eugene of Savoy* by Nicholas Henderson (London, 1964), on which I have drawn.

I should also like to acknowledge my debt to three unpublished works, all in the National Library at Vienna: *Die kulturellen und Sozialen Reforme unter der Regierung der Kaiserin Maria Theresia in Tirol* by Frida Reitböck (phil. Diss.; Innsbruck, 1943); *Hofreisen Maria Theresia's* by Maria Kollreider (phil. Diss.; Vienna, 1965) from which I have taken the details of Maria Theresa's journey to Prague in Chapter Nine; and *Elisabeth von Friz* by L. von Frizberg (privately printed; Vienna, 1954).

E. C.

INDEX

Index

Index

Index

Index

Hadik, 244

Haen, de, 200, 204

Handel, 19, 87, 171–2

Hanover, 38, 280–1; George II's concern for security of, 22, 46, 58, 77; visited by George II (1741), 58; and the War of Austrian Succession, 84; Kaunitz's policy towards, 208; and build-up to Seven Years War, 233–4, 236; and events of the Seven Years War, 242, 244

Harington, Sir John, 103–4

Harrach, Aloysius, 32, 61–2

Harrach, Count Friedrich, 192, 194

Harrach, Joseph, 32, 61–2

Harrachs, the, 130–1, 143, 159, 160, 163, 228

Hasse, Johann Adolph, 20, 165, 172–3, 183, 312

Haugwitz, Wilhelm, Count, 205, 277, 317; Tarouca's opposition to, 116; his reforms, 188–96, 225, 228, 254, 307, 315; his character, 189–90, 210; his early career, 190; his death, 271

Hawke, Admiral, 84, 238

Hayberger, 154

Haydn, Joseph, 143, 167, 171, 174; and the Harrach family, 130–1, 159, 160, 163; and the Esterházy family, 131–3, 159, 161, 177–9; his early life, 139, 158–66; Maria Theresa's attitude towards, 169, 179; his residence in England, 178; his relationship with Mozart, 179–80

Haydn, Matthias, 160–2, 164

Haydn, Michael, 163

Heberstein, Count, 62–3

Heinisch, Theresia, 143–4

Hennendorf, Battle of, 99

Henry, Prince (brother of Frederick the Great), 51, 242, 291

Hesse, 244

Hieronymus, Charlotte, 151–3

Hildebrandt, Lukas von, 17, 125–6, 154, 272

Hitler, Adolf, 32, 180, 282

Hochkirch, Battle of, 243

Hoe, 84

Hogarth, 311–12

Hohenberg, J. F., 138

Hohenfriedburg, Battle of, 97, 98

Hohenzollerns, the, 47, 66, 179

Holdernesse, 232

Holland, 108, 200; and the War of the Spanish Succession, 9; and the Pragmatic Sanction, 37; and Prussia's seizure of Silesia, 41, 56, 65; and the War of the Austrian Succession, 84–5, 97, 99, 100; and the Barrier Treaty, 215; and the Seven Years War, 233

Hungary, 3, 37, 43, 57, 284, 324; incorporated into the Habsburg Empire, 5, 6, 8, 68, 191; under Ferdinand I, 8, 68; under Joseph I, 11, 68; under Charles VI, 13, 68; disaffection in, 33–4, 68–71, 73, 75–6, 160; and Prussia's first Silesian campaign, 50, 53; Maria Theresa's coronation in, 58, 67–8, 70–3, 187, 267; history of, 67–70; Maria Theresa's compact with (1741), 77–81, 89, 107, 111, 318; her loyalty to Maria Theresa, 80, 105; Maria Theresa's affection for, 80; and the War of the Austrian Succession, 92, 93; Turkish invasions into, 121; her border with Austria, 130, 138, 159, 314; status of Esterházys in, 131–2, 143; independence of nobility in, 134; Michael Haydn's residence in, 163; and taxation, 192–3; and the 1848 uprising, 194; products of, 197; and the Seven Years War, 244; and Albert of Saxony, 304; peasants in, 306; penal laws in, 316

355

Index

Index

Born in 1909, Edward Crankshaw was one of Britain's premier journalists, reporting primarily on Soviet affairs for the *Observer*. The author of some twenty books, including *Vienna: The Image of a Culture in Decline* (1938), *The Habsburgs* (1971), and a critical study of Joseph Conrad, his last was *Putting Up with the Russians* (1984), which the *Times* (London) praised as "salutary, informative, and very good reading." He died in 1984.